English
A Level

MACMILLAN

Acknowledgements

The author and publishers wish to thank the following who have kindly given permission for the use of copyright material: The Associated Examining Board, Oxford and Cambridge Schools Examination Board, Southern Universities' Joint Board and University of London School Examinations Board for questions from past examination papers; The Guardian for the material from 'King for a TV Day', *The Guardian*, 30 June 1994, and Hugh Herbert, 'Programme from Heaven', *The Guardian*, 8 June 1994; The Hogarth Press for an extract from *Cider with Rosie*, by Laurie Lee (1959); International Creative Management, Inc., on behalf of the author for an extract from *Beloved*, copyright © 1987 by Toni Morrison; The Lord Chamberlain's Office for Court Circular, *The Times*, 30 July 1981; The Marvell Press for the poem 'I Remember, I Remember', by Philip Larkin, from *The Less Deceived* (1955); *The Morning Star* for an extract on the Royal Wedding, 30 July 1981.

Every effort has been made to trace all the copyright-holders, but if any have been inadvertently overlooked the publishers will be pleased to make the necessary arrangement at the first opportunity.

The University of London Entrance and School Examinations Council accepts no responsibility whatsoever for the accuracy or method in the answers given in this book to actual questions set by the London Board.

Acknowledgement is made to the Southern Universities' Joint Board for school Examinations for permission to use questions taken from their past papers but the Board is in no way responsible for answers that may be provided and they are solely the responsibility of the author.

The Associated Examining Board wishes to point out that worked examples included in the text are entirely the responsibility of the author and have neither been provided or approved by the Board.

First edition (*English Literature*) 1986
Reprinted four times
Second edition (*English A Level*) 1995

Published by
MACMILLAN PRESS LTD
Houndmills, Basingstoke, Hampshire RG21 6XS
and London
Companies and representatives
throughout the world

ISBN 0–333–64379–8

A catalogue record for this book is available from the British Library.

Printed in Great Britain by Biddles Ltd,
Guildford and Kings Lynn

10 9 8 7 6 5 4 3 2 1
04 03 02 01 00 99 98 97 96 95

Contents

Topic

Topic

Exam Board Addresses

Exam Boards Addresses
Syllabuses and past examination papers can be obtained from:

The Associated Examining Board (AEB)
Publications Department
Stag Hill House
Guildford Surrey GU2 5XJ

University of Cambridge Local Examinations Syndicate (UCLES)
Syndicate Buildings
1 Hills Road
Cambridge CB1 2EU

Northern Examinations, and Assessment Board (incorporating) Joint Matriculation Board (JMB)
12 Harter Street
Manchester M16 HL

University of London Examinations and Assessment Council (incorporating) University of London School Examinations Board (L)
ULEAC Publications
Unit 3
River Park Industrial Estate
Billet Lane
Berkhamsted
Hertfordshire
HP4 1EL

University of Oxford Delegacy of Local Examinations (OLE)
Ewert House
Ewert Place
Summertown
Oxford OX2 7BZ

Oxford and Cambridge Schools Examination Board (O & C)
Purbeck House
Purbeck Road
Cambridge CB2 2PU

Scottish Examination Board (SEB)
Robert Gibson & Sons (Glasgow) Ltd
17 Fitzroy Place Glasgow G3 7SF

Welsh Joint Education Committee (WJEC)
245 Western Avenue
Cardiff
CF5 2YX

Northern Ireland Council for the Curriculum, Examinations and Assessment (incorporating) Northern Ireland Schools Examination Council (NISEC)
Examinations Office
Beechill House
42 Beechill Road
Belfast BT8 4RS

Introduction

How to use this practical guide to English A Level

All the principal features of an English A Level course are present in this book. The questions selected for discussion have been taken from (or modelled on) those set by the various examining boards. The material on which the worked examples and guided practice are based is of the same nature as that specified for close study in the various English A Level syllabuses. Its time span extends from Chaucer to the present day (including contemporary writing in English that is international in origin and repute); and it contains examples of all the major literary forms (or 'genres').

Because it is so closely geared to syllabus requirements this book provides its readers with help of a very practical kind. It describes the varied demands that English A Level makes on candidates – and it demonstrates how those demands can be met.

As I shall now explain, the worked examples have an especially important part to play in preparing you for the various papers you will be taking. No single book could include worked-out answers to questions set on every one of the texts specified by each of the examining boards. The limited amount of space available compelled me to make a selection. I made my choice with the following considerations in mind: authors and texts that are most frequently set by most of the examining boards; texts representing each of the major literary genres – the novel, lyric poetry, drama (tragic and comic), and so on.

Consequently, you will find that some of the worked examples are based on authors and texts specified for close study in your own syllabus, but that others are based on authors and texts that are not included in your list of set books. But, because each of the worked examples is designed to show you *how to answer a particular kind of question*, those based on authors and texts not included in your set book list are just as useful to you as the others.

For instance, by studying the critical commentary on the passage from *The*

Prelude in Chapter 5 you will learn how to answer examination questions *of that kind*. The *method* of studying that passage by Wordsworth and of writing the commentary can be applied with equal success to a passage taken from the work of any other poet.

Similarly, in the same chapter, the worked example from *Much Ado About Nothing* shows you how to write a critical commentary on a scene in that particular play, but the demonstrated procedures will produce a good commentary on a scene in any other play, whether by Shakespeare or by another dramatist.

Again, the critical commentary on a passage from *Middlemarch* shows you how to deal with an examination question of that kind, whether set on that particular novel or any other (see also *Guided Practice 3*, in Chapter 2).

Turning to another kind of question, the essay on *Hard Times* (in Chapter 6) demonstrates an approach and a method that will help you to write a good essay on any novel you are studying. Then, in that same chapter, essay questions set on different kinds of literature are analysed and answered.

To sum up: the guided practice and worked examples provided in this book show you how to answer *the different kinds of questions* that your examiners will ask about *the various kinds of writing* that are included in your English A Level syllabus.

Pay careful attention to the background material ('What you need to know') in Chapters 4, 5 and 6. It is especially useful in two ways. First, it provides explanatory notes on the authors and texts discussed and thus helps you to study the worked examples critically. Second, it enables you to judge the progress you are making with your own set book studies. To get a good grade in English A Level your knowledge, understanding and appreciation of the texts you are studying should measure up to the standards set in these notes.

There are two further points that I want you to bear in mind while you are using this book.

When you are studying the guided practice and the worked examples pay close attention to my use of text references in support of my judgements and to the reasoning on which my conclusions are based. Then, if you disagree with my views, say so – and say *why* you disagree with them.

The second point concerns the style in which my answers to the examination questions are written. The issues raised by these questions are important to anyone who is interested in language and literature. I enjoy exploring them and expressing my critical responses to them. I could not do that properly unless I wrote about them in my own way, drawing on the resources of vocabulary and sentence structures made available to me by long experience of reading literature and writing about it. I make no apologies for assuming that my readers are capable of appreciating serious discussions of books and authors expressed in an appropriate – and therefore, of course, a lucid – style of writing. Apologies would be due if I had patronised my readers by writing in an artificially 'simplified' way, in which the critical issues could not have been adequately discussed.

I hope that the way in which I have presented my answers to the questions will help you to develop your own powers of expression, but do not think that you are expected to imitate my style of writing. As you extend your own vocabulary and command of language structures you will learn to express reasoned arguments *in your own way* – in clear and persuasive language that reflects *your* interests and *your* opinions.

You have much to gain by adopting the approach to examination questions and the methods of answering them set out here; but do remember, the guided practice and the worked examples are not meant to be used as 'copybook' material.

Revision

Most English A Level candidates are aware of the importance of revision, but because they generally do most of their revising towards the end of their course, when the date of their first examination paper is rapidly approaching, they do not get full value from it.

A frantic attempt to go back over all the work you have done – some of it recently, some of it much longer ago – is not an effective way of preparing for the kinds of questions set in English A Level papers. Some of those questions do, of course, test your knowledge of the texts prescribed for close study. Checking that knowledge and closing any gaps you discover is a useful way of revising in the period immediately preceding the examination. Thorough knowledge of prescribed texts is the bedrock requirement for success; but the questions set on those texts are designed to test the *use* you can make of your knowledge. They probe your understanding and appreciation of the books you have studied; and the questions set on 'unseen' passages require you to exercise the critical sense you are expected to develop through studying your prescribed texts. Additionally – and obviously – set book questions and those on 'unseen' passages require you to show that you can use written English correctly, clearly and appropriately.

For all of these reasons, revising for English A Level is not simply a matter of consolidating factual knowledge. It is also a matter of reinforcing your question-answering techniques, of refining your critical judgement, and of exercising your writing skills – none of which can safely be left until the end of your course, or achieved by intensive 'cramming'. Frequent revision is an essential part of your preparation for the various examination papers. Make time for it *during your course*, going back over the different kinds of work (essays, critical commentaries, summaries, comprehension and appreciation of 'unseen' passages, and so on) to make sure that you understand their demands and that you know how to meet them.

The structured approach to English A Level studies presented in this book makes it easier for you to plan your revision efficiently and to tackle it in manageable quantities and at times of your own choosing, when you feel best able to profit from it. The comprehensive overviews provided in Chapters 1 and 3 and in the preliminary sections of the other chapters draw attention to matters of basic importance: the nature of the examination as a whole, and in particular papers; the qualities and skills that it tests; the examiners' requirements; and the criteria by which your work will be assessed. The different kinds of work included in your syllabus are then described, discussed and *practised* in successive chapters.

Because it explores syllabus requirements in this methodical, step-by-step way, the book provides you with a ready means of revising any aspect of your course at any time. You know where to find the help you need to refresh your understanding of that particular kind of work – to get to grips with the kinds of questions set on it, and to improve your methods of answering them.

For special attention

In every chapter (and especially in Chapters 4–8, each of which concentrates on a particular aspect of English A Level work) detailed help is given with the following matters that are of crucial importance when you are taking your examination papers:

- Spending on each question the amount of time you can afford – and no more than that.
- Planning how to present your answers in an orderly manner – before you begin to write.
- Avoiding the mistakes that are commonly made by candidates when answering the kinds of questions you are considering.
- Making sure that you write each of your answers in good English.

Those are matters that require special attention and frequent practice throughout your course.

Whichever syllabus you are following, this book will help you to get a good grade in English A Level – most of all, I believe, because it suggests ways of looking at language and literature that will greatly increase your enjoyment of your subject.

S. H. BURTON

How to make a good start

1

1.1 Facing the facts

English is a popular A Level choice. It attracts a lot of students who get a good result in their GCSE examination and who like the idea of continuing to study a subject which they have enjoyed and in which they have already been successful. If it was those sensible reasons that led you to choose English as one of your A Level subjects, you have made a good decision. You are suited to the course and you should do well in the examination.

Sometimes, however, students who start with justifiably high hopes are dismayed by the demands that an A Level course soon makes. The work seems more difficult than they expected. There is such a lot to do – so much to read; so many topics to be thought about and discussed; and such a variety of written assignments to be tackled. Faced with these challenges, students get disheartened and begin to wonder whether they have chosen the wrong subject.

If, just now, you are finding it hard to get to grips with your English A Level course, that is probably because you do not yet understand its aims. You have lists of the books you must study and you know which papers you will be taking in the examination, but you are not really clear about what is required of you. Discovering your sense of direction is the key to success.

1.2 Different boards – different syllabuses

As I write, I have the A Level syllabuses of all the examining boards in front of me. Placed one on top of the other, they make a hefty pile; and it takes a long time to study them all. Of course, you need not do that. The only syllabus that concerns you is the one that applies to the English A Level course you are following. However, there is a good reason to refer here to the fact that there are many different English A Level syllabuses.

You may know people who are also studying English as an A Level subject but are working to different regulations from yours. They have different set books

1

and they are preparing for different papers. It may even be that the subject they are taking is given a different name in their syllabus. It may be called 'English' or 'English Literature' or 'English Language and Literature' or 'English – Syllabus 1' or 'English – Syllabus 2' (and that is not a complete list of the various names given to the subject).

You need not be disturbed if you find that your syllabus and other students' syllabuses do not match. Bear two things in mind. First, (*I repeat*) it is only *your* syllabus that matters to you: if you know its regulations and work to them, you will not get any nasty surprises in the examination. Second, like all other candidates, you are working towards an A Level examination. Whatever name the subject is given in your syllabus and whichever papers you are taking, your performance will be judged by the same criteria as everyone else's. The grade you get will be an A Level grade and it will be of equal status to the grade obtained by students who are working to a different A Level syllabus.

The English department at your examination centre has entered you for the particular English A Level examination that it considers to be most suited to its candidates. The choice has been made after due consideration of all the options available and in light of the department's own teaching strengths and preferences. It is a case of 'horses for courses', as the old saying goes, and you can be sure that the English syllabus you are following has been chosen carefully as being the best for you.

1.3 Finding your way

Although they prescribe different books for detailed study and different examination papers, all the syllabuses are based on similar views of what students should achieve as a result of following an English A Level course.

Consequently, your examiners will look for the same *kinds* of knowledge and the same *kinds* of skills in your work as other examiners will look for in the work of their candidates.

Your aims

As a student of English A Level, you are required to pursue the following aims:

- To learn to enjoy and appreciate a wide range of literature.
- To learn to pay close and critical attention to the contents and to the style of various kinds of literary and non-literary writing (for example, in newspapers and magazines).
- To learn to be a proficient writer – which means being able to use written English clearly, accurately and appropriately for a variety of purposes.

The nature of these aims explains why an English A Level course includes so many different kinds of reading and writing, for close study and frequent practice.

Because the contents of the course are so wide-ranging, a varied work programme is a necessary feature of English A Level studies. For example, a typical day's work might well include the following activities: participating in group study and discussion of a scene in a Shakespeare play; spending a private study period comparing and making notes on two modern poems linked by a common theme; and working on a written assignment to summarise a leading article in a newspaper and comment on the writer's arguments.

No doubt, your own course of study has provided you with similar experiences. You are preparing for an examination that will test the range and the quality of your reading and writing. Variety of subject-matter, topic and approach is an essential element of your preparation.

What your examiners will look for

Your examiners will require you to show them that:

- You have accurate and detailed knowledge of your set books (or 'prescribed texts', as they are often called).
- You have made a personal response to the books and authors you have studied.
- You have a critical sense and can comment sensibly and sensitively on the contents and the style of prescribed texts and of 'unseen' material.
- You recognise effective presentation and can identify its features, such as: logical argument; firm structure; clear, fluent and (where appropriate) evocative language.

To demonstrate these qualities is a stiff test of your own ability to use written English, but your course work will give you ample opportunities to learn and to practise the skills you need.

The practice sections of later chapters provide detailed explanations of the examiners' requirements and show you how to satisfy them. Here, however, I want to consider two challenging features of English A Level work which have been referred to earlier in this chapter and which will now be looked at more closely under the headings of 'wide reading' and 'deep reading'.

1.4 Wide reading

It is unlikely that you would have chosen to study English A Level if you do not enjoy reading. Even so, you may find your list of prescribed reading formidable at first. Not primarily because it is lengthy, but because it includes different kinds of writing (some of which you may not have encountered before) by past and present authors (some of whom you may not have heard of before). You knew that you would have a lot of reading to do, and you are keen to get on with it; but you may not feel confident of finding your way through the unknown territory you are being asked to explore.

What may seem at first to be a bewildering mixture of required reading has a pattern. Each prescribed text is part of a planned course of study that introduces you to areas of knowledge in which students of English A Level are expected to become well informed and to skills that they are expected to acquire.

Prescribed texts are therefore listed in groups: texts to be studied for Paper 1; texts to be studied for Paper 2, and so on. Generally, each paper is given a descriptive title as well as a number (for example: 'Paper 1 – Shakespeare'; 'Paper 2 – Major Authors'; 'Paper 3 – Poetry'). The titles of the papers vary from syllabus to syllabus, but whatever names are used to describe the various papers, and whichever books are set for detailed study, all lists of required reading serve the same overall purpose. Your reading list, like those of all other students of

English A Level – is designed to help you to increase your appreciation of literature by directing your attention to the following fields of study.

Major authors

You are required to study some of the 'classics' of literature – works that have stood the test of time. At least one (generally two) of Shakespeare's plays will be prescribed, together with works by several other major writers, from Chaucer onwards.

There is usually a separate paper on Shakespeare. Sometimes, however, the Shakespeare texts are examined in one section of a paper, with questions on selected works by other major authors (Chaucer, perhaps, and Milton) in other sections.

Sometimes, too, writers who are undoubtedly of major status are listed for study under some other heading. For example, Wordsworth is certainly a major poet, but his work may be studied, not for a 'Major Author' paper, but for a paper with some such title as 'The Romantic Poets' or 'Early Nineteenth-Century Writing'.

For whichever paper they are prescribed, works by several great writers of the past will be included in your list of prescribed reading.

Some living (or recently dead) authors are also prescribed: writers who may achieve 'classical' status in the future. Their work seems likely to endure. Consequently, it is considered to merit the same close study and critical attention as are given to the great writing of the past.

The inclusion of contemporary works encourages you to recognise the continuing vitality of literature: its capacity to reflect and to influence the way we live. Now, as in the past, there are some writers who strive to voice the permanent concerns of humanity in memorable language. That is why some of today's poems, plays, biographies, novels and short stories will be among the classics of tomorrow.

Form (or 'genre')

Your required reading includes examples of several (perhaps, all) of the various literary forms just mentioned, study of which contributes to your appreciation of prescribed texts. The point can quickly be illustrated. You can neither understand a Shakespeare text nor appreciate its qualities unless you approach it as a *drama*. It is a playscript, written to be performed by actors for an audience: and that is the light in which it must be studied.

Similarly, Milton's *Paradise Lost, Books I and II* and Keats' *Hyperion* (often 'set' for A Level study) are to be considered as examples of the *epic* form of poetry. To appreciate them fully, it is necessary to compare and to contrast the ways in which Milton and Keats use (and modify) the in-built features of that particular genre.

Detailed study of prescribed texts includes consideration of the various literary forms in which they are written. It is important to recognise those forms; and it is important to recognise that writers handle them in their own ways and with distinctive results. For example, the formal features of a novel by Henry Fielding are as strikingly different from those of a novel by Jane Austen as the formal features of a novel by her are from those of a novel by Virginia Woolf. A student who is alert to those differences has discovered 'a way in' that can lead to a fuller understanding and appreciation of three novelists whose views of life – and therefore of literature – are far apart.

> Your awareness of the literary forms (and of the variations of those forms) that are exemplified in your prescribed texts helps you to develop the critical sense that your examiners will look for (see page 9).

In some syllabuses, the descriptive titles of the examination papers draw attention to the critical significance of literary form – for example: 'Approaches to Narrative'; 'Aspects of Comedy'; 'Prose Fiction'. The titles of the papers you are taking may not be so explicit, but it is always assumed that you will not neglect this essential aspect of English studies. (It is discussed in more detail in the 'What you need to know' sections of later chapters.)

Period

By definition, no enduring work speaks solely to its own age. (Time soon sweeps away writing that is of merely topical interest.) Nevertheless, however original and innovative it may be, all literature is necessarily marked by features characteristic of the period in which it is written. Authors employ the vocabulary and the grammar current in their day – although their own use of language may extend its boundaries and initiate change; they are influenced by prevailing ideas and attitudes – although they may do much to modify them; and they write within the dominant political and social structures of their time – although they may call them into question.

Each of your prescribed texts is the product of a strongly individual and creative mind. It is also, to some degree, the product of its period. Directly or indirectly, its contents reflect historical influences such as those just described. Your recognition of the author's response to those influences leads to a fuller appreciation of the intellectual, moral and aesthetic qualities of the text.

Texts by major authors are drawn from several different periods and exemplify a wide range of historical features and influences. Here are some examples.

A work by Geoffrey Chaucer (1340?–1400) introduces the reader to the vocabulary and grammar of late Middle English – not so profoundly different from Modern English as to present insuperable difficulties, but sufficiently different to require frequent reference to a glossary and to grammatical notes. Background reading is also needed to supply relevant information about medieval life and thought, as reflected in Chaucer's writings.

Contemporary theories of kingship are explored in the history plays of William Shakespeare (1564–1616). Knowledge of these theories increases appreciation of his dramatic presentation of men and women: some corrupted by the struggle for power; and others scrupulous to uphold the moral integrity of legitimate authority.

Explicitly and implicitly, the poetry of Alexander Pope (1688–1744) expresses the spirit of the Augustan Age. Like his contemporaries, Pope believed that order and proportion are of supreme importance in society and in literature: 'Order is Heaven's first law', he said. Adherence to those twin virtues had brought about an advanced state of civilisation (so he held) and it was the duty of writers to proclaim that achievement. In his choice and treatment of subject matter, he embodies the social values of his time. In the clarity and polished elegance of his style, he epitomises the literary ideals then prevailing. More than any other poet of his day, Pope represents what he confidently described as 'the present purity of writing'.

Readers living at a time when these ideas and attitudes are no longer current may, at first, find the contents of Pope's poetry remote from their concerns, and its style not much to their taste. Nor do his frequent allusions to the history and literature of Ancient Rome (and, but less often, of Ancient Greece) make him easy to read. Added to which is the troublesome fact that the meanings of some of the key words he uses when discussing society and literature (for example: 'nice'; 'wit'; 'nature'; 'science') have changed since his day. Yet for students prepared to make an informed and imaginative effort to put themselves into an Augustan frame of mind (as far as that is now possible) there is much enduring pleasure and good sense to be got from the poems of Pope.

These few examples are sufficient to indicate the importance of recognising and taking account of the ways in which a prescribed text may reflect the period in which it was written. At this stage, I have done no more than touch on some of the matters that must be considered. Detailed discussion of particular instances is left to the practice work in later chapters.

Bear in mind, too, that present-day texts are likely to be as strongly marked by period features and influences as those written in the past. Because their more obvious 'period indicators' (vocabulary, grammar, material circumstances and social setting, for example) are to a large extent familiar to you, contemporary texts may seem to present fewer difficulties initially. Yet no less than their predecessors, modern writers explore current – and often complex – issues that are of urgent concern to them and to their times.

Since the beginning of the twentieth century, literature has voiced the uncertainties of a troubled age, questioning former beliefs, attitudes, social systems, codes of morality and modes of conduct. Here are just some of the contemporary issues that may confront you when studying modern texts: race; gender; the lot of minorities and 'outsiders' (for example, aliens, exiles, refugees); the relative nature of truth (scientific, philosophical, psychological or religious); the function of art; the 'failure' of language; the dangers of advanced technology; and the pervasive influence of the mass media.

Some of the techniques commonly employed (in prose, in poetry and in drama) are as challenging as the subject matter. Many of the presentational devices of modern writing are closely allied to those used in film. For example: deliberately fragmented narrative; time gaps, and leaps backwards and forwards; recurring images, the symbolical significance of which is not always clear at first; shifting (and often, conflicting) angles of vision.

The response that writers make to the spirit of their age is a driving force that finds expression in their choice of subject (and in their attitudes to their subject), in their handling of form, and in their use of language. When, as often happens, a group of writers express similar views of and attitudes to their age (whether as 'conformers' or as 'rebels'), it is generally the case that their work is marked by shared stylistic features. Collectively, the writers in the group become the voice of a powerful 'movement' which – in later years, if not in their own time – is recognised as having been the outstanding literary achievement of their age.

That is why prescribed texts are often listed under 'period' and/or 'movement' headings, such as: 'Literature of the Early Nineteenth Century'; 'Poets of the First World War'; 'Writing in the Thirties'.

A summary of the main points made in this section will be helpful:

- Your list of prescribed reading covers a wide range of authors, past and present.
- It includes texts written in various literary forms and representing various literary periods and movements.
- You are required to make a detailed study of your texts. That necessarily includes close consideration of: (a) literary forms, and the distinctive ways in which different writers use them; and (b) period influences, and the distinctive ways in which different writers respond to them.
- Awareness of their formal and period features leads to a fuller appreciation of the texts you are studying.

1.5 Deep reading

Detailed knowledge

'Candidates are required to show that they have detailed knowledge of the prescribed texts.' A statement to that effect (if not in precisely those words) appears in every syllabus. It does not mean that straightforward 'knowledge' questions are set – the examination is not a quiz. It means that the kinds of questions set cannot be answered satisfactorily without detailed knowledge of the texts.

To illustrate that point, here is a typical examination question: '*Gulliver's Travels* includes a lot of political and social satire. Where did Swift stand on these issues, and how do you know?'

That is a searching question; but it is a perfectly fair one to put to candidates who are assumed to have made a detailed study of *Gulliver's Travels*. It probes their knowledge of the text. More importantly, it tests their ability to make use of that knowledge to form sound opinions and to construct reasoned arguments.

The questions set on your prescribed texts will be of a similar nature and they will therefore make the same demands. That is why it is so important to get down to close study straight away. You will have to show your examiners that you have 'gone into' the texts very thoroughly; and your opinions and arguments will not carry much weight unless you support them with accurate and detailed references to the texts.

To put it very simply:

If you want people to be interested in what you are saying, show them that you know what you are talking about.

Apt use of relevant details signifies that you have made a personal response to your prescribed texts and that you have developed a critical sense by studying them. There is more to be said about this; but first an important warning.

Access to prescribed texts in the examination

Each examining board has its own rules about taking copies of the prescribed texts into the examination room. Some *allow* their candidates to do so; others *require* them to. Some stipulate that only *plain* texts are allowed; others permit the use of *annotated* texts. You must, of course, observe the regulations of your own board.

Permitting candidates to have access to their prescribed texts during the examination is a comparatively recent development – and a sensible one. After all, students use texts when they are writing essays (as do critics and scholars when they are writing articles and books). A ban on the use of texts during an examination is an artificial and unnecessary handicap. Candidates who have their own familiar copies of the texts to hand are less likely to be affected by 'examination nerves'. Knowing that they can check the accuracy of any quotations and references they may want to use, they can concentrate on planning and writing their answers to the questions.

But *beware!*

Unless you know the texts thoroughly, it will not be much help to have them with you in the examination.

When you are planning your answer to an examination question, you should be able to draw on a fund of knowledge and understanding built up beforehand. Of course, it is an advantage to have copies of the texts for immediate reference; but only if you know exactly *what* you are looking for, and *why* you need it, and *where* to find it.

A vague recollection that 'there is something about this, somewhere' is no use at all. While you are turning over the pages, hunting for text material that you *think* you *might* be able to use in your answer to the question, time is running out.

If your previous studies have been skimped, you will not be able to hide the gaps in your knowledge and understanding by using copies of the texts when you are answering the examination questions.

Text study: aims and methods

As your syllabus describes them, these should be your two principal aims: (a) to make 'a personal response' to the prescribed texts; and (b) to develop 'a critical sense' by studying them closely. That tells you what you should try to do; but it does not tell you how to do it. Here, then, is some practical advice to help you make a good start.

First, a reminder:

What you get out of text study depends very largely on what you bring to it. In the words of R. W. Emerson (poet, philosopher and critic, 1803–82): ' 'Tis the good reader that makes the good book.'

Try to see text study as a continuing discovery, to be undertaken with an enquiring mind and a lively imagination. So when you are reading a text (poem, play, novel, short story or whatever it is) for the first time:

- Get involved.
- Let the events carry you along, and let the people come alive.
- Give your imagination free rein, and don't worry if your first impressions are challenged as you read on. It is the liveliness of your reactions that is important, not their 'correctness'. Be ready to take sides, to like or dislike people, to approve or disapprove of their behaviour and opinions – just as you do in a 'real life' experience.
- Let the writer work on your feelings and thoughts. If a particular passage, line or phrase (especially in a poem) makes a strong impression, pause; then read it again – and again. Let it sink in.
- Don't be afraid of being 'wrong'. In later readings and discussions, you will be reconsidering your initial reactions. Some will be confirmed and strengthened; others will be modified; still others will be scrapped and replaced by more mature reflections.

Text study is a two-way process: an interchange of thoughts and feelings between the author and the reader. It requires sustained effort, but if you approach it in the spirit and the manner just described, you will find it an enjoyable and rewarding experience.

Your other aim – to develop 'a critical sense' – is achieved as a consequence of making a thoughtful and sensitive response to a text.

Note, first, that developing a *critical* sense does *not* mean developing a fault-finding disposition. It means learning to recognise what the writer is trying to do, and appreciating the qualities of the text in light of that recognition. (The terms 'critical' and 'criticism' are discussed at greater length in Chapter 5.)

As you enlarge and deepen your response to a text, you will be drawn increasingly into the experience that the writer is offering – more aware of its nature and more alert to the literary skills with which it is conveyed.

Finding yourself strongly affected by some aspect of its contents and some features of its style: characters, events, ideas, language, as the case may be, you naturally look for the cause: 'Why do I feel this?' 'What makes me think that?' 'How do I know that this is true (or false)?' To find the answers, you return to the writer's words, testing your reactions, reassessing your opinions and scrutinising details to try to account for the impact they make on you. As you search out and weigh the evidence, you are enabling yourself to form and express worthwhile judgements, based securely on your thorough and imaginative exploration of the text.

The value of the text study methods outlined here is confirmed by the nature of the questions set in the examination. However the instructions are worded (and they vary greatly in that respect) they have certain features in common. A particular topic is presented for discussion. It bears on one (or more than one) important aspect of the contents and/or style of one (or more than one) of the prescribed texts; and candidates are expected to grasp its significance and to have plenty to say about it. They are invited to express their own reasoned opinions and to support them with detailed references to the text (or texts).

To underline the points made in this section, here is an extract from a report on the work of two candidates. It tells you very clearly what the examiners are looking for when they are marking the scripts.

Text study: knowledge – understanding – appreciation	
Assessment	*Criteria*
Good	Genuine interest – close involvement with texts – sensitive personal response – thorough knowledge and understanding – reasoned arguments – ample and apt textual references – evidence of critical insight
Weak	Thin in substance – dull – little to say – lack of detail – sketchy textual references – tendency to narrate and describe – no deep involvement – little evidence of genuine appreciation

1.6 Preparing for the 'unseen'

It may sound like the title of a ghost story! In fact, it refers to one part of the examination which causes a lot of anxiety. Many candidates approach the 'unseen' with unnecessary fear, and consequently do themselves less than justice.

What is it?

To explain as briefly as possible: 'unseen' is the term used to describe a test in which candidates are given passages of writing to study. They are then required to answer questions about them and/or to comment on particular features of their content and style to which the examiners draw attention.

The given material is 'unseen' in the sense that candidates are unlikely to have read it before they encounter it in the examination. If, by chance, they have come across it previously, they will probably not have studied it closely. It will certainly not be taken from one of their prescribed texts.

The unseen passages are derived from a great variety of sources: they may be poetry or prose; they may be literary or non-literary; they may be extracts from past or contemporary poems, plays, novels, short stories, biographies or essays; or they may be extracts from magazines, newspapers, advertising copy, political speeches, public relations hand-outs, radio and television scripts or verbatim reports of everyday conversation. But whatever their source and form may be, they have been chosen to illustrate some of the many different ways in which language is used in different contexts and for different purposes.

Although the various syllabuses describe this part of the examination in their own words, its *basic* nature and aims do not vary. Whichever syllabus you are following, the questions set and the comments required test your ability to read carefully and critically.

Having studied an unseen passage, you are asked to do three things.

(i)   Show that you have understood its contents. For example, you may be asked to explain the meaning of particular words and phrases; to summarise the meaning of a particular section; to trace the successive stages through which an argument is developed; or to express the meaning of the whole passage briefly and in your own words.

(ii)   Show that you have identified the passage as an example of a particular kind of writing or speech. In other words, show that you have recognised the context in which it operates and the purposes it is intended to serve. For instance, you might identify a given passage as a descriptive, 'scene-setting' piece of writing, taken from a novel or a short story. You might recognise that it provides the background against which a leading character is introduced. You might also recognise that it is intended to create an 'atmosphere' which will colour the reader's first impressions of that character and exert a continuing influence as the narrative progresses. Or, having studied a non-literary passage, you might identify it as a piece of advertising copy, the purpose of which is to extol the merits of a product. You might recognise that it was written to persuade its readers that they have a pressing need for that product, and to explain how they can satisfy that need quickly and without worrying about the expense.

(iii) Show that you have paid close attention to the ways in which language is used in the passage; and that you have considered whether they are well- or poorly-suited to the context within which it operates and to the purposes it was intended to serve. (**NB**   Basing your judgement on purely linguistic grounds, you might quite rightly consider that the second of the two examples given in (ii), above, is well written, though you might not approve of its aims.) Matters to be considered under 'uses of language' include: appropriate choice of words; aptness of phrasing; firmness of sentence and paragraph structures; use (if any) of figurative expressions; clarity and fluency of style; logical deployment of argument; and overall effectiveness of presentation.

Detailed help with examination questions of this kind is provided in Chapters 2 and 8, together with ample practice material. But you can (and should) start now to prepare yourself for that more advanced work.

Taking the first steps

If you compare what was said earlier about text study (see pages 8 to 10) with what has just been said about work based on unseen material, you will realise that these two areas of an English A Level course have many features in common. That is why you are, in fact, beginning to prepare for tests based on unseen material as soon as you get down to text study. Your work on the prescribed texts teaches you to read carefully and critically; and that is how you must read the unseen passages in the examination.

According to which syllabus you are following, the unseen passages will appear in a paper called by a name such as 'Practical Criticism' or 'Understanding and Appreciation' or 'Comprehension and Comment' or 'Varieties of English'. Whatever title the paper is given, it is a test of your ability to:

- Take in the meaning of a passage.
- Recognise the writer's purposes.
- Judge whether the ways in which language is used in the passage are suited to achieve those purposes.

The reading skills acquired through text study will be there for you to draw on when you tackle the unseen tests in the examination, but it would be a great mistake not to practise using them beforehand. Your coursework will include exercises on unseen material (see, too, Chapters 2 and 7), but do not restrict your practice to the tasks you are given by your teachers or to those provided in this book. Use your everyday reading to test and to develop your ability to read attentively and discerningly.

We all do a lot of 'skim-reading' – and rightly so. Some of the material we read can be taken in quickly and it would be a waste of time to do more than glance through it. Much that we read, however, cannot be understood or appreciated unless we give concentrated attention to its content, its purpose and its style.

So, from time to time, and as a deliberate exercise, after you have read a newspaper article, or a chapter in a book, or a poem:

Pause. Take a sheet of paper and write comments on what you have just read. Use the following headings to guide your thoughts: What? Why? How?

Extending the range of your reading

Because the unseen passages are drawn from such a variety of sources, wide reading is an important aspect of your preparation. Even though it is unlikely that you will have read any of the examination pieces beforehand, you will deal with them much more confidently if you have had previous experience of the kinds of writing they represent. So, in addition to doing the necessary 'background reading' directly associated with your prescribed texts (see Chapter 3), try to extend your reading range.

Be adventurous. Read new authors and new kinds of books – new to you, that is – and see how you get on with them. Approached in the ways described earlier in this chapter, this experimental reading will greatly improve your prospects of doing well in the examination – and some of it will prove to be unexpectedly enjoyable. It is not unusual to discover interest and pleasure in material that seems to be heavy going when first attempted.

Your non-literary reading should include sampling the various periodicals and newspapers ('broadsheet' and 'tabloid') available in college and public libraries. Note their varied (often contrasting) treatment of news items and their sometimes 'loaded' presentation of public issues. Have a look at the pages you have, perhaps, previously ignored: the sections covering the arts (cinema, theatre, television, radio, painting, architecture) and those discussing social questions. Read some of the book reviews: it can be an interesting exercise to compare one critic's opinion of a newly-published volume with that of another.

Those are just a few hints to help you to make the most of your opportunities to read widely and, in so doing, to prepare for the different kinds of unseen material that you will have to comment on when you take the examination.

1.7 Well-written answers

Many examination papers carry a 'health warning'. The wording varies, but the message is always the same. Here is a typical example:

> You are reminded of the necessity for good English and clear presentation in your answers.

Note the word *necessity*. A high standard of written English is not an 'optional extra'. It is a basic requirement. Unless your answers are well-written, you cannot get a good grade.

If the examination papers you take do not include such a reminder, it makes no difference. Like all other English A Level candidates, you will be rewarded for writing well and penalised for writing badly.

As the example just quoted makes clear, your examiners will judge the quality of your written English by these two considerations: (a) Are these answers expressed in good English? and (b) Are they clearly presented?

Good English

Note If you need further help with any of the points made in this section, it is available in the books listed under the heading 'English Language' in the reading list on page 168.

- *Grammar* Not surprisingly, the examiners require correct grammar. English is one of your specialist subjects, so it is reasonable to expect you to use the language without making elementary mistakes. While not demanding 'perfection', examiners deduct marks from candidates who break the basic rules of grammar. (Examples of this would be: using the 'case forms' of the personal pronouns incorrectly, such as writing 'I' where 'me' is required; or 'we' where 'us' is required, and so on; or using a singular verb with a plural subject, or vice versa.) Marks are also deducted, of course, from candidates who write badly-constructed sentences (see page 15).
- *Punctuation* Poor punctuation costs marks. (Examples of this would be: full stops omitted at the ends of sentences; commas omitted where they are needed, or used where they are not needed.) Like grammar, punctuation is an essential means of conveying meaning. When it is under-used, over-used or misused, meaning is lost.
- *Spelling* Although an *occasional* spelling mistake is not regarded as a major weakness, written work that is disfigured by frequent blunders is penalised. (Be especially careful not to misspell the names of the authors you have studied or the names of characters in prescribed texts. To do so is rightly seen as a grossly careless mistake.)

Those three aspects of good English (grammar, punctuation and spelling) constitute 'the mechanics' of writing. If your written coursework is spoilt by errors falling under that heading, your attention will be drawn to them. Study your mistakes and make a determined effort to avoid repeating them. You cannot afford to lose marks in the examination by writing English that does not reach the expected standard of literacy.

Regard each piece of written work as an opportunity to practise your present skills and to acquire new ones. You are serving an apprenticeship to writing and you should work at each task until you are satisfied that it attains the highest standard you can reach.

- *Vocabulary*   Good written English has two basic qualities: (a) correct grammar, punctuation and spelling (see pages 13 and 14); and (b) well-chosen words. Whatever kind of writing you are doing (for example: an essay on a prescribed text; a commentary on an unseen passage; a summary), you need to find words that will convey your meaning accurately, clearly and appropriately. That is why it is so important to have a large vocabulary. (Your vocabulary is the stock of words that you have at your command: you know what they mean; and you know how and when to use them.) Obviously, the larger your vocabulary, the greater the choice of words available to you. You can select the words that are exactly right (that is, accurate, clear and appropriate) for the context in which you are using them. By enlarging your vocabulary, you will quickly raise the standard of your written English (and as a bonus, find much more pleasure in your work). Here are some practical tips: (i) Look up in your dictionary the meaning of any word that you do not understand when you hear or read it; (ii) When you hear or read a word that is being used in a sense that is new to you, look up that particular usage; (iii) If you are in any doubt about the meaning or usage of a word that you are going to use, check it; and (iv) Don't be afraid to experiment when you are writing. Try to find synonyms for the words that first come into your head. One of these may convey your meaning better – more precisely and/or more appropriately – and it will certainly help you to avoid monotonous and unenterprising repetition. If you misuse a 'new' word, your mistake will be pointed out, and you can learn a lot by discussing diction (choice of words).

As that last point suggests, your progress will depend very much on how you approach your written assignments. If you regard them as a necessary but tiresome chore, you will learn little from them. As a student of English, you ought to be able to adopt a much more constructive attitude than that. You are (or you should be) learning to appreciate good writing and taking an interest in the ways in which skilled writers use language for their own particular purposes. A written assignment (of whatever kind) gives you scope to practise skills you admire in other people's writing and to show that you can use language effectively for your own particular purposes. Given that attitude, the importance of correct grammar, punctuation and spelling and the benefit of an extensive vocabulary become self-evident.

A sustained effort to improve your written English will pay off handsomely when you take the examination. Well-written answers make an immediately favourable impression. They identify you at once as a thoughtful and interesting candidate.

Clear presentation

Notes   (i) Detailed advice on planning and writing essays is given in Chapter 6; (ii) Structured writing (with special emphasis on paragraphing and sentence construction) is discussed at length in the books listed in the 'English Language' section of the reading list (page 168). These will provide you with any further help you might need.

The examiners' instructions quoted on page 13 reminded candidates of the necessity for '*clear* presentation'. When giving their candidates a similar reminder, other examiners may prefer to use the term '*orderly* presentation'. In this context, 'clear' and 'orderly' are used as alternatives. They describe two sides of the same coin, so to speak.

> *Orderliness* is the essential basis of *clarity*. To present your answers clearly you must set them out in an orderly way.

Dictionary definitions of the word *orderly* include: 'well arranged'; 'in good order'; 'well regulated'; and 'disciplined'. They all fit the sense in which the word 'orderly' is used in the term 'orderly presentation'. It is helpful to gather all those definitions together and express them in one compound adjective – thus: 'orderly presentation' means '*thoroughly-thought-out-beforehand* presentation'.

- *Well-structured answers*   Whenever you have a piece of writing to do, be guided by this golden rule: 'Don't start writing until you have thought out where you are going and how you are going to get there.' Assemble your 'raw material', then sort it out by deciding where to start; what to say next; and next; and where to finish. Then draw up your plan. Consider it closely. Have you left out anything that ought to be included? Have you included anything that ought to be left out? Is your material arranged in a sensible and clear sequence, moving forward smoothly and steadily from the opening point to the next, and then to the next, and on to the closing point?

- *Well-structured paragraphs*   Here is another golden rule: 'One *main* topic and *only* one in each paragraph.' Announce that topic clearly in the key sentence (often, and better, called 'the *topic* sentence'), which is generally best placed at or near the beginning of the paragraph. The contents of the other sentences should then have a direct bearing on the main topic (this is what is meant by 'paragraph *unity*'). However, while each paragraph should be a self-contained unit of expression, it is at the same time a step or a stage in the larger structure and makes its own distinctive contribution to the whole piece of writing. It is therefore important to show how the main topics dealt with in successive paragraphs are connected with each other. This you can do, either by concluding a paragraph with a 'linking sentence' that leads into the main topic of the next paragraph; or by beginning a paragraph with a 'linking sentence' that connects with the main topic of the preceding paragraph. In this way, you will ensure that your readers recognise the carefully thought-out sequence in which you are presenting your material.

- *Well-structured sentences*   A sentence is 'an independent utterance'. That is to say, it is a word or a group of words that makes complete sense *on its own*. The first word of a written sentence begins with a capital letter. The last word of a written sentence is followed by a full stop. The clarity of your written English depends on your ability to express your meaning in well-made sentences. That is the fundamental writing skill. Test the structures of your own written sentences by reading them aloud. When you hear them you can tell at once whether they make complete sense. You will also know whether they sound pleasing or not. If a sentence does not pass both those tests, reword it. Another benefit of reading aloud what you have written is that it reminds you to vary the structure of your sentences. A succession of sentences that are all constructed on the same pattern is monotonous. Varied sentence lengths and structures help you to express your material in a lively way and to hold the reader's attention. Finally, when you read your own writing aloud, faults of style become apparent. Long-winded phrases, pompous expressions, jargon and slang stand out when you *hear* them. They can then be rewritten in plain, direct and appropriate language.

1.8 Summing up

This introductory chapter has provided an overview of English A Level which will help you to work with a clear sense of direction (see Section 1.1 on page 1). The various areas of study and practice that are included in your course have been identified and described. Constructive ways of approaching them have been suggested; and effective methods of answering different kinds of questions have been outlined. (These methods are explained in more detail in later chapters, where they are used to answer questions taken from examination papers.)

Although the contents of your course and the questions set on them are varied and wide-ranging, they all make similar basic demands and require you to engage in similar mental activities.

(The arrows indicate that these activities are interconnected. The box highlights *organising* to remind you that this plays a crucial role.)

Guided practice 2

2.1 Introduction

These preliminary exercises introduce the kinds of work which may seem especially difficult when you first meet them. The questions are similar to those you will be required to answer in the examination, but they are worded in simpler and more explanatory language. They are also accompanied by notes.

The notes do two things. They explain the particular demands that each kind of question makes; and they show you how to meet those demands. They do not do all the work for you. You still have to arrive at your own answers, but the 'signposts' provided by the notes point you in the right direction.

Working through these exercises will help you to learn an effective question-answering technique based on the approach and the methods demonstrated in the notes.

One final point. Examination questions are often worded in the form of instructions: 'Give an account of . . .' or 'Comment on . . .' or 'State your reasons for . . .' – and so on. For convenience, whatever form they take they are referred to as 'questions'.

2.2 Exercises – with notes

1

Read this poem carefully. Then answer the questions.

Paying Calls

I went by footpath and by stile
    Beyond where bustle ends,
Strayed here a mile and there a mile
    And called upon some friends.

On certain ones I had not seen
  For years past did I call,
And then on others who had been
  The oldest friends of all.

It was the time of midsummer
  When they had used to roam;
But now, though tempting was the air,
  I found them all at home.

I spoke to one and other of them
  By mound and stone and tree
Of things we had done ere days were dim,
  But they spoke not to me.

                                        Thomas Hardy

Questions

1. Give an account of the content of the poem. Brief quotations and detailed references to the poet's words will help you to express your understanding of the content clearly.
2. What seem to you to be the chief features of its style? Give at least one example of each stylistic feature to which you draw attention.
3. Do you think the title is apt? Give reasons for your answer.
4. Describe your response to the poem, illustrating your description with brief quotations and/or close references to the text of the poem.

Notes

Reading the poem carefully

(i)   For the purpose of this exercise your attention is concentrated on one particular poem, but the advice given here applies to your reading of any passage (whether of poetry or prose) on which you have to answer questions.

(ii)   More than one reading is necessary before you start to answer the questions:

- First, read the poem right through. Don't gallop, but don't stop and start. Keep going steadily, taking in the overall meaning and getting involved with the experience that the poem offers. Let it work on you.
- Next, read it again – slowly. Pause at and dwell on any line, phrase or word that you didn't understand at first reading. Having taken in the overall meaning, you will probably understand 'the difficult bits' this time because you can now see what part they play in the poem as a whole.

- Finally, another 'whole' reading. This is when your general understanding (first reading) and your grasp of detail (second reading) come together to complete your *comprehension* of the poem.

Answering the questions

Question 1

(i)   Be sure you understand exactly what you are required to do. 'Give an account of' means 'describe'. What is the meaning of *content*? When that word is used in examination questions (and it often is), it is used in this sense: 'that which is contained in'. So, the instruction is: 'Describe what is contained in the poem.'

(ii)   Having read the poem carefully, you have recognised that what it contains (its *content*) is an account of a personal experience.

(iii) That experience, as set out in the poem, is made up of two elements:
- the narrator's account of what took place; and
- the narrator's emotional response to what took place.

You must include both when you describe the content of the poem.

(iv)   *Check! Are you sure that you have understood what took place? Are you aware of the emotional undertones present in the poem?*

One particular (and dominant) feature of the way in which language is used in this poem makes it essential to carry out those checks. The experience contained in the poem is unfolded in a succession of *apparently* plain and simple statements. But many of those statements are so worded as to suggest another meaning, arising from and going beyond the bare, 'factual' language. The 'basic meaning' of the words is charged with *implications*. Here are some key examples: 'The oldest friends of all' . . . 'I found them all at home' . . . 'By mound and stone' . . . 'But they spoke not to me'.

- **Remember**
  Content = what is stated + what is implied.

Question 2

(i)   Think of 'the *style* of the poem' as meaning: 'the particular ways in which language is used in the poem'. When you are required to consider the chief features of the style (of this poem or of any other passage of writing) bear this simple explanation in mind:
- Content = *what* is expressed.
- Style = *how* it is expressed.

(ii)   You will probably want to comment on two noteworthy features of the style of this poem:
- the choice of words (the *diction*); and
- the verse structure (the *versification*).

(iii) *The choice of words:* the plain, unadorned language in which, by statement and implication (see previous notes), the poet tells of a personal experience that moved him deeply.

(iv)   *The verse structure:* like the language, it is simple. There are four short stanzas (verses), each consisting of: a 4-beat line/a 3-beat line/a 4-beat line/a 3-beat line. A quiet, steady rhythm is maintained – there are no metrical 'fireworks'. There is, however, one striking change in the rhyme pattern. Stanzas 1 and 2 have two pairs of rhyming lines. (The rhyme scheme in both those stanzas is a-b-a-b.) But stanzas 3 and 4 have only one pair of rhyming lines. (The rhyme scheme in both those stanzas of a-b-c-b.) The poet made that change deliberately. (It certainly didn't just 'happen' on its own!) What is its effect? You may not find it easy to answer that question, but keep trying. It is worth the effort because it will involve you very closely with the experience contained in the poem and it will deepen your appreciation of the ways in which that experience is conveyed.

(v)   You are not obliged to make use of everything included in the previous note, but consider all the suggestions made there before writing your answer.

Question 3

(i)   The meaning of 'apt' (as the word is used in this question) is 'fitting' or 'suitable'.

(ii)   Consider the following suggestions:
  ● The title is brief – and so is the poem.
  ● It is simply worded, as is the poem – its basic meaning is easy to grasp, as is the basic meaning of the poem.
  ● *But* the wording of the title, like that of the poem, carries emotional undertones: 'paying calls' is an activity generally associated with sociable interchange, but *here* it refers to a sad and lonely experience.
  ● The contrast between the 'surface meaning' and the 'deep meaning' of the title echoes the ironical tone of the poem.

Question 4

(i)   'Describe your response to the poem.' What is meant by *response*? Think of it like this. You are often asked to describe your response to an experience, though probably not in quite those terms. For example, when people want you to tell them about a film you have seen, they ask questions such as: 'Did you enjoy it?' 'Is it a good film?' 'What did you make of it?' 'Is it worth seeing?' They are, in fact, asking you to describe your *response* to the film.

(ii)   When you are asked such questions you don't just give 'yes' or 'no' answers. (Well, if you do, your questioners soon make it plain that they want to hear some details.) If you say 'Yes' (or, of course, 'No') when asked if you enjoyed it, you go on to tell them *why*. If you say that seeing the film was a worthwhile experience, you go on to describe what you got out of it – what it meant to you – what thoughts and feelings it left you with. In other words, you tell them *how* you responded to the film and you explain *why* you responded to it as you did.

(iii)   When the examiners ask you to describe your response to this poem (or to any other) they want you to tell them whether reading it was (or was not) an interesting, enjoyable and valuable experience for you – and they want you to tell them why.

(iv)   Like everyone else, you have made your *own individual* response to the poem. No two readers of this poem (or of any other) will respond to it in quite the same way – though many will respond to it in similar ways.

(v)   Because your response is essentially a personal matter, it cannot sensibly be judged as being 'the *right* response' or 'the *wrong* response'; and the examiners will not see it in those terms. They have asked you to describe *your* response – the response *you* have genuinely made – and that is what they are interested in.

(vi)   Even so, although they will not judge your response as being 'right' or 'wrong', they will take notice of its *quality* (see note vii below) and they will mark your answer accordingly.

(vii)   When they read your description of the way in which you have responded to this poem (or to any other) the examiners will not be impressed favourably by hasty impressions and snap judgements. They want you to show them that your response is based on close and thoughtful study of the poem.

●   Most importantly, they want you to show them that you have opened your mind to the poet's words and have allowed them to work on your imagination.

(viii)   In addition, the examiners will, of course, assess the quality of your writing and award marks for a well-expressed and well-organised answer (see pages 13–16).

2

This is a test of your skills in summary writing, for which a maximum of 40 marks will be given.

Using the following article as your source, write an account of Dennis Potter's work as a television dramatist. You are restricted to 300 words.

Using your own words as far as possible, you should include (though not necessarily in this order):

(a)   Potter's major plays and their content;
(b)   the artistic ideals to which he was committed;
(c)   the controversial nature of his work; and
(d)   a brief assessment of his work as a writer.

Up to 30 marks will be given for the inclusion of appropriate material.
Up to 10 marks will be given for accuracy and appropriateness of expression.

Dennis Christopher George Potter
born 17 May 1935; died 7 June 1994

In that brave and famous last interview Dennis Potter, who has died aged 59, made what he almost seemed to see as a confession to his audience: 'I do have a sense of vocation . . . I'm proud of it . . . I'm no longer ashamed of saying I have it.'

That sense of being driven by a quasi-religious dedication to his vision and his craft lies under almost everything he has said about the torrent of plays he has poured on to our television screens for nearly 30 years. He described *The Singing Detective*, his most autobiographical work, written in 1985 at the peak of his powers, in directly biblical terms. It was, he said, about a man who picks up his bed and walks. The refrain running though the serial is 'Am I right, or am I right?' a phrase adopted from the pulp of American private eye thrillers, but no less of an aggressive moral challenge for that.

His first television play, *Vote Vote Vote for Nigel Barton*, was produced in 1965. It was the result of two key events: his failed attempt to become a Labour MP in that crucial 1964 election; and the disabling onset of psoriatic arthropathy, the disease that dominated his physical life up to the point earlier this year when he was told that he had terminal cancer.

He was born in 1935, the bright son of a poor miner in the Forest of Dean, and he went up the hill to chapel twice every Sunday. The post-war revolution of the Education Act took him, like many of his generation, to grammar school and then to New College, Oxford, where he edited *Isis*, took his degree in PPE, and wrote his first book, *The Glittering Coffin*. It was a classic young man's state-of-the-nation analysis that still, in parts, sends out shivering echoes: 'We are seeing something akin to a moral disintegration; we are seeing a greater amount of chauvinism, both in the little things like sport and personal relationships, and in the inability to face up to some of the politics of decline, and we are suffering from the collapse of some of the great beliefs of the past decades. The atmosphere is one of polite decay and immense self-deception.'

He went from university to the BBC current affairs department, moved to the *Daily Herald* as a feature writer and then television critic, and was briefly a leader writer when the *Herald* turned into the (pre-Murdoch) *Sun*. Thwarted political ambition, then his worsening physical condition, drove him to write the two *Nigel Barton* plays, because he was unable to do anything else, and he had a wife and three children. He lived by and for writing ever after.

He often felt misunderstood – both by professional critics and by those outraged by his work, most recently and most bitterly over *Blackeyes*, which he saw as a protest against the exploitation of women's bodies and beauty. Others saw only the exploitation itself of an inexperienced actress.

An earlier play, *Brimstone and Treacle*, was banned by the BBC from 1976 to 1987. Despite Mary Whitehouse's threat to have him arraigned for blasphemy, the problem was not that it was about a devil incarnate. The problem was that this ambiguous figure tried to rape a mute, handicapped young girl. The effect was to give her back her voice, which she used to accuse her father, and Potter saw the play as a parable about how evil deeds can have good consequences, and vice versa.

Despite the ban, the BBC in the late seventies when Potter wrote two of his finest plays – *Blue Remembered Hills* and *Pennies From Heaven* – remained his icon of what a public service broadcasting organisation should be.

The rows over both *Brimstone* and *Blackeyes* were partly caused by that tunnel vision a sense of vocation induces. He saw his plays in the crystal purity of his conception of them. And because he was without question the most innovative and at his best the most brilliant television writer of his time, his vision was respected, and was usually right.

In the early Thatcher years some plays, like *Blade On The Feather* and (despite its Prix Italia) *Cream In My Coffee*, seemed flat and sour. And adapting other writers' texts was rarely a success, except in keeping him going: neither Scott Fitzgerald's *Tender Is The Night* nor Christabel Bielenberg's story of her war years in Germany added to Potter's reputation.

But his best work changed television drama for ever, because it expanded the medium and defied its dogged naturalism. He was lucky to be writing for the small screen as television drama emerged from the restrictions – or creative challenges – of studio production and live transmission. More important, his innovations were not driven by technical changes, but by the need to find metaphors for what he most urgently wanted to convey.

So the adults acting the roles of children in *Blue Remembered Hills* both magnified the cruelty of childhood behaviour and signified our inability to grow out of it. The popular songs of *Pennies From Heaven* were not period decoration. They expressed exactly how a class-ridden society in the Depression found a way to comfort itself by singing out its hopes and its repressed emotions. 'Cheap songs, so called,' he said, 'do have something of the Psalms of David about them. They do say the world is other than it is.'

The Singing Detective was more complex. It used the songs ironically, chuckling at itself as *Pennies* did not. And the third serial of dramas-with-music, last year's *Lipstick On Your Collar*, though not as successful or as enthralling, did what was most needed after the disaster of *Blackeyes*. It proved that Potter could not stand still. It gave a political edge to the form he had developed to combine popular entertainment with social comment. From what he has said about his two plays yet to be seen, *Karaoke* and *Cold Lazarus*, Potter never did stand still. He was climbing the hill to the chapel right to the end.

Hugh Hebert: *The Guardian*, 8 June 1994

Notes

Check your instructions

(i) Write an account of Dennis Potter's work *as a television dramatist*. Because the article from which you are to draw your material is an obituary, it includes a brief account of Potter's life as well as an appraisal of his work for television. Consequently, you have to decide which (if any) of the biographical material in the article is relevant to the task you have been set.

- The biographical material referred to by Hugh Hebert *when discussing Potter's plays* is relevant.
- None of the other biographical material is relevant and it should *not* be included in your answer. For your purpose, it is not 'appropriate material' (see the marking scheme on page 21).

(ii) You are to use the article *as your source*. The material used in your account of Potter's work for television must be drawn solely from the article.
- Do not add to it, alter it, or comment on it.
- 'Straight reporting' of the relevant material in the article is what is required.

(iii) Your account *must not exceed 300 words*. Be sure to keep within that word limit.
- You will lose marks if you exceed the word limit.

There are approximately 1400 words in the article, but because only some of the material is relevant to your task (see note i) 300 words is a reasonable limit.

(iv) Your account must be written *in your own words* as far as possible. Find your own way of expressing the material you take from the article.
- Do *not* copy out Hebert's words.

You may, however, use words and short phrases from the article for which there is no brief and accurate equivalent. Examples of expressions it would be permissible to use are: 'social comment'; 'naturalism'; 'innovations'; 'dramas-with-music'.

An effective method of working

Study the article carefully (see the advice about reading on pages 18 and 19). Then proceed step-by-step, in this manner:

First: Select from the article all the relevant material and note it down.
Next: Decide on the order in which it can best be presented.
Next: Write a draft of your answer.
Next: Revise the draft – check the accuracy of its content, prune it if it is too long, make sure it is clearly and correctly expressed.
Finally: Write a fair copy of the revised draft.

Each of these steps will now be considered in detail.

Selecting the relevant material and noting it down

(i) The instructions list four subjects that you should include in your account of Potter's work. Use that list as the framework for the notes you make on the content of the article.

(ii) Write down on your working sheets four headings, each corresponding to one of the four listed subjects. Leave plenty of space below each heading. Divide that space into two columns.

(iii) Select from the article all the material that is relevant to each of the four listed subjects and note it down under its appropriate heading. Enter in the first column material that you decide *must* be included in your account of that particular subject. Enter in the second column material that you decide *might* be included in your account of that particular subject *if there is room for it.* (Remember that you have a limited number of words to use in your summary.)

This example illustrates the recommended method.

Subject (d): A brief assessment of Potter's work

Material that must be included	*Material that might be included*
He changed the nature of television drama – permanently enlarged its scope – refused to conform to its rooted naturalism . . . etc.	Comparative failure of his dramatisations of other people's work – not what he will be remembered for . . . etc.

- *Caution 1*
  When noting down the relevant material put it in your own words as far as possible. If you copy out the writer's words you risk repeating them in the draft and again in the fair copy.
- *Caution 2*
  Bear in mind that material relevant to each of the four stipulated subjects is spaced out in the article. For example, material relevant to 'Subject (b)' (Potter's artistic ideals) appears in several places – at the beginning, again later, and again at the end. Search through the article thoroughly when collecting the material for each subject.
- *Caution 3*
  Check that you are placing each item under its appropriate heading. For example, where should Hebert's comments about *Blade On The Feather* and *Cream In My Coffee* be placed? *Not* under 'Subject (a)'. Perhaps under 'Subject (d)'? And, if that is the place for them, should they be classified as 'essential' material or as 'if-space-permits' material? It is very important to make the right decisions at this stage of the work. You are now collecting and *sorting out* material on which you will base an *accurate* and *balanced* account of Potter's work.

Deciding on the order in which you will present the material

(i)   The instructions make clear that it is for you to decide on the order of presentation.

(ii)   Because a summary should be a passage of *continuous* prose, it would not be suitable to include the headings used in your notes. You have to present the required subject matter in a clear, logical sequence – in well-constructed paragraphs, but without internal headings.
   - Your aim should be to *shape* the summary so that it progresses smoothly: *from* its beginning, *through* its middle, *to* its end.

(iii) The order in which the stipulated subjects are listed in the instructions suggests a suitable shape for the summary, but it requires some adjustment:

Beginning of summary:	Subject (a).
Middle of summary:	Subjects (b) and (c).
End of summary:	Subject (d).

The suitability of beginning with 'Subject (a)' and of ending with 'Subject (d)' is self-evident. It then follows that 'Subject (b)' and 'Subject (c)' must be covered in the middle section.

- *But* careful planning and *distribution of emphasis* are needed to cover both subjects in one section *while giving due weight to each*.

You are bound to meet this kind of problem when writing a summary. The need to express the *gist* of a much longer passage in comparatively few words compels you to decide on *priorities*. In this particular instance, given the fact that all four listed subjects must be included in the summary, how can they be covered adequately within the permitted length?

- By paying careful attention to the degree of emphasis given to each subject in the article. Which subjects does the writer treat as being of more importance and which as being of less importance?
- By then giving more emphasis (and more space) in the summary to the more important subjects. Remember that there is little (if any) room in the summary for material that the writer of the article uses to introduce, support or illustrate its main points.

(iv)   If you have noted the content of the article accurately you will recognise that Hugh Hebert links the controversial nature of Potter's work ('Subject (c)') with his commitment to his artistic ideals ('Subject (b)'). He maintains that audiences were bound to be shocked by plays written in accordance with those ideals. Although he describes the controversies at some length, he puts more *emphasis* on Potter's ideals. Note, too, that it is 'the controversial *nature* of Potter's work' (*not* the controversies themselves) that you are instructed to include in the summary. Bearing those points in mind, it would be suitable to include both 'Subject (b)' and 'Subject (c)' in the middle section of the summary, giving more emphasis (and space) to (b) than to (c). Refer explicitly, but very briefly, to 'Subject (c)', but exclude the illustrative details provided in the article.

(v)   Having sorted that out, you might plan your summary like this:

Beginning   'Subject (a)'.
    Include only the *major* plays (as instructed). Exclude those that Hebert regards as less important.

Middle   'Subject (c)' *followed by* 'Subject (b)'.
    Reverse the order as listed in the instructions. This reflects the respective emphasis given to these two subjects in the article. The middle section of the summary might then start something like this: 'The violent controversies aroused by some of Potter's plays (notably *Brimstone And Treacle* and *Blackeyes*) were the inevitable outcome of his artistic ideals. He did not write to offer his audiences cosy entertainment, but to confront them with a disturbing view of human nature and society . . .'. Express it in your own way. The wording suggested is simply an illustration of how the two subjects might be combined, giving due weight (but few words) to (c) by emphasising its essential connection with (b).

End   'Subject (d)'.
    Handling the middle section of the summary in the way just suggested provides a suitable lead-in to the brief assessment

of Potter's work with which you will end. Give it a paragraph to itself and be sure to include the chief points made in the article: that Potter's commitment to his artistic ideals drove him to develop new ways of writing; and that his innovatory techniques transformed television drama.

The plan outlined there would be effective, but you may have other and better ideas. In any case, further material is needed to complete each section of the plan before the draft summary can be written.

It takes time to prepare a well-considered plan in the way just demonstrated, but you cannot write an accurate and balanced summary until you have collected *and sorted out* the material you need.

Writing a draft of the summary

(i) Begin by writing out the title of the summary in full: 'An account of Dennis Potter's work as a television dramatist: based on the obituary by Hugh Hebert in *The Guardian*, 8 June 1994.' (The words used in the title will not be included in the word count.) The title of a summary (of this article or of any other passage) should indicate very briefly its content and identify its source.

(ii) Then write the draft from your notes. If your plan is well-ordered and sufficiently detailed, you will not need to extract any more (or any different) material from the article. If you are in doubt about the accuracy of an item in your notes (you shouldn't be!) you can, of course, check it. But it is not a good practice to re-read the passage while you are writing your draft summary. First, because you might start using the writer's words instead of your own. Second, because you might give undue emphasis to a point you have gone back to, and that would unbalance the summary.

(iii) Write the draft in plain, direct and *concise* language – no figurative expressions or 'frills' of any kind, no superfluous words, and no long-winded phrases. Use short sentences wherever possible. Pay careful attention to grammar, punctuation and spelling.

Revising the draft

(i) Count the number of words (excluding those used in the title).

(ii) If the draft is too long (by even one word) you must shorten it.

(iii) If it is just a few words too long you can probably reduce it to the permitted length by pruning and polishing its style, cutting out superfluous words, condensing phrases and tightening sentences.

(iv) If it is much too long revise its content as well as its style. Have you included inappropriate material? Have you included unnecessary details?

(v) If your draft is well *below* the permitted length, that is a danger signal. Look at its content again. Have you omitted essential material? If so, it must now be included (in its appropriate place – *not* simply tacked on at the end).

Writing a fair copy

Do this when you are satisfied that your draft of the summary meets the following requirements.

- It is within the permitted length.
- It is an accurate and balanced account of the material you were instructed to summarise.
- It is a readable piece of writing: well-organised, clearly and correctly expressed.

3

The passage below is taken from the opening of a novel, *Beloved*, by Toni Morrison.

Read the passage carefully, and then write a critical analysis of it. Consider such matters as the presentation of the characters, the description of period and place, the way in which the passage develops, the appropriateness of the passage as the opening of a novel, and the style in which the passage is written.

124 was spiteful. Full of a baby's venom. The women in the house knew it and so did the children. For years each put up with the spite in his own way, but by 1873 Sethe and her daughter Denver were its only victims. The grandmother, Baby Suggs, was dead, and the sons, Howard and Buglar, had run away by the time they were thirteen years old – as soon as merely looking in a mirror shattered it (that was the signal for Buglar); as soon as two tiny hand prints appeared in the cake (that was it for Howard). Neither boy waited to see more; another kettleful of chickpeas smoking in a heap on the floor; soda crackers crumbled and strewn in a line next to the door-sill. Nor did they wait for one of the relief periods: the weeks, months even, when nothing was disturbed. No. Each fled at once – the moment the house committed what was for him the one insult not to be borne or witnessed a second time. Within two months, in the dead of winter, leaving their grandmother, Baby Suggs; Sethe, their mother; and their little sister, Denver, all by themselves in the gray and white house on Bluestone Road. It didn't have a number then, because Cincinnati didn't stretch that far. In fact, Ohio had been calling itself a state only seventy years when first one brother and then the next stuffed quilt packing into his hat, snatched up his shoes, and crept away from the lively spite the house felt for them.

Baby Suggs didn't even raise her head. From her sickbed she heard them go but that wasn't the reason she lay still. It was a wonder to her that her grandsons had taken so long to realize that every house wasn't like the one on Bluestone Road. Suspended between the nastiness of life and the meanness of the dead, she couldn't get interested in leaving life or living it, let alone the fright of two creeping-off boys. Her past had been like her present – intolerable – and since she knew death was anything but forgetfulness, she used the little energy left her for pondering color.

'Bring a little lavender in, if you got any. Pink, if you don't.'

And Sethe would oblige her with anything from fabric to her own tongue.

Winter in Ohio was especially rough if you had an appetite for color. Sky provided the only drama, and counting on a Cincinnati horizon for life's principal joy was reckless indeed. So Sethe and the girl Denver did what they could, and what the house permitted, for her. Together they waged a perfunctory battle against the outrageous behavior of that place; against turned-over slop jars, smacks on the behind, and gusts of sour air. For they understood the source of the outrage as well as they knew the source of light.

Baby Suggs died shortly after the brothers left, with no interest whatsoever in their leave-taking or hers, and right afterward Sethe and Denver decided to end the persecution by calling forth the ghost that tried them so. Perhaps a conversation, they thought, an exchange of views or something would help. So they held hands and said, 'Come on. Come on. You may as well just come on.'

The sideboard took a step forward but nothing else did.

'Grandma Baby must be stopping it,' said Denver. She was ten and still mad at Baby Suggs for dying.

Sethe opened her eyes. 'I doubt that,' she said.

'Then why don't it come?'

'You forgetting how little it is,' said her mother. 'She wasn't even two years old when she died. Too little to understand. Too little to talk much even.'

'Maybe she don't want to understand,' said Denver.

'Maybe. But if she'd only come, I could make it clear to her.' Sethe released her daughter's hand and together they pushed the sideboard back against the wall. Outside a driver whipped his horse into the gallop local people felt necessary when they passed 124.

'For a baby she throws a powerful spell,' said Denver.

'No more powerful than the way I loved her,' Sethe answered.

Notes

A student's answer; with comments

Number 124 Bluestone Road – the house in which Sethe and her sons, Howard and Buglar, and her daughter, Denver, lived, together with the children's grandmother, Baby Suggs – is troubled by a spiteful presence. At the beginning of the passage we learn that it is the ghost of a baby (the house is 'full of a baby's venom'). At the end, when she tells Denver how powerfully she loved the baby, it becomes clear that the dead infant was Sethe's child.

True – but is it relevant? You were asked to write a critical analysis of the passage not to re-tell the story.

It is perhaps not quite accurate to refer to the presence as 'a ghost'. We are not told that it has been seen, and the malicious tricks it plays (the shattered mirror, the overturned slop jars, and so on) are the spiteful activities of a poltergeist rather than 'hauntings' in the strict sense of that term.

An interesting 'aside' – but way off the point; and you have forgotten that the presence is referred to as 'the ghost that tried them so.'

Whatever it was, the presence drove Sethe's sons out of the house. By the time they were thirteen both boys had run away from home to escape 'the lively spite the house felt for them'. Soon after they went, their grandmother died. By 1873 Sethe and ten-year-old Denver were left alone in the house to face the intermittent terrors of its supernatural visitations.

A well-expressed description of the opening situation, but it doesn't get you anywhere. You were not asked to summarise the content of the passage.

The account of Baby Suggs' last days makes us keenly aware of the past and present sufferings of this afflicted family. From her bed she heard her

Yes; but now does our awareness of this affect our response to the passage? You are not <u>using</u> your insight to make a critical point.

An imaginative comment on a difficult part of the passage. Well done! This could be developed into a major critical point.

Careful! You are simply re-telling the story here – <u>and</u> relying far too much on copying out the author's words.

Here – at last – you are getting to grips with the question. Some important critical points made, which should have been introduced and <u>developed</u> earlier. The space wasted on side issues should have been given to the matters raised in this final para.

grandsons departing, but made no attempt to stop them. Her own experience had been so wretched that she was now uninterested 'in leaving life or living it, let alone the fright of two creeping-off boys'. In the time remaining to her she found what solace she could in contemplating the colour that life had denied her. The fabrics that Sethe and Denver brought for her to touch and gaze upon afforded her some distraction from the bleakness of existence, symbolised by the harsh and colourless Ohio winter during which she died.

The passage ends with a description of the two survivors attempting to bring the troubled spirit out of the darkness in which it hides. Sethe believed that if she could see her dead child and talk to her she could help her to understand. The hauntings would then cease. Their challenge ('Come on. Come on. You may as well just come on.') is fruitless: 'The sideboard took a step forward but nothing else did.' Sethe and her living daughter are the helpless victims of her dead daughter's 'powerful spell'.

This passage is a very good opening of a novel. It introduces the characters and sets them in vividly-described surroundings. The situation in which they are trapped grips the reader's interest and is made the more tense by being conveyed in hints rather than being fully explained. By so skilfully creating and maintaining suspense in this way, the author calls on us to use our imagination. After reading this passage I wanted to learn more about the people in the story and to discover what happened to them. I think that anyone who reads this passage will want to read the book.

<u>Overall comment</u>
This is well written, and it shows that you have read the passage carefully and imaginatively. But because much of what you say is irrelevant to the task you were set, the examiners would not be able to give you a good mark. Have another go; and this time, <u>organise</u> your answer so that it explores the ideas introduced (but not developed) in the last paragraph.

Because the writer did not carry out the instructions that was not a satisfactory answer – although it had some good qualities. Try now to write a better answer, but study the next two sections of these notes before you do so.

Study the instructions: note the key points

(i)   Reminders
- As they are used in English A Level studies, the terms 'criticism' and 'critical' signify *appreciation*. (See Chapter 1, especially page 9. See also Guided Practice 1 in this chapter.)
- An appreciation (or criticism) of a passage of writing is a *reasoned* statement of the critic's opinion of its merits.
- Recommended procedure: (a)   Decide what the writer's aims were; (b)   Study the content and the style of the passage closely *in the light of those aims*; and (c)   Consider whether the writer's choice and treatment of subject matter and use of language persuade you to respond to the passage in the way you were intended to.

(ii)   The instructions for answering this question are similar to those you will be given in the examination. They are lengthy, but they are meant to be helpful – as, indeed, they are, *provided* that you study them closely and follow the guidelines they suggest.

(iii)   Note, first, that you are to write 'a critical analysis' of the passage. The meaning of 'critical' should be clear to you by now. The term *analysis* is used to indicate that you should identify the leading features of the content and of the style of the passage, and consider carefully what each contributes to the overall impact that the passage makes on you.

(iv)   If you pay close attention to the next sentence in the instructions ('Consider such matters as . . .') you will recognise that it provides the basis of the plan on which you should construct your answer. One of the matters listed for consideration is: 'the *appropriateness* of the passage *as the opening of a novel*'. Take that as the key point of your critical analysis, then consider the other matters in relation to it.

Thinking it out: some suggestions

Consider the following points. Make use of any you agree with, developing and expressing them in your own way. Add to and alter them as you think fit.

(i)   The appropriateness of the passage as the opening of a novel

(a)   How is that to be judged? By its success in exciting our interest and making us want to read the book.

(b)   Does Toni Morrison do that? If so, how?

(c)   Consider the matters listed in the instructions to explore the means by which she draws us into the experience embodied in this passage, engaging us with her characters and with their situation.

(ii)   The presentation of the characters

(a)   Note how little there is by way of 'static' description of their appearance and personality. They are presented abruptly: named, identified by their family relationships, and that is all. Yet we are intensely aware of them. They enter our minds.

(b)   Perhaps it is because we cannot separate them from their terrible situation that we are so affected by them? It is in relation to the 'outrage' that we know them. Even the two 'creeping-off boys' who so soon depart from the story are memorable – not as individuals but as victims, escaping from the unendurable 'insult' – but at what cost to themselves and to those they leave behind?

(c)   The others, their lives dominated by the malign presence, do what they can, bonded by their family ties, by their shared suffering, and by their courage in enduring.

(d)   Striking individual attributes begin to emerge as events unfold. *Baby Suggs*: Our awareness of her is intensified by the account of her dying – the poignant symbolism of her contemplation of colour (see the comment on this in the student's answer studied earlier) – this helpless old woman, made indifferent by her sorrows to both living and dying, commands our attention, our respect and our grief – the origins of her suffering lie deep in her past, long preceding the present outrage and its cause – her fearful knowledge that death 'was anything but forgetfulness' (echoed by her granddaughter) – the past invades the present, maiming the affections of the living and their memory of the dead. *Sethe*: begins to assume a leading role – decisive action (with Denver) 'to end the persecution' – courage (dares to confront the source of tribulation) – endurance – great capacity for love – a moral stature here which will surely influence the development of events – a hint of ruthlessness? Is her love for her dead child a threat to her living daughter? *Denver*: Although only ten, she has much of her mother's strength – courage to act and to endure – keenly aware of the loss of her grandmother – angered by sense of desertion – did she see her as an ally? – Against the dead child? Against her mother? Burdened by a terrible inheritance of which we (and she) have as yet only partial knowledge.

(iii)   The description of period and place

(a)   Specific information about period and place is provided. We are told that Sethe and Denver were the sole living occupants of the house by 1873; that the two sons left by the time they were thirteen; that Baby Suggs died soon after that, in winter. The house is identified as 124 Bluestone Road. It is situated in the distant outskirts of Cincinnati in the State of Ohio, USA. We are given two more pieces of precise 'historical' information: when the boys left, the house did not have a number because Cincinnati had not by that time expanded so far as to include Bluestone Road; and Ohio had been calling itself a State for only seventy years.

(b)   What purpose does this 'factual' description of period and place serve? It anchors the story in 'the real world' – assures us of the *actuality* of the setting – helps to persuade us to accept the 'reality' of events that might otherwise strain our credence. 'At such a time and in such a place,' the writer affirms, 'such things as these happened to people such as these.'

(c)   Note, too, how the 'facts' themselves become embedded in the imaginary world created in the passage – 124 Bluestone Road encloses its inhabitants in its spite – and is itself enclosed in a harshly implacable environment, surrounded by a winter landscape, bounded by a Cincinnati horizon –

distanced from the city's inhabitants, whose attitude we do not yet know, but fearfully guess at: the driver who whips his horse to a gallop is doing 'what local people felt necessary when they passed 124.'

(iv)   The way in which the passage develops

(a)   It opens with two stark and shocking statements, seizing our attention.

(b)   Then, partly by 'flashback', it provides sufficient (but no more than just sufficient) information about setting, situation, characters and past and present events to excite our interest and arouse our expectations. This 'expository' section of the passage draws us into the lives of people whose terrible situation compels our concern for them.

(c)   Then comes the dying of Baby Suggs (see note iii).

(d)   After Baby Suggs' death (and, it seems, as a consequence of it) there follows the tense incident when Sethe and Denver challenge the tormenting spirit, whose identity is now revealed to us. The passage opened with a shock and it closes with another.

(e)   Its development through the phases just described helps to make this passage an effective opening of the novel. Seeming at first to offer the excitement of a ghost story, it quickly makes us aware of deeper concerns, stirring our pity and fear for people caught up in a terrifying situation. It intensifies suspense by progressively isolating Sethe and Denver. Then, at the end, it reveals that the surviving victims are linked with their tormentor, to whom Sethe feels compelled to make something clear. Our wish to discover what that is gives us a strong incentive to read the book.

(v)   The style in which the passage is written

(a)   What features of Toni Morrison's writing help to make this passage an effective opening of her novel? (Consider the following suggestions. Do not accept them uncritically. Refer to the passage to check that there is evidence to support them. Use those you agree with as the starting point for your own comments on the style.)

(b)   Packed with material – about the setting, about the people and their situation, about past and present happenings (see previous notes) – the passage makes considerable demands on our attention – there is a lot to take in; and much of the material refers to circumstances remote from our experience.

(c)   To be effective, this material must be presented in such a way that we are intrigued, but not baffled. The writer must excite our interest without overloading it.

(d)   Pursuing that aim, she writes *lucidly*: short sentences; careful punctuation; no superfluous words; no 'clutter'.

(e)   Very few adjectives; and those she uses are precise. Nouns and verbs do most of the work.

(f)   No 'word-painting' – short, crisp descriptions and bare, 'undecorated' statements work on our imagination.

(g)   Quiet, restrained but compelling 'story-teller's' voice – we *listen* to her – and we listen to the few words her characters utter, and we note the striking idioms of their speech.

(h)   Economy and compression of language – yet it is suggestive and dynamic – the pace is remarkable, but never breathless or forced.

3 Reminders

3.1 What English A Level examinations test

Because each examining board has its own syllabus for English A Level, candidates for the examinations of the various boards study different set books. The contents of the examination papers also vary from board to board. For example, whereas one board may set questions on the specified Shakespeare plays in Paper 1, another board may set its questions on Shakespeare in Paper 2, reserving its Paper 1 for questions on Chaucer and Milton. One board may combine questions involving critical commentary on passages from the set texts with context questions. Another board may set critical commentary questions in a separate paper.

Candidates must therefore be familiar with the syllabus and regulations of their own board, studying the texts prescribed by that board and aware of which texts and which authors will appear in each paper.

Despite their differences, all English A Level examinations are based on similar views of the attainments, aptitudes and skills which should be fostered by its study and which, therefore, may be expected of its students. In consequence, as the various syllabuses and the kinds of questions set make clear, all the examining boards design their papers and questions to test their candidates in certain common areas of knowledge, judgement and skills, good performance in which is proof of a successful course of study.

● All English A Level examinations are tests of:

    (i) *Knowledge* – of the set books and, where relevant, knowledge of the particular circumstances (personal and/or historical) in which they were written.

    (ii) *Understanding* – ranging from straightforward factual comprehension to awareness of the deeper meanings and subtler significances conveyed by the texts.

(iii) *Analytical skill* – the ability to recognise and describe literary effects and to explain how an author uses language to bring those effects about.

(iv) *Judgement* – the capacity to discriminate in matters of value (both those arising from content and those arising from style), and to support such value judgements with close references to and quotations from the texts under consideration.

(v) *Awareness of literary tradition* – recognition of the continuing vitality of the past as an influence on later writers: the ability to place a text in its historical as well as its contemporary context.

(vi) *Personal response* – the capacity to respond individually to the experience afforded by a text and to write about it in such a way as to reveal that there has been a 'meeting' – an interplay of minds – between author and student.

(vii) *Writing skill* – the ability to write clear, cogent English prose and to confine the contents of each answer to those matters that are relevant to the question set.

These are difficult tests; and rightly so, because the examinations measure your capacity to profit from an *advanced* course of study. Even so, there is nothing in their nature to dismay any student who works hard to acquire the necessary knowledge of set texts, authors and periods and learns how to *use* that knowledge in the ways taught by the guided practice and worked examples in this book.

3.2 The kinds of questions set

Different boards have their own distinctive ways of wording their examination questions. Nevertheless, since all English A Level examinations are based on common attitudes to the subject and make similar demands on their candidates, every question belongs to one or another of certain well-defined groups, according to the particular area of knowledge, judgement and skill which it is designed to test.

● English A Level examination questions are of the following kinds:

(a) context questions on set books, with questions on the meaning of particular words and phrases;
(b) critical commentaries on passages from set books;
(c) essay questions;
(d) 'unseen' passages for critical appreciation; and
(e) 'unseen' passages for comprehension, with questions on 'varieties of English'.

Each type of question is dealt with in a separate chapter of this book, where its problems are discussed, and ways of solving those problems are demonstrated step-by-step.

3.3 The time factor

The time allowed for each paper and the number of questions to be answered vary from board to board and from paper to paper. Four questions to be answered in a three-hour paper is the most common requirement, but you must find out what your own board expects of you in each of its papers, and you must practise writing answers within the permitted time span. Too many candidates spread themselves on the first answers they write and leave insufficient time for the later ones.

During your preparation – and, of course, in the examination room – pay attention to the marks allotted to each question, or to each part of a question. They tell you the relative amount of time you should spend on each. Your answer to a question carrying four marks does not merit the same time and space as your answer to a question carrying ten or twenty marks. It is surprising how often candidates ignore that obvious fact.

Never omit a question. However well you answer the others, you cannot score more than the maximum number of marks allotted to each, and a missing answer costs you all the marks allotted to that. If you have allowed yourself to spend too much time on your first answers, try to jot down at least an outline of your answer to the last question. That is much more sensible than writing the first few lines of your answer and then breaking off. A clear indication of the contents of the answer you would have given – even if you have only a minute or two in which to sketch in the main points – may earn you a precious mark or two. But it must be emphasised that a well-prepared and well-organised candidate does not get rushed into a hasty salvage operation.

The time factor causes much of the tension that many candidates experience. It is often the reason for a performance that is well below the standard of which they are capable when free from its pressures.

But the time factor exists as an inescapable condition under which examinations are taken, so you must learn to think and write against the clock, making the best use of the limited time at your disposal. Subsequent chapters of this book provide detailed advice on coping with the problem as it arises in answering questions of each different kind. Here are some general hints to help you during preparation and when you are sitting in the examination room, whatever the paper and whatever the kind of question in front of you.

- Thorough knowledge of your set books, authors and periods is the surest shield against panic. A well-informed candidate is likely to be a confident candidate, not easily rattled by examination pressures.
- As you study, learn by heart brief quotations from your authors and from the critics you find most illuminating. Use them to support your statements of fact and of opinion. A short, relevant quotation makes a point swiftly and authoritatively. (But be careful. Having learnt a lot of questions, some candidates drag them into their answers by the scruff of the neck, regardless of their relevance to the point being made or the question being answered. You won't gain any marks merely by showing the examiners that you have memorised chunks of your set books. The worked examples in this book show you how to make telling use of quotations. Note, too, the advice in Chapter 9 on how to handle prose quotations, especially when writing about novels.)
- Practise writing answers within the allotted time span, not merely in the last few days before you take the examination but throughout your period of preparation. Train for it systematically, just as an athlete trains to run a given distance in a given time. Careful and protracted thought about your books and authors is needed throughout your preparation, and frequent,

timed practice in answering examination questions is just as important. At first, you will find it hard to cover the ground at the required pace but, if you begin regular and disciplined training early on in your course of study, you will speed up and learn how to keep your head when the pressure is on.

- Never confuse quantity with quality. The examiners will not weigh your answers! – or award any marks for sheer bulk and length. Many candidates think that they are losing marks unless they are scribbling furiously all the time. Not a bit of it. Time spent in thinking out your material and planning the best way of presenting it is an essential preliminary to writing a good answer. Throughout your preparation, you must take time to think and plan before you begin to write. Similarly, you must allow time for reading through and correcting your answer.

3.4 Common mistakes

Ignorance! Not knowing your subject is the surest way to get a poor grade. But some candidates who do know quite a lot about their books and authors still find it hard to reach a high standard in the examination. In later chapters, you will be shown how to avoid the mistakes that are made most frequently when answering particular kinds of questions. Before we consider specific problems, however, it will be useful to look at a check-list of the general weaknesses present in many A Level scripts. The list that follows has been compiled from examiners' reports. (As you will see, it overlaps with some of the points made earlier in this chapter.) While you are studying it, bear in mind that these are not traps cunningly laid by the examiners: they are traps that candidates set for themselves and into which, carelessly, they fall.

- *Badly planned answers*, the contents of which are set out haphazardly. Candidates do not keep separate points separate; nor do they arrange their material in a clear and sensible order. Their answers stand still or – worse – go round in circles. The importance of a clearly structured answer, with a beginning, a middle and an end, is not generally appreciated.
- *Careless paragraphing*. Candidates have little sense of paragraph unity on the one hand, and of the need to supply paragraph links on the other. Lack of clear 'turning points' and 'connectives' make their answers hard to read.
- *Reliance on quantity rather than quality*. Candidates cram their answers with a mass of unsorted, undigested material, much of which is irrelevant to the question set.
- *Lack of quotation or close reference to the text* weakens the arguments advanced and the views expressed. By failing to provide textual evidence in support of their answers, candidates too often appear ill-informed about their subject and shallow in their judgements.
- *Poor sentence construction, incorrect grammar, faulty punctuation, limited vocabulary*. Many scripts fail to reach the standard of literacy expected of English A Level candidates.
- AND – commonest of all the common errors – *the cardinal mistake of **narrating** the contents of a set book instead of **commenting** on them*. Candidates most often make this fatal blunder when they are writing about plays and novels.

3.5 Background reading

Close study of your set books is your first concern, but you must also find time to read round them. The range and the nature of the questions set in the examination give you the opportunity of putting wider reading to good use, and your answers will get higher grades if you can do so.

You may find it difficult to plan a useful and manageable programme of extra reading, so here are some practical tips.

Keep it short. It is better to read a few books thoughtfully than to read a lot superficially, so don't be too ambitious.

The editorial matter (introduction and notes) in your set books will probably suggest some further reading on your authors and texts. Use those suggestions as your starting point. Then look round your local bookshop and dip into the various critical commentaries now readily available on a great many writers. You will soon see which of them are likely to be most useful to you and worth getting. You will also need to refer to a history of English Literature and one or two other standard reference books. (You will find further details in 'Further Reading'.)

Plan your reading methodically. You should aim to cover some ground in each of these areas: comparative reading; critical reading; historical and biographical reading; and technical studies.

Comments now follow on each of those four areas of additional reading. You can adapt the examples given to suit the requirements of your own list of set books.

(i) *Comparative reading* Read as much as you can of other work by each of your set book authors. For example, if Keats' *Hyperion* is a set book, read *Endymion, The Fall of Hyperion* and the *Odes* too. If *Hamlet* is a set book, read at least two of Shakespeare's other tragedies as well. Detailed study is not required, but your understanding and appreciation of your set book will be greatly increased by thoughtful reading of some of its writer's other work.

(ii) *Critical reading* Do not overload yourself by attempting too much. In any case, you will learn more by comparative reading than by studying critics. If *The Return of the Native* is a set book and you have to choose between finding time to read another of Hardy's novels and reading what critics have written about Hardy, read Hardy. Nevertheless, on each set book and author, you can find some critical reading that will increase your understanding and add to your pleasure. The editors of your set books will point you in the right direction.

Critical reading should include study of the *genre* of each set book. For example, if you are studying *Paradise Lost*, you need to know something about the characteristic features of an epic poem, and of how Milton's treatment of this genre is both similar to and different from that of other epic poets. All writers work within literary traditions of which they are fully aware; and their writing is shaped by those traditions, whether by conforming to them or by modifying them.

(iii) *Historical and biographical reading* Literature is written by gifted people who are, as a rule, strongly individual; but it is also, in part, the product of an age. It bears the marks of its period. That is why this kind of background reading is so illuminating. If a novel by Dickens is a set book, you will get much more out of it if you know something about his life and times and about the work of his contemporaries.

(iv)   *Technical studies*   Papers on critical appreciation and papers on varieties of English, like all critical commentaries and many essay questions, require you to explore the ways in which specific uses of language affect your thoughts and feelings. That is why you need to have some knowledge of the 'mechanics' of verse and prose writing. You do not have to be an expert prosodist or grammarian, but it is much easier to write clearly and to make your points pithily if you can use the standard (and, therefore, unambiguous) technical terms. For example, you should be familiar with such terms as 'blank verse', 'heroic couplets', 'end-stopped lines', 'onomatopoeia' and 'assonance'. (See 'Further Reading', where books that provide definitions and illustrations of literary terms are listed.)

But never – ever! – imagine that you are adding to the merits of your answers merely by sticking technical labels on an author's words. It is pointless to identify, say, internal rhyming, or a particular metre, or alliteration unless you have something illuminating to say about the writer's use of such devices: *why* they were used – their effect on you – the part they play in furthering the writer's immediate and/or overall purposes. It is as futile to say, 'This passage is written in heroic couplets' *and to leave it at that* as it would be to say, 'This passage is printed in black ink on white paper'. Close study of the guided practice and worked examples in this book will show you how to make good *critical* use of your technical studies.

4 Context questions and text explanations

4.1 What these questions test

Passages taken from set books are printed on the examination paper. Each passage is accompanied by a series of questions designed to test:

- your detailed knowledge of the context from which the passage has been taken;
- your understanding of the meaning of the passage as a whole;
- your ability to explain the meaning of particular words, phrases or whole sentences in the passage;
- your understanding of the writer's purposes in the passage, and of the ways in which the language is used to achieve those purposes; and
- your understanding of ways in which the passage relates to the set book as a whole.

4.2 Recognising the point of each kind of question

Note   Read through *all* the questions set on the passage before beginning your answers. Overlapping answers cause confusion. Repetition wastes time.

Each question tests your knowledge and understanding of a set book in a particular way. Examples of typical questions, grouped according to their 'targets', illustrate how this is done.

(a) *Knowledge of the context*   'Who speaks these words and at which point in the play (or poem)?'/'To whom are these words spoken and in what circumstances?'/'What happens immediately after these words are spoken?'/'Who is the person addressed in line 13?'/'State the precise references of *He* and *it* in line 6.'

(b) *Understanding the passage and the writer's purposes*   'What does this passage tell you about the character of the speaker?'/'How do you think we are intended to react to the speaker?'/'Compare and contrast the two points

41

of view expressed in the passage.'/'What do we learn from this passage of the writer's attitude to this character?'/'What is the dramatic significance of the resolution expressed by the speaker?'

(c) *The writer's use of language* 'Show how the imagery in lines 10–13 suggests that the speaker's true position differs from the one he proclaims.'/'What do the successive adjectives in line 5 imply about the situation?'/'What is the dramatic effect of the striking variations of line length and rhythm?'/'How does the figurative language in the last line influence your attitude to the speaker?'

(d) *Relationships between the passage and the set book as a whole* 'In what way is the speaker's attitude here unrepresentative of her character as revealed in the poem as a whole?'/'Show that the contrast on which this speech is based is central to the theme of the play.'/'Discuss the significance of the italicised phrase in line 7, referring in your answer to two comparable statements in the poem.'/'What characteristic qualities of the style of the poem are represented here?'/'Comment on the relationship between day and night established in this passage, bringing out its significance in the theme of the play.'

(e) *Text explanations* 'Put the meaning of lines 17–20 in your own words.'/ 'Paraphrase lines 3–9.'/'Translate the italicised words in lines 2, 5 and 10.'/'Explain any expressions that would not be readily understood today.'

Note Be prepared for questions in which those categories overlap. For example: 'Explain the meaning of the italicised lines and show that the use of language is characteristic of the style of the poem. Support your answer by referring to two comparable examples.' That question requires you to: (i) explain the meaning of the text; (ii) show that you understand how language is used in those lines; (iii) relate the use of language in those lines to its use elsewhere in the set book.

4.3 Common mistakes

There is no point in discussing errors of fact. Candidates have only themselves to blame if they do not know their set books thoroughly.

The common mistakes that arise from failure to carry out instructions and from faulty examination techniques are a different matter. Analysis of examination scripts and of examiners' reports reveals the nature and causes of errors made even by well-informed candidates. These you can learn to avoid.

Failure to obey instructions

Note The mistakes that crop up time and again are listed below in groups, according to the particular targets at which the questions are aimed. However, one very common mistake is liable to occur in any answer, whatever the particular nature of the test. The questions on passages from set books are one of two kinds:

- questions that require answers *restricted to* the material supplied by the passage; or
- questions that require answers *based on* the material supplied by the passage, but *reaching out* to *include* material derived from elsewhere in the set book.

The instructions indicate which kind of answer is required, and failure to supply this is penalised. If you write a 'restricted' answer to a 'reaching out' question, you are throwing half your marks away. Equally, if you write a 'reaching out' answer to a 'restricted' question, the superfluous material in your answer will be ignored.

Placing the passage in its context

Straightforward 'recognition' questions such as: <u>To whom are these words addressed?</u> *and* <u>Identify the speaker</u>

Do not give a sentence answer unless you are told to do so. A sentence answer ('Hamlet speaks these words.') where a one-word answer ('Hamlet') is perfectly acceptable wastes precious time. (It also irritates the examiner – and that is not to your advantage!)

Do not provide more information than you are asked for. If the question is *To whom are these words addressed?* and the correct answer is 'Casca', you will not score any extra marks for adding, 'He and Cicero have met in a street near the Capitol, and a storm is raging', even though that superfluous material may be factually correct. Another time-waster.

More difficult 'context probing' questions such as: <u>To what event that has just occurred is the speaker referring?</u> *and* <u>What is the immediate result of the decision announced here?</u>

The key words are *just occurred* and *immediate result*. Confine your answer strictly to the precise point raised by the question.

Do not attempt to summarise all that has gone before or all that takes place afterwards. The examiner has asked you to identify one particular event and one particular result to which the given passage is directly connected.

'Placing' questions such as <u>State briefly where the passage occurs in the play</u> (or *in the poem*) *and* <u>In what circumstances are these words spoken?</u>

Do not be misled by the deceptively simple wording of such questions. They test your knowledge of the set book in some depth. Questions framed in this way indicate that the passage occurs at some particularly important moment in the set book, involving plot development, character portrayal, the expression of a key idea, mood or theme, and so on.

Your answer must: (i) identify the precise moment at which the passage occurs; (ii) indicate the nature of the importance of that moment; and (iii) show how the passage relates to that moment. And all must be done in a few words.

Explaining the author's purposes in the passage

Questions such as *How do you think you are intended to react to the speaker at this moment?* and *What does this passage tell us of the poet's attitude to the event described here?* are 'restricted' questions demanding restricted answers. The examiner is asking you, 'What exactly is the author doing here?'

Do not go outside the passage for your answer. You may know that the speaker's mood as expressed in the passage is not typical of his/her personality as a whole. You may know that the views expressed in the passage conflict with the overall philosophy of the poem. Keep that knowledge to yourself. It is irrelevant here.

Establishing relationships between the passage and other parts of the set book

Questions such as *Show that the speaker's attitude is untypical of his/her true character* and *In relation to later developments what is surprising about this decision?* are 'reaching out' questions demanding answers that go beyond the material supplied in the passage.

Do not fail to base your answer on the material in the passage to which the question directs attention.

Do not fail to bring into your answer material from elsewhere in the set book.

Do not fail to show the *relevance* of the 'outside' material to the passage-based material.

Commenting on the writer's use of language

Note   These questions presuppose your ability to recognise literary qualities and devices such as apt or striking diction (choice of words), imagery, figures of speech, rhythm and rhyme. Like all other questions set on passages from set books, they may require either 'passage-restricted' answers or 'reaching out' answers.

Here is a typical question: *What does the sudden change of rhythm in line 3 suggest about the speaker's state of mind at that moment?*

Too often, the answer given consists of a generalised account of the rhythm of the passage as a whole. For example: 'Written in iambic pentameters, the passage varies its basic rhythm occasionally, as in line 3, where there is a sudden change in the pattern.'

That, even if accurate, does not answer the question. To get the marks, your brief answer must: (i) show that you recognise *how* the rhythm changes in line 3; (ii) identify the speaker's state of mind at that moment; and (iii) show *how* the change of rhythm helps to express that state of mind.

Similar considerations apply to use of language questions that require 'reaching out' answers. For example: *In not more than 50 words, comment on the use of alliteration in lines 10 and 11. Develop your answer by referring to two other examples drawn from elsewhere in the poem.*

Guard against these common mistakes:

(a)   Failure to show the *use* to which alliteration is put. You get no marks for simply identifying the alliteration. (Though, of course, you cannot explain its effects unless you know what alliteration is!)

(b)   Failure to provide *two* other examples (not one; not three) crisply and clearly. This can be done either by quotation or by close reference. Quotation is quicker, clearer and more authoritative. There is no need (and no time) to quote at length. Quote just the introductory words that pinpoint your examples.

(c)   Failure to show that the use of alliteration in your examples is strictly comparable to the way it is used in the passage.

Exactly the same kind of answer is required whatever the stylistic feature singled out in the question – use of rhyme, use of compound words (or any other striking aspect of the diction), rhythmic effects, imagery, and so on.

Explaining difficult words in the passage

(i)   Difficult words (and phrases or whole sentences) must always be explained *as they are used in the passage*. This may not be expressly stipulated by the instructions, but it is *always* expected. Words can have multiple meanings. You must explain the sense in which the author used them in the passage, *not* the sense in which they could be used elsewhere. Words can change their meaning in the course of time. You must explain the sense they had in the author's time, *not* the sense they have acquired later.

(ii)   Answers must be set out clearly, so that the examiner can see at once which explanation refers to which word. Wherever possible, set your explanations out in a form that matches the form of the question. There must be no possibility of confusion. A list of explanations without 'markers' to point each to its 'target' is no good. Something along these lines is recommended:

Question: Explain the meaning of *orts* (1.3) and *levell'd at* (1.11).
Answer: <u>orts</u> = 'scraps'
             <u>levell'd at</u> = 'guessed at'

There is no need to write sentence answers unless you are explaining a sentence; or, of course, unless the instructions tell you to.

(iii)   Be especially careful when the instructions are worded in ways such as these: *Bring out the force of the verb 'spaniel'd' in line 21* and *Explain the image underlying the adjective 'fretted' in line 8*. A good answer to such questions does two things: (i) it explains the meaning of the word singled out; and (ii) it shows your appreciation of the way in which the word is used. Candidates often write half an answer to such questions, supplying the meaning, but omitting the appreciation.

(iv)   Instructions such as *Paraphrase lines 10–15* and *Paraphrase the italicised lines* are often not properly carried out. When you paraphrase, you must substitute *your own words* for the original words, reproducing their *full* and *exact* meaning. Nothing must be left out or altered. Where the language of the passage is figurative, do not attempt to provide figurative expressions of your own invention; but include the literal meaning of the figurative words when it makes an essential contribution to the meaning of the passage.

(v)   The instruction *Put into your own words* means 'paraphrase'.

(vi)   When you are told to *Make clear the meaning* of a whole line or of a sequence of lines, a paraphrase is often the best method.

(vii)   Sometimes, the 'third person' method of explanation is the appropriate response to the instructions. For example: *Explain clearly and briefly the advice that Warwick gives in lines 14–18*. Answer: 'Likening England to a sick person, Warwick advises the king to play the part of a doctor and to administer the painful remedies needed to restore his kingdom's health.'

Poor time-keeping

Note   Poor time-keeping is a frequent cause of lost marks in context questions. The total time available for the whole question must be shared out between the separate parts, according to the marks allocated to each.

Working out a schedule

1. Three hours allowed for the whole paper.
2. Four questions to be answered, including a compulsory context question.
3. Equal marks allocated to each of the four questions.

   - Allow 45 minutes ($180 \div 4$) per question.

4. Two passages from set books to be selected from those printed on the paper.

   - Allow $22\frac{1}{2}$ minutes ($45 \div 2$) per passage.

5. Four questions are set on each passage, so you can think in terms of about five minutes ($22\frac{1}{2} \div 4$) per question.
6. *But* the four questions on each passage do not carry equal marks, so you must spend less time on some than on others.

   - *Apply, as a rule of thumb, an allowance of two minutes per mark.*

7. A typical schedule will then be:

(i)	1 mark	2 minutes
(ii)	3 marks	6 minutes
(iii)	4 marks	8 minutes
(iv)	$4\frac{1}{2}$ marks	9 minutes
Totals:	$12\frac{1}{2}$ marks	25 minutes

8. *But*, if you applied that schedule to both passages, you would spend 50 minutes (25×2) on this question as a whole. That is more time than you can afford.
9. So time must be shaved off somewhere. In practice, you will find that you can explain the meaning of single words and short phrases (generally, 1 mark and $1\frac{1}{2}$ mark questions) in considerably less than two minutes each. You then have adequate time for the questions carrying more marks: those requiring paraphrases and those concerned with the author's intentions and use of language in the passage.

Naturally, you must work out a schedule to fit the particular requirements of the questions set by your own examining board; but, if you proceed along the lines just laid down, you will use your time efficiently.

- Unless you strike the right balance between questions and keep up with the clock, you are bound to lose marks.

4.4 Worked examples

Note   The notes on the answers given here draw attention to particular problems as they arise. Advice on dealing with a specific problem is not repeated each time that problem occurs. Consequently, you should refer to the earlier notes as you study each new set of questions and answers.

1

    A We were, fair queen,
Two lads that thought there was no more behind,
But such a day tomorrow as today,
And to be a boy eternal.

(5) **B** Was not my lord
The verier wag o' the two?

    A We were as twinn'd lambs that did frisk i' the sun,
And bleat the one at the other: what we changed
Was innocence for innocence; we knew not
(10) The doctrine of ill-doing, nor dream'd
That any did. Had we pursued that life,
And our weak spirits ne'er been higher rear'd
With stronger blood, we should have answer'd heaven
Boldly 'not guilty'; the imposition clear'd
(15) Hereditary ours.

    B By this we gather
You have tripp'd since?

    A O my most sacred lady!
Temptations have since then been born to's: for
(20) In those unfledg'd days was my wife a girl;
Your precious self had not then cross'd the eyes
Of my young play-fellow.

    B Grace to boot!
Of this make no conclusion, lest you say
(25) Your queen and I are devils.

(i)   Identify the two speakers.   [2]
(ii)   What important development occurs just before these words are spoken?
    [2]
(iii) Paraphrase lines 11–15 ('Had we pursued . . . Hereditary ours.'). [3½]
(iv) Bring out the dramatic significance of the passage.   [5]

What you need to know about the passage

This dialogue (from *The Winter's Tale*) between Polixenes, King of Bohemia, and Hermione, Queen of Sicilia, is crucial to the plot of the play. Leontes, King of Sicilia, is a suspicious bystander, and he draws false and fatal conclusions from the demeanour of his wife Hermione and of his life-long friend Polixenes as they talk together. Leontes' misconceptions are confirmed a moment later, when Hermione tells him that she has persuaded Polixenes to stay on as their guest. 'He'll stay, my lord,' she announces. 'At my request he would not,' Leontes bitterly reflects, before publicly and extravagantly congratulating her on her success. He then – while talking to his little son, Mamillius – reveals the full extent of his murderous, jealous rage, though neither Hermione nor Polixenes hears his words. In the given extract, Polixenes' knotty and difficult language contrasts with Hermione's light-hearted, bantering responses to the somewhat pompous sentiments he so weightily expresses.

All those points should be familiar to a candidate for whom *The Winter's Tale* is a set book. They provide the material needed to answer each question as it explores a particular aspect of the context, the meaning, and the significance of the passage.

Answers – with notes

(i)   A is Polixenes. B is Hermione.

Notes   That straightforward recognition question, carrying two marks, can and must be answered very briefly. The two speakers must be separately and clearly identified: 'Polixenes and Hermione' would *not* be a satisfactory answer. An answer in the form of two very short sentences enables the examiner to see at once that you know which speaker is which. Other forms of answer would be acceptable (e.g. 'A – Polixenes; B – Hermione') but save hardly any time.

(ii)   Polixenes yields to Hermione's persuasion and agrees to prolong his stay in Sicilia.

Notes   It is tempting to provide more information than is asked for. The results of Polixenes' decision are so momentous that you feel you must show the examiner that you understand how important this development is. Resist the temptation! Only two marks are available for (ii), so you can gain nothing by expanding on the single and precise piece of information asked for. Also, if you have read through all the questions, you should realise that these larger issues are raised in (iv), where five marks are available.

(iii)   If our lives had continued in that way, and our frail virtues had never been challenged by the sinful impulses of adulthood, we would have remained untainted by our inheritance of original sin and fearlessly proclaimed our innocence when charged by heaven.

Notes   When paraphrasing, you must reword the original, yet retain its full meaning. Do not attempt to imitate the figurative expressions or the compressed grammatical constructions. Concentrate on conveying the full and plain sense. Not an easy task here, for the language is condensed and some of the expressions (e.g. 'Hereditary ours') introduce concepts more familiar in Shakespeare's day than in ours. Only if you have studied the text closely (taking full advantage of your editor's notes) can you paraphrase these lines clearly and accurately. This question is harder than either (i) or (ii); hence the extra marks.

(iv)   This passage is full of dramatic irony. Neither speaker is aware that Leontes is becoming insanely jealous and that he sees Hermione's success in persuading Polixenes to stay as proof of her adulterous relationship with his life-long friend. Consequently, Polixenes' nostalgic reminiscing about his boyhood days with Leontes, and Hermione's light-hearted banter are unwittingly exchanged in the shadow of murderous rage. Immediately after this conversation, we hear Leontes giving brutal expression to his savage suspicions, while talking to his little son, Mamillius; but neither his wife nor his friend hears what he says. Estrangement and death are the outcome of the happy and innocent conversation between Hermione and Polixenes. Thus, this passage initiates the violent development of the action. It is an ironical prelude to the shocking 'wintry' events that dominate the first movement of *The Winter's Tale*.

Notes   Assuming you have spent half a minute on (i), about a minute on (ii) and about seven minutes on (iii), you have left yourself about fourteen minutes for (iv). This kind of question cannot be answered properly in much less time than that. To *bring out* the *dramatic significance* of a passage, you must show that it contributes something of importance to the set book as a whole. First, establish the writer's aims as the passage reveals them. Does it develop the plot? Does it generate/relax tension? Does it deepen/resolve conflict? Does it develop character? Does it arouse emotion? Does it embody a leading theme, idea, mood? (It may do all, or some, or one of those.) Then, you must relate the aims and impact of the passage to the larger aims and the overall impact of the whole work. Only by knowing and understanding the set book can you have access to the required material. And only by writing clearly, briefly and relevantly can you compress a good answer into the limited time available for this searching question. Do not start to write until you have thought out the main points *and* an effective order in which to present them.

2

Ay, sir: where lies that? if 'twere a kibe,
'Twould put me to my slipper: but I feel not
This deity in my bosom: twenty consciences,
That stand between me and Milan, candied be they,
(5)   And melt, ere they molest! Here lies your brother,
No better than the earth he lies upon,
If he were that which now he's like, that's dead;
Whom I, with this obedient steel, three inches of it,
Can lay to bed for ever; whiles you, doing thus,
(10)   To the perpetual wink for aye might put
This ancient morsel, this Sir Prudence, who
Should not upbraid our course. For all the rest,
They'll take suggestion as a cat laps milk;
They'll tell the clock to any business that
(15)   We say befits the hour.

(i)   Name the speaker; and say where this passage occurs in the play.   [2]

(ii)   Explain 'if 'twere a kibe, 'Twould put me to my slipper' (ll. 1–2).   [2]

(iii)   Rewrite lines 5–9 ('Here lies your brother . . . bed for ever') in your own words.   [3½]

(iv)   What striking linguistic qualities of the original lines are missing in your version?   [2]

(v)   Specify three aspects of the speaker's character that are revealed in this passage.   [3]

What you need to know about the passage

In this extract from *The Tempest*, Antonio (Prospero's usurping brother) is speaking to Sebastian (brother of Alonso, King of Naples). A spell has been put upon Alonso and his courtiers by Ariel, Prospero's spirit, and they lie asleep. Neither they nor the two conspirators (Antonio and Sebastian) are aware that they have been shipwrecked on Prospero's magic island and that they have been in his power since he raised the storm that drove their vessel to his shores. Alonso believes that Ferdinand, his son and heir, has been drowned. This belief is shared by Antonio and by Sebastian, who now regards himself as heir to Naples. Ferdinand, however, is safe. He has been guided to Prospero's cell and has fallen in love with Prospero's daughter Miranda. It is their eventual union, destined by Prospero, that heals the discord of the past. Just before these lines occur, Antonio has suggested to Sebastian that the murder of the sleeping Alonso would make him King of Naples. Sebastian recalls that Antonio himself is a usurper, having expelled Prospero from the Dukedom of Milan. Rather weakly, he asks Antonio whether his conscience has troubled him. This speech is Antonio's cynical reply. He dismisses conscience contemptuously, and proposes that he shall kill Alonso, while Sebastian puts paid to Gonzalo ('This ancient morsel, this Sir Prudence'), who would denounce them if allowed to live. The other courtiers, he says, will collaborate readily and find it expedient to go along with whatever Sebastian and Antonio suggest. This speech ended, they are about to attack their intended victims, when Ariel wakes Gonzalo, whose cries of alarm arouse the sleeping king. Full realisation of the wickedness revealed here is a necessary part of our understanding of Prospero's character and motives. His stern, sometimes harsh, words and actions must be weighed against the sheer evil that he combats. His eventual forgiveness of enemies such as these is a hard-won spiritual triumph. It is also his fitting, final blessing bestowed on the young lovers, to whom the future now belongs, and from whom he lifts the burden of the past.

Answers – with notes

(i)   Antonio is speaking to Sebastian. Alonso and his courtiers are lying under Ariel's sleepy spell. Antonio and Sebastian are planning to murder the king and Gonzalo. Ariel wakes Gonzalo and thwarts the plot.

Notes   You must pinpoint *exactly* where the passage occurs, specifying the events and/or situations that immediately precede and follow the extract. Choose your words carefully to get the maximum effect as briefly as possible. Can you improve on the answer given? For example, would 'Alonso and his courtiers are asleep' be an improvement on 'Alonso and his courtiers are lying under Ariel's sleepy spell'? It saves four words, so it is worth thinking about.

(ii)   Having dismissed his conscience as a mere figment ('where lies that?'), Antonio says that if it were an ulcerated chilblain on his foot, he'd be forced to take notice of it and wear his slipper to ease the pain.

Notes   The problem here is to decide what is meant by 'Explain'. Since you are not asked either to paraphrase the whole expression or to give the meaning of single words or phrases (say, 'kibe' or 'put me to my slipper'), a different kind of answer seems to be called for. The suggested answer attempts to make clear exactly what was in Antonio's mind when he spoke those words; his meaning *and* his attitude. Of course, you cannot do that unless you know the meaning of 'kibe' and 'put me to my slipper'. You must also know what 'that' (1.1) refers to, and understand that 'if 'twere' (1.1) means 'if it (my conscience) were'. Just so, you must know that 'Twould' (1.2) means 'It (a kibe) would'. This kind of question cannot be answered without a thorough knowledge and understanding of the text.

(iii)   Your brother lies here, and I can kill him with a jab of my dagger. He looks dead now, and – if he were what he looks like – he'd be of no more account than the ground he's lying on.

Notes   When you are substituting your own words for the original words, you may need to change the order and the grammatical structure of the passage. (Pay close attention to the original punctuation, or you will be in danger of distorting the meaning.) Here, the single sentence of the original passage became two sentences in the paraphrase. That change was made to establish very plainly the connection between 'Whom' (1.8) and 'your brother' (1.5). Lines 5, 8 and 9, reworded, were combined into a single sentence and placed first in the paraphase. Lines 6 and 7, reworded, became the second sentence of the paraphrase.

(iv)   The compressed vigour of the blank verse and the vivid figurative language cannot be reproduced in plain prose. Contrast, for example, 'this obedient steel' (rhythmic and metaphorical) with 'my dagger' (flat and literal).

Notes   Your answer must identify the 'striking linguistic qualities' referred to in the question. The first sentence does that. The second sentence provides an illustration of those qualities, proving that you understand and appreciate the material you are using to answer the question.

(v)   Cynical: 'if 'twere a kibe . . .'
         Ruthless: 'twenty consciences . . . ere they molest!'
         Sneeringly witty: 'This ancient morsel, this Sir Prudence'.
                          '. . . take suggestion as a cat laps milk'.

Notes   The instructions limit your answer to the contents of the passage. Nothing outside it is relevant. Three aspects of the speaker's character are asked for, so specify three only, even if you can find more. Present them in a time-saving (but clear) form. Provide brief evidence for each point you make.

3

       Greet chiere made oure Hoost us everichon,
       And to the soper sette he us anon.
       He served us with vitaille at the beste;
       Strong was the wyn, and wel to drynke us leste.
(5)   A semely man OURE HOOSTE was withalle
       For to han been a marchal in an halle.
       A large man he was with eyen stepe –
       A fairer burgeys is ther noon in Chepe –
       Boold of his speche, and wys, and wel ytaught,
(10)   And of manhood hym lakkede right naught.
       Eek therto he was right a myrie man,
       And after soper pleyen he bigan,
       And spak of myrthe amonges othere thynges,
       Whan that we hadde maad oure rekenynges,
(15)   And seyde thus: 'Now, lordynges, trewely,
       Ye been to me right welcome, hertely;
       For by my trouthe, if that I shal nat lye,
       I saugh nat this year so myrie a compaignye
       Atones in this herberwe as is now.
(20)   Fayn wolde I doon yow myrthe, wiste I how.
       And of a myrthe I am right now bythoght,
       To doon yow ese, and it shal coste noght.

(i)   Suggest modern English synonyms for 'leste' (1.4) and 'stepe' (1.7).   [1]
(ii)   Bring out the full meaning of 'For to han been a marchal in an halle' (1.6) and 'A fairer burgeys is ther noon in Chepe' (1.8).   [3]
(iii) Paraphrase lines 15–20 ('Now, lordynges, trewely ... myrthe, wiste I how').   [4]
(iv) What can be deduced from the passage about Chaucer's attitude to this character?   [4½]

What you need to know about the passage

Taken from near the end of 'The General Prologue' to Chaucer's *Canterbury Tales*, these lines describe the Host of the Tabard Inn. The pilgrims are staying there for one night before starting on the long journey that they are undertaking for piety's and pleasure's sake. Chaucer – who arrived before the others – has mingled with them, delightedly observing their varied characters and motives. He has described each in turn, and now presents the imposing figure of the Host. Harry Bailey (we learn his name later in the poem, in 'The Prologue to the Cook's Tale') announces, a few lines further on, that he has decided to accompany the pilgrims, acting as their guide, yet paying his own expenses. Chaucer watches and listens with detached amusement as the pilgrims readily agree to fall in with the Host's further proposals, all of which are greatly to his own advantage as well as to the pilgrims'. This mixture of good fellowship and a shrewd eye to the main chance accounts for Harry Bailey's success as a famous hotelier. He appoints himself the pilgrims' Master of Ceremonies. It is his idea that each pilgrim shall tell stories to beguile the tedium of the outward and return journeys. He decrees that there shall be a prize for the best story-teller, who will be their guest of honour at a great supper at the Tabard on their return, the cost of which shall be split between them all. In this way, the Host ensures that he will make a good profit out of them, amply rewarding himself for the time and money he will spend in conducting them to Canterbury and back. Thus he secures for himself a well-paid, pleasant break from his busy life as proprietor and manager of a large and prosperous inn. (Moreover, as is hinted later, he is not sorry to have a break from his wife's company.) Before they go to bed, the pilgrims unanimously request the Host to be their 'governour', and pledge themselves to be 'reuled . . . at his devys/In heigh and lough'.

Answers – with notes

(i)   leste = 'pleased'; stepe = 'bright'

Notes   An easy question (provided you know your set book), to be answered quickly and clearly.

(ii)   1.6   The Host was qualified in every way to be the Master of Ceremonies in the establishment of some nobleman and to preside over his great hall. (1.8)   He could have held his own in the heart of the City. There was not a finer turned-out or more prosperous-looking burgess in any of London's business centres – not even in Cheapside.

Notes   See notes to Question 2 (ii) on page 51. You have to try to bring out the *implications* of the words, as well as their literal meaning. No need to explain 'burgess' (*burgeys*): it is still used in Chaucer's sense.

(iii)   Ladies and gentlemen, I give you a most sincere and hearty welcome. Without a word of a lie, I can assure you that I have not seen, in the whole of this year, such a pleasant, happy-looking crowd of guests in this tavern. If I knew how, it would give me a lot of pleasure to think up some special entertainment just for you.

Notes   See Section 4.3 (page 45), and the paraphrases in Questions 1 and 2.

(iv)   Chaucer admires the Host's striking appearance and imposing presence. He is impressed by the excellent way in which he runs the Tabard; but he also notes with shrewd amusement what an astute businessman he is. The Host relaxes ('pleyen he bigan') after the guests have finished supper, turning his mind to 'myrthe' – but *not* before they have paid their bills (1.14).

Notes   See answer and notes to Question 2 (v) on page 51.

4

        If thou beest he; but O how fallen! how changed
        From him, who in the happy realms of light
        Clothed with transcendent brightness didst outshine
        Myriads though bright: if he whom mutual league,
(5)   United thoughts and counsels, equal hope
        And hazard in the glorious enterprise,
        Joined with me once, now misery hath joined
        In equal ruin: into what pit thou seest
        From what highth fallen, so much the stronger proved
(10)   He with his thunder: and till then who knew
        The force of those dire arms? Yet not for those,
        Nor what the potent victor in his rage
        Can else inflict, do I repent or change,
        Though changed in outward lustre, that fixed mind
(15)   And high disdain, from sense of injured merit,
        That with the mightiest raised me to contend,
        And to the fierce contention brought along
        Innumerable force of spirits armed
        That durst dislike his reign, and me preferring,
(20)   His utmost power with adverse power opposed
        In dubious battle on the plains of heaven,
        And shook his throne.

(i)   Who is 'thou' (1.1)?   [1]

(ii)   What is the meaning of 'the happy realms of light' (1.2) and 'In
        dubious battle' (1.21)?   [3]

(iii)   Paraphrase lines 17–22 ('And to the fierce contention . . . And shook
        his throne').   [4]

(iv)   What do lines 1–11 ('If thou beest he . . . those dire arms?') tell us
        about the speaker?   [2½]

(v)   Describe any remarkable feature that you notice in the sentence
        construction of lines 11–22 ('Yet not for those . . . And shook his
        throne').   [2]

What you need to know about the passage

In these lines from Book I of *Paradise Lost*, Satan addresses Beelzebub. For nine days and nights, the fallen angels have lain in the burning pit of Hell, racked by its torments. Satan, their leader, his 'obdurate pride' and 'steadfast hate' unquenched by defeat, now prepares to rally his followers, who are as yet overwhelmed by the shock of their defeat and the pains of their eternal punishment. He turns first to Beelzebub, second only to himself in power and in crime. In this first speech to his principal confederate, he reminds him of former glories and of their comradeship in the great enterprise they dared together against the tyrant, God, whose throne they shook. Though defeated by a power whose might none could know until it had been tested, Satan asserts his own unyielding resolve. The lines of this passage lead in to the tremendous outburst of defiance beginning: 'What though the field be lost?'. Beelzebub soon responds to the inspiring leadership of his 'matchless Chief'. Together, they instil new heart into their comrades; build their infernal capital, Pandemonium; and, as the outcome of the great debate (in Book II), set in train the fearful plot to revenge themselves on God by contriving the Fall of Adam. Milton's style in this passage (notable for its majestic rhythm, complex constructions and sonorous diction) is typical of this great epic poem, the theme of which is the destiny of the human race, caught up in the eternal war between Good and Evil.

Answers – with notes

(i)   Beelzebub.

Notes   A one-word answer saves the examiner trouble, and you time. (*And* you score the single mark available – provided it's the right word!)

(ii)   (1.2)   The Kingdom of Heaven, where happiness and light were their lot – as opposed to the miseries and 'darkness visible' of Hell, just described.
(1.21)   In armed struggle, the outcome of which was, for a time, in doubt.

Notes   It is not enough merely to supply the literal meaning. You must bring out the implications of the expressions – but as briefly as possible.

(iii)   And led to the deadly struggle a numberless army of angels who had the temerity to object to God's supremacy, advancing my right to rule before his. So, in the heavenly fields, we confronted his ultimate might in a contest of doubtful outcome in which we threatened to overturn his sovereignty.

Notes   The order and sentence structure of the original passage are modified in the paraphrase – see notes to Question 2 (iii) on page 51. Milton often uses compendious words for which plain substitutes are not easily found. His vocabulary is strongly Latinised, and the paraphrase has to bring out in modern English the sense which Milton intended (and which he assumed his reader would instantly comprehend). See, for example, how 'me preferring' is reworded in the paraphrase. A good answer to this question depends on close and sustained study of the text. Nobody can paraphrase Milton 'off the cuff'.

(iv)   Satan is an inspiring and cunning leader. He understands how to rouse Beelzebub to revenge and how to forge even stronger links of loyalty at this disastrous time.

Notes   This is the kind of question that tempts you to overrun your time. The lines in question are packed with relevant material; but only two and a half marks are available for the answer, so you must be brief. Try to present the *essence* of what the lines reveal, and make every word of your answer tell.

(v)   There is only one sentence in these lines, but the complex structure is under strict control. Every modifying phrase and subordinate clause is firmly and clearly linked to the main statement: 'Yet not for those do I repent or change that fixed mind and high disdain'.

Notes   Again, it is tempting to write at greater length than the allotted two marks can justify. The lines are an outstanding example of disciplined eloquence, and they merit detailed analysis and extensive comment – neither of which time or marks will permit. You have to deal only with the basic point and, in doing so, show that you appreciate this characteristic aspect of Milton's style. You do not have to be a grammarian to answer this question, but you are expected to be able to distinguish between a main statement and extensions and elaborations of that statement. In other words, you are expected to be an intelligent and careful reader. If you think my suggested answer is too long, shorten it; but do not lose the main point.

5 Critical commentaries on passages from set books

5.1 What these questions test

Note Bear in mind the meaning of *critical*, as used in the term 'critical commentary'. In general speech, 'criticism' is often synonymous with 'fault-finding'. In the language of literary studies, 'criticism' and 'critical' denote *appraisal*. To criticise is to judge. Good criticism is as sensitive to strengths as to weaknesses; and, since the books set for study at A Level are noteworthy for their literary merit, your critical commentaries will be concerned largely with the analysis and appreciation of successful writing. However, you should comment on any weaknesses you may detect.

Many examining boards ask for critical commentaries on passages from set books, preferring this form of test to the more traditional context question. The examiners' instructions to candidates are worded in various ways, each board having its own phrasing. Even so, whatever the particular wording, all critical commentary questions cover the same ground, testing your knowledge, understanding and appreciation both of the passage itself *and* of the work from which it has been taken.

The tests posed by critical commentary questions are, in fact, scaled-up versions of the tests posed by context questions of the kinds discussed in Chapter 4.

A good critical commentary is based on:
- Your recognition of the exact place in the set book from which the passage has been taken.
- Your knowledge of the particular developments of plot, characterisation or theme occurring at that place in the set book.
- Your understanding of the connections between the passage and developments of plot, character or theme, both in the immediate context and in the set book as a whole.
- Your understanding of the meaning of the passage, as a whole and in detail.

57

- Your understanding of the writer's intentions, as revealed by the passage; and your appreciation of how the writer's use of language in the passage helps to achieve those intentions.
- Your appreciation of the stylistic qualities of the passage; and your ability to draw comparisons and/or contrasts between those qualities and the style of the set book as a whole.

The overlapping of critical commentaries and context questions should now be apparent. If you still have any doubts about their common ground, revise Section 4.1, Section 4.3(a) and Section 4.4.

5.2 Timing and planning answers

The questions worked out in Section 5.4 demonstrate how timing and planning are affected by the different requirements of the various examining boards. All critical commentary questions test similar areas of knowledge, understanding and appreciation, but the length of answer required varies greatly. Some boards want a brief answer (a paragraph in length); others want an extended answer (anything from 1 to 2 sheets long, according to the time allowed).

Again, some instructions specify the critical topics to be covered in the answer, thus providing a ready-made plan. Others are so worded that all decisions about planning the answer (its contents and the order in which to present them) are left to the candidate.

So, despite their essential similarities, critical commentaries pose varying problems of scale, proportion and organisation. Study past papers so that you can recognise the particular demands your own examiners will make. The answers and notes in Section 4.4 will then show you how to tackle the commentaries they set.

5.3 Common mistakes

Note Because critical commentaries go over some of the ground covered by context questions, many of the most frequent mistakes are common to both. Revise Section 4.3 (pages 42–6) before proceeding.

Three particular features of critical commentaries cause special problems:

(i) The essence of a critical commentary is the appreciation and analysis of a writer's use of language to achieve intended effects. The commentary must show your understanding of *what* is done. It must also show *how* it is done. Failure to bring out both the 'what' and the 'how' reflects inadequate knowledge of the set book and/or the absence of the literary judgement and skills expected of A Level candidates.

(ii) A critical commentary must be written as a piece of *continuous* and *connected* prose. This applies both to paragraph-length answers and to the extended answers so often required. Therefore careful attention to the planning of the answer is necessary. This is especially the case when the instructions call for a critical commentary (or a critical essay) without specifying the particular topics to be covered. Your response to such general wording must be to plan out your answer with particular care. You have to look for the relevant material in the passage, classifying it under headings such as diction, imagery, verse, prose style and so on. Then, having found your material and sorted it into coherent groups, you must work out a sensible order in which to present it, taking care to link the various parts of your answer to establish a smooth progression of ideas.

(iii) The points you make must be supported by evidence. Provide this by means of close reference to or brief quotations from the text. Unsupported opinions and observations do not carry much weight.

5.4 Worked examples

1

Antony and Cleopatra

Attendant. News, my good lord, from Rome.
Antony. *Grates me*; the sum.
Cleopatra. Nay, but hear them, Antony:
Fulvia, perchance, is angry; or, who knows
If the scarce-bearded Caesar have not sent
His powerful mandate to you, 'Do this, or this;
Take in that kingdom, and *enfranchise that*;
Perform't, or else we damn thee.'
Antony. How, my love!
Cleopatra. Perchance? nay, and most like;
You must not stay here longer; your dismission
Is come from Caesar; therefore hear it, Antony.
Where's Fulvia's process? Caesar's I would say? Both?
Call in the messengers. As I am Egypt's queen,
Thou blushest, Antony, and that blood of thine
Is *Caesar's homager*; else so thy cheek pays shame
When shrill-tongued Fulvia scolds. The messengers!

(i) State briefly where the passage occurs in the play;
(ii) comment on the content and style; and
(iii) give a brief, clear explanation in modern English of the italicised sections of the selected passage.

(A.E.B.)

Note The time schedule worked out for the whole paper allowed $22\frac{1}{2}$ minutes for this question. The passage selected was one of four passages on offer. It took a couple of minutes or so to read them all and choose this. That left about 20 minutes in which to carry out the tasks specified by the instructions. The notes on the answers explain how the available time was divided between the three tasks, leaving just adequate time for reading through the answers and correcting mistakes.

What you need to know about the passage

It is taken from the beginning of *Antony and Cleopatra*. Philo, one of Antony's followers, in a short speech to his companion Demetrius, has just denounced Antony's 'dotage' – for so he describes what he sees as Antony's enslavement to

Cleopatra's beauty. The great captain and leader ('the triple pillar of the world'), says Philo, has been 'transformed into a strumpet's fool'. As he speaks, Antony and Cleopatra make a brilliant entry with their courtiers. Cleopatra is teasing Antony to tell her how much he loves her, when the attendant breaks in to announce that news has come from Rome. Antony's impatient response ('Grates me; the sum.') shows him outwardly defiant of Rome and all it stands for, but secretly ill at ease.

But Cleopatra will not let him hide from reality, for Rome cannot be shrugged off. She taunts him: perhaps Fulvia (his wife) is angry; perhaps the youthful Octavius Caesar has commands for him. He reacts angrily, but she continues to goad him. Caesar or Fulvia, or both – it hardly matters which, she implies – have decided that he must return to Rome and duty. Regally ('As I am Egypt's queen'), she asserts that his angry colour is a deferential blush because his master speaks, or a token of shame because his wife scolds.

Her command (at the end of the passage) that the messengers shall be heard provokes Antony to the passionate outburst that immediately follows: 'Let Rome in Tiber melt, and the wide arch/Of the ranged empire fall! Here is my space'. To the listening Romans, Antony's words are sacrilege. To Cleopatra, they are a longed-for affirmation that he will stay with her; though she knows that her hold on him is precarious. 'A Roman thought' will always threaten to tear him from her side.

The passage plunges the audience at once into the conflict on which the whole action turns. At the very outset of the play, we are made vividly aware of the complex characters and tangled relationship of the two lovers, whose worldly greatness and responsibilities are at odds with their mutual passion. Their tragedy is implicit in this dialogue.

Answer – with notes

(i) Taken from the opening lines of the play, this passage immediately follows Philo's bitter description (to Demetrius) of Antony's transformation into 'a strumpet's fool'; and immediately precedes Antony's vehement rejection of Rome and all it stands for: 'Let Rome in Tiber melt . . .'.

Notes   The instructions stipulate a brief answer. In a few words, you must pinpoint the context and indicate its importance. By using brief quotations, you can slot the passage back into the play and, at the same time, bring out its dramatic significance. Note that the omission marks in the second quotation tell the examiner that you consider the whole speech (of which these are the first words) to be relevant to the point you are making. Note, too, the careful choice of words (for example, 'bitter description' and 'vehement rejection') to maximise the impact of a brief answer. Drawing on a thorough knowledge and understanding of the play, you should be able to think out and write this answer in about two minutes.

(ii) Antony's impatient reaction to the attendant's words is an attempt to hide his own unease. He tries to carry the situation off with a high hand; but Cleopatra will have none of this. She knows that Rome cannot be brushed aside. Her taunting supposition that his wife, Fulvia, is angry with him, or that young Octavius Caesar has sent orders for him, is designed to make him face up to the issues.

Angered even more, he tries to rebuke her ('How, my love!'), but she intensifies her mockery. Only by stinging him can she force him to recognise the precariousness of his – and, therefore, of *their* – position. As Egypt's queen, she understands the power politics involved ('Caesar's *homager*'). As Antony's mistress, she realises Fulvia's legal and moral strength as Antony's wife. It would be pleasant to pretend that their Alexandrian revels can continue unmindful of Rome and its pressing demands; but she rejects that illusion. Antony cannot be allowed to temporise, so she risks his anger.

Antony says little: just two short, rather stumbling attempts to play the strong man. The inadequacy of his language here is in striking contrast to the magnificence of his utterances elsewhere.

Cleopatra's vivid language reflects her passionate concern with and her deep understanding of Antony and of their true situation. Without wasting a word, she exposes his self-protective evasions mercilessly, shooting dart after dart into his self-esteem: 'scarce-bearded Caesar'/'Do this, or this'/'your dismission'/'Fulvia's process'/'Thou blushest'/'thy cheek pays shame'.

Notes   The instructions tell you to 'comment on the content and style'. The time schedule allows 10–12 minutes for this, provided (i) is answered in about two minutes and (iii) in about five.

First, you must decide what points you want to make about the content of the passage: *What is going on here? What character/plot/theme matters are in hand?* Then, you must look for ways in which the language of the passage is used to get those issues through to the audience.

Having considered the material you want to use, you have to decide on the order in which to present it. Here, a ready-made plan is provided by the instructions, which put content before style. So it is sensible to follow that order.

Finally, you must write your answer, taking care to make your points clearly and to support them with brief references to and quotations from the text.

As you can see, you need every moment of your allotted 10–12 minutes, so it is vital not to overrun on (i) and (iii).

Now consider the answer given above and see whether you can improve on it.

(iii)   <u>Grates me</u>: 'it offends me'.
<u>enfranchise that</u>: 'set that [kingdom] free'.
<u>Where's Fulvia's process?</u>: 'Where is Fulvia's legal summons?'
<u>Caesar's homager</u>: 'Caesar's vassal'.

Notes   No need for sentence answers. Concentrate on brief, accurate explanations. Take the necessary time and trouble to set out the answers clearly, so that the examiner can see at once which expression you are explaining. If you know your set book as thoroughly as you should, this question can be answered in less than five minutes, and a bit more time can be given to (ii), if you need it.

2

Write a critical commentary on this passage from *Middlemarch*, paying particular attention to George Eliot's use of humour in the extract.

MY DEAR MISS BROOKE, — I have your guardian's permission to address you on a subject than which I have none more at heart. I am not, I trust, mistaken in the recognition of some deeper correspondence than that of date in the fact that a consciousness of need in my own life had arisen contemporaneously with the possibility of my becoming acquainted with you. For in the first hour of meeting you, I had an impression of your eminent and perhaps exclusive fitness to supply that need (connected, I may say, with such activity of the affections as even the preoccupations of a work too special to be abdicated could not uninterruptedly dissimulate); and each succeeding opportunity for observation has given the impression an added depth by convincing me more emphatically of that fitness which I had preconceived, and thus evoking more decisively those affections to which I have but now referred. Our conversations have, I think, made sufficiently clear to you the tenor of my life and purposes; a tenor unsuited, I am aware, to the commoner order of minds. But I have discerned in you an elevation of thought and a capability of devotedness, which I had hitherto not conceived to be compatible either with the early bloom of youth or with those graces of sex that may be said at once to win and to confer distinction when combined, as they notably are in you, with the mental qualities above indicated. It was, I confess, beyond my hope to meet with this rare combination of elements both solid and attractive, adapted to supply aid in graver labours and to cast a charm over vacant hours; and but for the event of my introduction to you (which, let me again say, I trust not to be superficially coincident with foreshadowing needs, but providentially related thereto as stages towards the completion of a life's plan), I should presumably have gone on to the last without any attempt to lighten my solitariness by a matrimonial union.

Note   This was one of three questions to be answered in a three-hour paper. The notes on the worked-out answer indicate how the available hour was divided between preparation, planning, writing and revision.

What you need to know about the passage

This is an extract from the letter in which the Reverend Edward Casaubon proposes marriage to Dorothea Brooke. There is 'a good 27 years' between them, and even Dorothea's easy-going, rather scatty-minded uncle (who is her guardian) is surprised and faintly troubled by her acceptance of this improbable suitor. Her younger sister, Celia, is saddened by it. She finds Casaubon physically repulsive. Her common sense tells her that the marriage cannot be happy, though she lacks the insight to understand the true nature of Dorothea's deep disappointment – were it ever confessed. Friends deplore the marriage of 'this blooming girl' to a man with 'no good red blood in his body', but – like Celia – they would be incapable of appreciating the sources of Dorothea's anguish when disillusionment rapidly dims the bright hopes she entertained. For Dorothea, an idealist, eager to find some great cause to which she can dedicate herself, saw in Casaubon a scholar devoted to the search for truth. She believed, too, that his selfless labours (for so they seemed to her) were the manifestation of a nobility of mind corresponding to the magnitude and worth of the task he had set himself.

Dorothea's state of mind on reading this letter is described by George Eliot in words that enable us to understand – even sympathise with – her motives for making her dreadful mistake. 'How could it occur to her to examine the letter, to look at it critically as an expression of love? Her whole soul was possessed by the fact that a fuller life was opening before her . . . Now she would be able to devote herself to large yet definite duties: now she would be allowed to live continually in the light of a mind that she could reverence . . . This hope was not unmixed with the glow of proud delight . . . she was chosen by the man whom her admiration had chosen.'

But, as Dorothea quickly and painfully discovers, Casaubon is a dried-up pedant. His proposed great work (to be called, if ever published, *Key to All Mythologies*) has for its subject dead issues long since resolved by scholarship of which he is wilfully and pig-headedly ignorant. In George Eliot's words, he spends his time 'carrying his taper among the tombs of the past'. He is not even capable of sorting out his ragbag of useless knowledge. An ever-growing pile of notebooks clutters his library, the repository of extracts and jottings for a tedious and useless book that will never be written.

Worse, he is a cold, self-centred, unimaginative man. He is incapable of responding to affection, suspicious of enthusiasm, narrow in sympathies, a prey to self-doubt which he dare not face, and intolerant of the least hint of criticism, actual or suspected. Autocratically possessive, he lays on Dorothea's life the dead hand of his own chilling jealousy: 'a blight bred in the cloudy, damp despondency of uneasy egoism'.

Answer – with notes

For neither Casaubon, its writer, nor Dorothea, its recipient, is there anything humorous in this letter. For the reader of *Middlemarch*, seeing people, events and motives through its author's eyes, it is a characteristic example of George Eliot's use of humour to bring out the moral issues implicit in the book.

The humour is complex, operating simultaneously on several levels and quickening our perceptions of many different aspects of human behaviour. Our first impression of this letter is simply how very funny it is. It is a silly letter, written by an overeducated fool. Casaubon reveals himself as a pompous ass: a sort of literate Dogberry (see *Much Ado About Nothing*). This is intended to be a love letter, written to propose marriage to the young woman he claims to love – if so tepid an emotion as an 'activity of the affections' can be described as 'love'. The language is wholly unsuited to his ostensible purpose. Its frigid, polysyllabic diction and convoluted constructions give the game away. This carefully composed exercise has neither warmth nor nature in it. A feeble attempt here and there to express an emotion he supposes he ought to be feeling serves only to emphasise the absence of true affection. Surely, nobody who can write in this wholly inappropriate manner can be taken seriously as a lover? The only possible response, we feel, must be derisive laughter at his presumption, insincerity and sheer hamfistedness.

Simultaneously, however, we are aware that the writer of this astonishing letter is wholly honest. He means every word he writes, and he intends the way it is written. For this letter is a blatant expression of Casaubon's monstrous egoism. He is open about it because he sees no reason to hide it. He is unashamed of it. This is how he is; and he does not pause to question whether this is how he ought to be.

The lofty position from which he so complacently addresses Dorothea becomes increasingly apparent. He says, in effect: 'I, Edward Casaubon, leading a life of learning and endeavour superior to that for which lesser beings are suited, had already felt the need for assistance in my great labours and comfort for my declining years when I met you, Dorothea. I at once came to the conclusion that you are young enough, docile enough, elegant enough and just about intelligent enough to supply what I need. It is no mere chance that you have come to my notice at precisely the right moment. Providence has so arranged matters that, as my wife, you will have the opportunity to assist in the fulfilment of my life's plan.'

Nor does the final paragraph of his letter (omitted from this extract) do anything to improve our opinion of its writer. It is an elaborate statement of the benefits he can confer on Dorothea and of his merits as a husband offering her 'an affection hitherto unwasted'.

The unassailable self-esteem is breathtaking. In this letter, Casaubon is truly comic, unconsciously revealing himself as a 'humorous' character, in the original sense of that term. He is dominated by a fixed idea (his conviction of his own importance and superiority), and so blinded by it that his attempts to relate to other people are ludicrous. He lives in a world of his own making, of which he is the centre. Others are permitted to enter that world only on his terms; and their roles in that world are strictly subordinate to his.

But all this is only a part of what we experience as we read the letter. If we could detach ourselves from Dorothea, or if we could hope that she would react to Casaubon's words as we do, then this proposal would be simply an amusing episode. In fact, we read it in the sickening knowledge that she is reacting in quite a different way. She has already told her guardian that if Mr Casaubon proposes marriage to her she will accept, for she 'admires and honours' him. By this time, we know her well enough to understand why she so completely and disastrously misinterprets his character.

Young, inexperienced, 'ardent and theoretic', Dorothea has 'childlike' views about marriage. Longing to escape from the pettiness of her present life into a larger world where she can devote herself to some noble cause, she sees Casaubon as a great man, selflessly dedicated to scholarly labours and the search for truth. To her sister, he appears a repulsive old bore. To Dorothea, he is 'distinguished-looking', and 'remarkably like the portrait of Locke'. She sees his 'great soul' in his face. Moreover, he says he needs her, and she experiences a 'glow of proud delight' because she has been 'chosen by the man whom her admiration had chosen'.

So it is that we read this ridiculous letter with double vision, simultaneously seeing Casaubon as he really is and Casaubon as he seems to Dorothea. Even as we dismiss him contemptuously as a preposterous pretender, we recognise his power over her eager, idealistic soul, which is 'possessed by the fact that a fuller life was opening before her'. She believes that she will 'live continually in the light of a mind that she could reverence'.

It is folly, of course – desperate folly. But it is a triumph of George Eliot's art that we do not withdraw our sympathy from a girl whose illusions are so great and whose consequent misery is so predictable.

The moral issue here, starkly raised by the fearful contrast between appearance and reality, is personal accountability. It is pointless to shift the blame onto Casaubon. Dorothea's mistake is hers, and hers alone. If she is to grow in moral stature, she must (and does) learn to accept responsibility for her own actions and, in doing so, learn to know herself.

Thus, our immediate perception of the absurdity of Casaubon's letter soon leads to an awareness of the deeply serious issues stemming from it. This is a use of humour familiar to us today. We call it 'black comedy'.

Notes   The wording of the question indicated that an essay-type answer was expected. The examiners stressed that the author's use of humour required particular attention, but no other topics were specified. All the planning of the answer was thus left entirely to the candidate.

Of the hour available, about 20 minutes were spent in studying the passage, thinking out the points to be made, and then working out a plan for the answer. Points were jotted down on rough paper and sorted out into a working plan *before* the answer itself was begun. Those essential preliminaries left about 40 minutes for writing the answer, reading it through and correcting mistakes. Because the preparation was thorough, the actual writing – based on carefully selected material and a clear plan – went smoothly. The full-length treatment required was completed within the time limit.

This is the plan on which that critical commentary was based:

Introduction   A clear statement of the main points to be made in the critical commentary. Briefly expressed (it is compressed into one short paragraph), this puts the examiner in the picture by showing that a clear line of argument and exposition has been thought out. There is no waffle. The issues raised by the question are grappled with at once.

Development   The use of humour in the passage (to which the question directs special attention) is explored in successive paragraphs (beginning: 'The humour is complex'; and ending: 'strictly subordinate to his.'). Each paragraph is confined to one aspect of the topic and kept short. Care is taken to link the paragraphs so that each new idea (or each illustration of an idea) is seen to follow on logically.

Qualification   The topic for special attention having been thoroughly explored, it is necessary to examine the other critical topics that arise from the passage *and* to show how they *relate to* the one already dealt with. This is done in the paragraphs beginning: 'But this is only a part'; and ending: 'learn to know herself.' (You will learn more about the 'qualification' and its function in Chapter 6.)

Conclusion   Here, all the threads of the answer are drawn together in a brief and conclusive statement. The theme (as announced in the *Introduction*) is rounded off. One paragraph suffices. A crisp 'punchy' ending is what is needed. All the necessary arguments and exposition (together with supporting evidence) have been deployed in the body of the answer.

Study the answer closely in the light of these notes. I think it is a good critical commentary, but it is unlikely to be entirely free from faults! Improve it wherever you think you can. For example, on re-reading, I hesitated about including the rewording of Casaubon's letter (beginning: 'He says, in effect . . .'), but I felt that the points I was illustrating were important enough to justify the space they took. What do you think? If you decide against me, you will still have to take those points into consideration, though you may find a more economical way of doing so.

One strong feature of the answer is the use of brief quotations from the novel to support the comments made on the passage. The quotations show that the set book has been studied thoroughly and understood. They also show that the *critical significance* of the passage has been appreciated. (It really does help to learn brief quotations by heart as you study your set books and come to grips with the critical issues.)

Note, too, that I tried to write in a lively fashion (for example: 'sheer hamfistedness': 'repulsive old bore'). A critical commentary is an account of ways in which *you* (the reader) have reacted to a piece of literature. You must, of course, be thoughtful about your judgements and give reasons for your opinions; and you must *not* write in a slangy or flippant manner. But do try to show that you have made a *personal* response to your set books.

3

Write a critical essay on the following passage, relating it to the rest of the play to establish its dramatic significance. Bring out its importance in plot development and characterisation, and show how its stylistic qualities contribute to the realisation of the dramatist's purposes, especially in communicating themes that lie at the heart of the play.

Much Ado About Nothing

Don Pedro   Come, lady, come; you have lost the heart of Signior Benedick.

Beatrice   Indeed, my lord, he lent it me awhile; and I gave him use for it, a double heart for his single one; marry, once before he won it of me with false dice, therefore your Grace may well say I have lost it.

Don Pedro   You have put him down, lady, you have put him down.

Beatrice   So I would not he should do me, my lord, lest I should prove the mother of fools. I have brought Count Claudio whom you sent me to seek.

Don Pedro   Why, how now, Count! Wherefore are you sad?

Claudio   Not sad, my lord.

Don Pedro   How then, sick?

Claudio   Neither, my lord.

Beatrice   The Count is neither sad, nor sick, nor merry, nor well; but civil count – civil as an orange, and something of that jealous complexion.

Don Pedro   I'faith, lady, I think your blazon to be true, though I'll be sworn, if he be so, his conceit is false. Here, Claudio, I have wooed in thy name, and fair Hero is won. I have broke with her father, and his good will obtained. Name the day of marriage, and God give thee joy!

Leonato   Count, take of me my daughter, and with her my fortunes; his Grace hath made the match, and all grace say Amen to it!

Beatrice   Speak, Count, 'tis your cue.

Claudio   Silence is the perfectest herald of joy: I were but little happy if I could say how much. Lady, as you are mine, I am yours; I give away myself for you, and dote upon the exchange.

Beatrice   Speak, cousin; or, if you cannot, stop his mouth with a kiss, and let him not speak neither.

Don Pedro   In faith, lady, you have a merry heart.

Beatrice   Yea, my lord; I thank it, poor fool, it keeps on the windy side of care. My cousin tells him in his ear that he is in her heart.

Claudio   And so she doth, cousin.

Beatrice   Good lord, for alliance! Thus goes every one to the world but I, and I am sunburnt; I may sit in a corner and cry 'Heigh-ho for a husband!'

Don Pedro   Lady Beatrice, I will get you one.

Beatrice   I would rather have one of your father's getting. Hath your Grace ne'er a brother like you? Your father got excellent husbands, if a maid could come by them.

Don Pedro   Will you have me, lady?

Beatrice   No, my lord, unless I might have another for working-days; your Grace is too costly to wear every day. But, I beseech your Grace, pardon me; I was born to speak all mirth and no matter.

Don Pedro   Your silence most offends me, and to be merry best becomes you; for, out o' question, you were born in a merry hour.

Beatrice   No, sure, my lord, my mother cried; but then there was a star danc'd, and under that was I born. Cousins, God give you joy!

Leonato   Niece, you will look to those things I told you of?

Beatrice   I cry you mercy, uncle. By your Grace's pardon.

[*Exit Beatrice*

What you need to know about the passage

Don Pedro, Prince of Arragon, has fought a brief and victorious war against his bastard brother Don John, and the play opens with news of his triumph and the information that he is coming to visit Leonato, Governor of Messina. Count Claudio of Florence and Signior Benedick of Padua, two of his friends, are with him. So, too, is Don John, officially reconciled with Don Pedro, but – aided by his henchmen Conrade and Borachio – on the lookout for any chance to get his own back.

Claudio wants to marry Hero, Leonato's daughter; and his patron, Don Pedro, woos her for him and obtains her father's consent to the marriage. Don John, however, has convinced Claudio that Don Pedro has tricked him by wooing Hero for himself. That is why Claudio is 'civil as an orange and something of that jealous complexion'. This first piece of trickery is soon thwarted and, as we see in this passage, everything is sorted out happily – for a time. Don John's next move has much more serious, though temporary, effects. Aided by Borachio, he persuades Don Pedro and Claudio that Hero is unchaste. They denounce her at the altar and leave her lying, apparently dead, in the church where she and Claudio should have married. Fortunately, the villains are exposed (by the blundering incompetence of Dogberry and the Watch). Hero is not dead. Claudio is suitably sorry for his 'mistake', and the wedding takes place after all.

Even as one plot development ends in this passage, another begins. Beatrice, Leonato's niece and ward, plays a prominent part in this scene. Indeed, she and Benedick are the leading characters and the centre of interest in the whole play – which was often referred to as 'Beatrice and Benedick'. We have learnt already that there is 'a kind of merry war betwixt Signior Benedick and her'. It has become plain to the audience (though not to any of the characters in the play) that their unremitting battle of wit, in which each ruthlessly upstages the other, is an elaborate game to hide their mutual attraction. Fiercely independent, each fears the other as a unique threat to that cherished independence. If they cannot have each other, they will have nobody else: and they *will not* have each other. As a mysterious undercurrent to this sex battle, there are suggestions (never explained) that Benedick has somehow tricked Beatrice in the past – or so she seems to believe ('once before he won it [my heart] of me with false dice'). Whatever the truth of that, she professes scorn for Benedick. He – a determined bachelor, by choice and by frequently expressed conviction – is equally vehement in demonstrating his hostility to her. He has left the company just before this passage opens because he has seen Beatrice coming and, as he tells Don Pedro, he 'cannot endure my Lady Tongue'. The fact is that, at their last encounter, Beatrice scored so many direct hits that he dare not risk another exchange until he has recovered his self-possession.

The shining qualities of this lovely, witty young woman, born under a dancing star, captivate Don Pedro in this scene. (His 'Will you have me, lady?' is on the edge of seriousness.) As soon as she leaves on her uncle's errand, the prince announces his intention of bringing her and Benedick 'into a mountain of affection th'one with th'other'. He is determined to 'have it a match', even though Leonato believes that 'if they were but a week married, they would talk themselves mad'. Although the ensuing plot does succeed (in a wonderfully comic scene) in making Beatrice and Benedick admit their love, Don Pedro is quite wrong in thinking that he, or anyone else, can 'make' them fall in love. They are not puppets to dance on the strings he pulls. Nor, though Benedick ruefully observes that they 'are too wise to woo peaceably', is Leonato's forecast very perceptive. Theirs is a marriage of true minds, though the way that leads to it is not smooth. Ironically, it is Claudio's callous treatment of Hero that brings Beatrice to full realisation of her need for Benedick; and he responds to her then with a total commitment of love and, if need be, of life itself.

Answer – with notes

Don John's spiteful attempt to drive a wedge between Claudio and Don Pedro is thwarted here. Claudio, sick with jealousy, is soon cured by Don Pedro's announcement that he has won Hero for him, followed by Leonato's bestowal on him of the heiress's hand.

But the spring of another plot is being wound up as this first trick of Don John's comes to an end. Captivated by Beatrice's wit and charm, Don Pedro decides to make a match between her and Benedick. As soon as she goes off on her uncle's errand, he tells the others that she would make 'an excellent wife for Benedick' and that he intends to bring them 'into a mountain of affection' for each other. Leonato, Hero and Claudio agree to help him. Ironically, as they leave to discuss the details of his scheme, we hear Don John and Borachio plotting a second and much more serious attempt to destroy Claudio's union with Hero.

It has never surprised an audience that Beatrice makes such a deep impression on the Prince of Arragon. In this scene, as throughout the play, she shines out in the company of the ordinary, conventional people with whom she lives. Only Benedick is her peer; and it is he, a little later, who speaks for us all when he exclaims, 'By this day, she's a fair lady!' Her sparkling wit – quicker, livelier, even than Benedick's – is the expression of her intelligent appraisal of people and society. So far from being 'born to speak all mirth and no matter', she is a deeply serious person, clear-sighted in her values, impatient of pretence and ostentation, warm and loyal in her personal relationships.

She has no great opinion of Claudio, but if Hero is content with him, Beatrice will do what she can to see that her cousin's happiness is unclouded. Here, she tries to stir Claudio into a happy, unconstrained expression of his sense of his good fortune. Knowing in her heart what love might be, she longs to see in the betrothed couple's demeanour a reflection of the joy that she would be feeling, were she the happy sharer of requited love.

Her self-mocking declaration that she is 'sunburnt' (a reference to her unfashionably dark beauty) and must 'sit in a corner and cry "Heigh-ho for a husband!" ' covers up her longing for the fulfilment that love could bring. But it must be love for and from the right man: a marriage of true minds, not the conventional made-match that satisfies her social world. There is only one man for Beatrice; but neither she nor Benedick will risk the scornful rejection that they have led each other to expect. Their 'merry war' protects them against each other.

Beatrice's enigmatic reference to 'false dice' affords a momentary glimpse of suppressed feeling. We are not given any details of the mysterious episode that has scarred her; and to her hearers at this moment, her words convey only a jest – as she intends. Whatever trouble it is that haunts her memory, it is exorcised in the church scene. There, when Benedick accepts the burden of her stark command, 'Kill Claudio', she knows at last that his heart is given, not lent.

Another facet of her character shows in her cool handling of a potentially embarrassing development in her relationship with Don Pedro. They are joking together on easy terms. Then, his response to her joke about a husband 'of your father's getting' threatens the delicate balance of their conversation. Carried away by his delight in their talk, he asks impetuously, 'Will you have me, lady?' In their hierarchical world, the lady Beatrice could be no fit match for the Prince of Arragon. His question has serious implications. It breaks the rules of the game they are playing, and he needs a way out of a situation that has suddenly got out of hand. Beatrice's good sense and quick wit provide him with a face-saving escape ('your Grace is too costly to wear every day.'). Light-heartedness is swiftly restored, for she makes it clear that his Grace was understood to be joking. No wonder he admires her!

This extract is written in the easy, flexible prose that is the characteristic language of this play. It sounds several distinctly different notes here: bantering; stately (Leonato's speech to Claudio); incisive (Don Pedro to Claudio). At moments, on Beatrice's tongue, it sounds a note of sheer poetry: 'No, sure, my lord, my mother cried; but then there was a star danc'd, and under that was I born'.

The quick disposal of the first of Don John's dirty tricks and the lead-in to the Beatrice/Benedick plot are typical of the spirit and the themes of this play. Successive plot developments, based on rumour, hearsay and deceit, give rise to 'much ado about nothing'. Each time, we – the audience – are tipped off that 'there's nothing in it', so we can sit back and watch the characters getting into quite unnecessary tangles. It is all very light-hearted and often melodramatic – with one exception. The Beatrice/Benedick plot explores a profoundly serious issue. The comedy of their 'gulling' is the starting point of their richly rewarding journey to self-knowledge and self-fulfilment.

Notes Candidates have 45 minutes for this question. Three passages (one from each of three set plays) were on offer. Reading them and making the selection takes two or three minutes. (Candidates can usually decide quite quickly which play they feel most at home with for their purposes here.) Allow another 10 minutes for studying the selected passage, gathering relevant material and planning out the answer. Because this critical commentary must be written as an *essay*, extended treatment is required, and points must be developed in some detail. However, planning is a straightforward job, for the examiners' instructions specify the topics to be covered.

In my answer, I presented the specified topics in the order in which the examiners listed them. This gave me a ready-made plan for my essay and helped me to make sure that I did not leave out any of the topics I was told to cover. Working along those lines, I found that I had a little more than half an hour for composing and writing the answer I had worked out, and a minute or so left for a quick read-through and the correction of a few minor slips.

As to the content of my answer, I spent more time on the revelation of Beatrice's character than on any other topic. I believe that is where the importance of the extract chiefly lies. Indeed, I found that everything I wanted to say about the topics specified by the examiners derived from my judgement of the dramatic significance of the Beatrice/Benedick plot in the play as a whole. This approach provided me with a thread to connect the various parts of my essay, for I saw the plot developments, the characterisation, the use of language and the expression of themes in the extract as being related to that centrally important issue of the play.

Of course, I could not have found all this material in the extract, or used it in the way I did, if I had not studied the play closely and thought about it a great deal before I came to this question. Also, several of my critical points – especially the one about Beatrice and Don Pedro – came out of my memories of Royal Shakespeare Company productions of this play both at Stratford and in

London. Do try to see your set plays on stage. Good actors and directors are better guides than academic critics. After all, Shakespeare wrote his plays to be acted; and he was himself an actor (and a 'fellow' of the great theatre company for which he wrote them).

4

Write a critical commentary on this passage, taking care to explain anything that would not be understood readily today, and showing the significance of the passage in relation to the whole work from which it is extracted.

The Prelude

If this be error, and another faith
Find easier access to the pious mind,
Yet were I grossly destitute of all
Those human sentiments that make this earth
So dear, if I should fail with grateful voice
To speak of you, ye mountains, and ye lakes
And sounding cataracts, ye mists and winds
That dwell among the hills where I was born.
If in my youth I have been pure in heart,
If, mingling with the world, I am content
With my own modest pleasures, and have lived
With God and Nature communing, removed
From little enmities and low desires,
The gift is yours; if in these times of fear,
This melancholy waste of hopes o'erthrown,
If, 'mid indifference and apathy,
And wicked exultation when good men
On every side fall off, we know not how,
To selfishness, disguised in gentle names
Of peace and quiet and domestic love
Yet mingled not unwillingly with sneers
On visionary minds; if, in this time
Of dereliction and dismay, I yet
Despair not of our nature, but retain
A more than Roman confidence, a faith
That fails not, in all sorrow my support,
The blessing of my life – the gift is yours,
Ye winds and sounding cataracts! 'tis yours,
Ye mountains! thine, O Nature! Thou hast fed
My lofty speculations; and in thee,
For this uneasy heart of ours, I find
A never-failing principle of joy
And purest passion

(S.U.J.B.)

What you need to know about the passage

Taken from near the end of Book 2 of *The Prelude*, this passage (ll. 419–451) is immediately before the direct address to Coleridge ('Thou, my Friend!' – l. 452) and leave-taking from him ('Fare thee well!' – l. 467) with which this book concludes. It comes immediately after a sustained outburst of thankful praise in which, looking back at his seventeen-year-old self, William Wordsworth recalls the revelation so wonderfully vouchsafed him and the ecstasy it gave:

> Wonder not
> If high the transport, great the joy I felt,
> Communing in this sort through earth and heaven
> With every form of creature . . .
> One song they sang, and it was audible,
> Most audible, then, when the fleshly ear,
> O'ercome by humblest prelude of that strain,
> Forgot her function, and slept undisturbed.
>   (Book 2, ll. 409–18)

It is to this passionate affirmation of his direct, personal communion through Nature with 'the Uncreated' that Wordsworth refers in the opening line of this extract: 'If this be error'.

The Prelude, as its title-page states, is 'an autobiographical poem' whose subject is the 'growth of a poet's mind'. Each of the 14 books into which it is divided has for its subject a particular stage of or period in Wordsworth's life. For example: 'Book 1   Introduction – Childhood and School-Time'; 'Book 2   School-Time (Continued)'; 'Book 3   Residence at Cambridge'. As those book titles indicate, the poem includes a good deal of direct autobiographical information and narration, but the dominant theme is everywhere the 'growth of a poet's mind'. It is a spiritual autobiography in which Wordsworth recalls and recreates his visionary experiences: those 'spots of time' at which he saw 'into the life of things'. He meditates on their significance and the 'life view' to which they led him. He traces the developing history of his imagination and the evolution of his poetic vocation.

Begun in the winter of 1799, the composition of the poem was interrupted frequently, partly by the pressure of other work (many of the great poems published in 1807 were written during this period), and partly by Wordsworth's initial uncertainties about the scope and scale of *The Prelude*. He paused for a long time after finishing Books 1 and 2; but by March 1804, when he had written three more books, he was clear that he must continue with the poem until he had traced the development of his mind up to 1798 – his twenty-eighth year, and the year in which *Lyrical Ballads* was published. This he did, working steadily until May 1805, when the task was completed.

The poem remained untitled and unpublished during Wordsworth's lifetime. He always referred to it as 'a poem on my early life' or as 'a poem on the growth of my mind' or as 'the poem to Coleridge'. It was Mary, his wife, who gave it the title *The Prelude* and sub-titled it 'Growth of a Poet's Mind: An Autobiographical Poem' when she sent it to the printer soon after his death in 1850. Both she and Dorothy, his sister, had copied out his drafts of the poem or taken down passages at his dictation. They were well aware of his intentions and knew what he wanted to be done with it.

Lifetime publication was not to be thought of, because – as Wordsworth said – it was unusual, and open to adverse criticism, for a poet to write at such length about himself. Also, the many passages dealing with 'more lowly matters' (such as the lines in Book 1 describing 'Our home-amusements by the warm peat-fire') might attract scoffing attention from hostile readers unable or unwilling to appreciate a range of subject matter that included the ordinary things of life as well as its 'visionary gleam'.

But posthumous publication would set the seal on his life's work. In this immense poem, he had tried to put into words those mystical experiences that had visited him during his youth and recurred in his early manhood. From them, he believed, all that was best in him – as man and as poet – was derived. It was their influence that – once Dorothy had restored him to the natural world – had brought him through a desperate spiritual crisis. To explore, understand, and pass on his experience was a duty he owed to the beneficent power that had imparted to him an intuitive apprehension of the wholeness and oneness of the universe. So richly endowed with blessings in his own life, he must – in simple gratitude – attempt to share them with his fellow human beings.

The Prelude was also and in deepest truth 'the poem to Coleridge'. He is the 'Friend' so often addressed; and Wordsworth was, in a very real sense, talking to Samuel Taylor Coleridge throughout the poem. With Coleridge in mind as his prime and original audience, Wordsworth was able to sustain his imaginative drive through the long task. Coleridge ('the only wonderful man I ever knew', Wordsworth said, years later) influenced him deeply, quickening his creative powers and giving him faith in his poetic destiny.

When, in 1839, Wordsworth completed his final revisions to this astonishing poem, he knew that his major work was done. Yet all the time he was writing it, he regarded it as an essential preparation for an even greater undertaking. In March 1798, before he had written his poems for *Lyrical Ballads*, he conceived the idea of a poem which he then called *The Recluse; or Views of Nature, Man, and Society*. Coleridge, Mary and Dorothy all knew of this ambitious project. For many years, Coleridge implored (sometimes badgered) him to write it. Mary and Dorothy for a long time confidently expected him to. As late as 1814, he referred to it and compared 'the poem about my early life' to *The Recluse* as 'the ante-chapel . . . to the body of a gothic church'. When he began to write what we now know as Book 1 of *The Prelude*, his intention was to take stock of his mind and powers; to examine his fitness to write *The Recluse*. He had been unable to make a start on that huge enterprise (or on any of the other large subjects described in lines 166–220 of Book 1). His frustration and perplexity are starkly apparent:

> This is my lot; for either still I find
> Some imperfection in the chosen theme,
> Or see of absolute accomplishment
> Much wanting, so much wanting, in myself,
> That I recoil and droop, and seek repose
> In listlessness from vain perplexity,

> Unprofitably travelling toward the grave,
> Like a false steward who hath much received
> And renders nothing back.
>
> (Book 1, ll. 261–9)

Out of this self-doubt *The Prelude* was born. 'Was it for this?' he asks that Nature had so blessed him (Book 1, l. 269).

And, in finding the answer to that question, Wordsworth wrote a poem now generally agreed to be one of the very greatest works of English literature. *The Prelude* places him in the front rank of literary genius, for the written masterpiece achieves all his ambitions for the great work that it was intended to precede – to be 'a prelude' to. Here, Wordsworth triumphantly explores those universal themes – 'prophetic, meditative, sometimes homely' – in a great song

> Of Truth that cherishes our daily life;
> With meditations passionate from deep
> Recesses in man's heart, immortal verse.
>
> (Book 1, ll. 229–32)

Answer – with notes

Introductory Note   From five passages offered (one from each of five set books), candidates had to select one for critical comment. The five set books were: *Hamlet, As You Like It, The Winter's Tale, The Franklin's Tale* and *The Prelude, Books 1–3*. For the purposes of this chapter, it was helpful to choose *The Prelude* passage. It is an extract from a literary work of a very different kind from any of those considered so far. Even so, the critical approach and methods previously demonstrated can be applied with equal success to *The Prelude* passage. That approach and those methods provide a sound basis for a critical commentary on any passage, from whatever kind of set book it has been taken.

As it happens, I might well have chosen to write on this passage had I been a candidate taking this particular paper. Though the extracts from *Hamlet* and *The Winter's Tale* would have suited me well, *The Prelude* passage, in both its content and its style, gave me the opportunity to comment on features that I particularly appreciate and enjoy in this great poem. So I felt that I had something of my own to say about it. Not that I claim any special originality for my views, but they are very much a reflection of my *own* experience of *The Prelude*. Consequently, I could tackle this passage with particular enthusiasm.

Always look for a passage from a set book which interests you deeply and gives you keen pleasure. You can then hope to communicate a lively and genuinely personal response to the work.

In the worked example that now follows, your knowledge of the information supplied on pages 72–4 is assumed. Refer to those pages if you need to refresh your memory while studying the worked example. (You would, of course, have acquired the necessary information during your A Level course if *The Prelude* had been one of your set books.)

Note   This is one of four questions to be answered in a three-hour paper, so you have 45 minutes for your answer. The recommended time to be spent on each part of the answering process is indicated in the worked example.

Select the passage that suits you best

If you know your set books as thoroughly as you should, *and* understand the qualities to be aimed at in writing a critical commentary (see Sections 5.1, 5.3 and the introductory note on page 74), you should not need to spend more than two or three minutes in making your choice. (For the reasons already given, I have chosen *The Prelude* passage.)

Study the chosen passage

As you do so, note those aspects of its content and style on which you will probably want to comment. Do this by underlining words and phrases in the passage, making marginal notes and/or jotting points down on rough paper. Do not worry too much at this stage about the order in which you will deal with your points. Planning your commentary comes next, after you have gathered your material. But you do need to have guidelines in your mind as you go through the passage: mental headings to direct your thoughts towards a comprehensive and cogent critical commentary. Ask these questions as you are looking for your material:

1. *Where* does this passage occur in the set book?
2. *What* is being said here?
3. *How* is it being said?
4. *Why* is it being said? and *why* is it being said in this way?
5. In what significant ways does this passage *relate to* the rest of this set book?
6. How am *I* reacting to this passage? What is it making *me* feel and think? Do I get *enjoyment* from it? If so, *why*? And *what kind* of enjoyment do I get from it?

You may not find relevant material in answer to each of those questions. According to the nature of the passage, some will be more fruitful than others. But, if you get into the habit of asking them, you will not leave out any critical points that ought to be made.

I spent six minutes studying the passage from *The Prelude* and making these notes.

his belief in revelation of his own unity with 'the Uncreated' through Nature – just affirmed

.orthodox religion easier for others

    If this be error, and another faith
Find easier access to the pious mind,
Yet were I grossly destitute of all
Those human sentiments that make this earth
So dear, if I should fail with grateful voice
To speak of you, ye mountains, and ye lakes
And sounding cataracts, ye mists and winds
That dwell among the hills where I was born.
If in my youth I have been pure in heart,
If, mingling with the world, I am content
With my own modest pleasures, and have lived
With God and Nature communing, removed
From little enmities and low desires,
The gift is yours; if in these times of fear,

love of man arises from love of Nature – the feelings – affection, pity, kindness – the human heart source of all his joy AND morality 'consequence of complete failure of French Rev.' (Coleridge)

This melancholy waste of hopes o'erthrown,
If, 'mid indifference and apathy,
And <u>wicked exultation</u> when <u>good men</u>
<u>On every side fall off,</u> we know not how,
To selfishness, disguised in gentle names

former friends betray ideals

Of peace and quiet and domestic love
Yet mingled not unwillingly with sneers
<u>On visionary minds;</u> if, in this time
<u>Of dereliction and dismay,</u> I yet

but still has faith – <u>faith</u> NOT mere stoicism

Despair not of <u>our nature,</u> but retain
A <u>more than Roman</u> confidence, a faith
That fails not, in all my sorrow my support,

'blessings spread around me like a sea'
deliberate repetition – echoes – hymn of praise – antiphony

The <u>blessing</u> of my life – the gift is yours,
Ye winds and sounding cataracts! 'tis yours,
Ye mountains! thine, O Nature! Thou hast fed
My lofty speculations; and in thee,

the common lot

For <u>this uneasy heart of ours,</u> I find
A never-failing <u>principle of joy</u>

joy – <u>feeling</u>

<u>And purest passion.</u>

(i)   Echoes of Coleridge – 'if in these times of fear' – addresses him immediately after this passage – always 'the poem to C'.

(ii)   The 3 'voices' of Prelude – visionary, meditative, homely – this, the meditative voice – asks and answers questions: What are my blessings? What kind of a man have my visitations made me? What has Nature taught me of Man? How ought I to live? How do I live?

(iii) **NB**   'human sentiments'/'principle of joy'/'the gift is yours' – sympathy with man as man – gifts *from* and *to* life – see (ii) above.

(iv)   The blank verse – unobtrusive – varied – ranges from thoughtful to eloquent – sadness and scorn – flexible – changing stresses – verse paragraphs and sentences.

(v)   Diction not difficult, though ideas expressed are profound – 'language of today and forever' (Col.)

(vi)   Effect of repetitions: 'gift' – 'winds' – 'mountains' – 'cataracts', etc.

(vii) Powerful impact of *quiet* poetry – how? – ideas and expression fused – *music* – deep conviction – moving – deeply satisfying.

(viii) Response to passage depends greatly on recollection of Book 1 and earlier lines of Book 2 – must carry his visions in mind if this passage to strike home – their emotional force re-created – W. makes demands on his readers – not an easy poet – but very rewarding.

Plan the commentary

If you have studied the passage along the lines just suggested, you have already gone a long way towards evolving an effective plan. With the guiding questions in mind (see previous section), your material has been gathered in meaningful and usable groups. You now have to decide on the order in which you will present the points you want to make. A sensible sequence suggests itself as you consider the ground that you must cover. You have to comment on:

(i)   The context, content and meaning of the passage.

(ii)   Its stylistic features, and how they further Wordsworth's aims.

(iii) The relationship between the content and style of this passage and the rest of the work.

(iv)   Your own response to the passage: your assessment of its literary qualities.

These four main topics must be covered in your commentary, but it is not necessary to devote a separate section to each one. Indeed, to take them one by one might well result in a wooden piece of writing. A good commentary is a readable, smoothly flowing prose composition; and, in any case, your thoughts and feelings about the passage do not come into your mind as separately packaged items. You must present your comments with ordered clarity, but it is important to give your reader a lively and unified account of what you experienced as you read the passage. It is necessary to *analyse* your thoughts and feelings in order to get to grips with your critical task, but you must try to put the pieces back together.

Consequently, you will probably want to interweave comments on the relationship between the passage and the work as a whole with comments on its content and its style. Those two topics emerge in a natural association as you read the passage. Similarly, your own response to content, style and passage/whole-work relationships in a continuing element in your study of the extract. It is right, therefore, that personal response should play its part throughout your commentary.

Those considerations underlay the three-part plan that I worked out for my commentary:

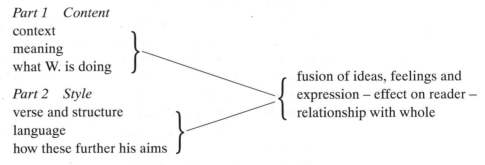

Part 1   Content
context
meaning
what W. is doing

Part 2   Style
verse and structure
language
how these further his aims

fusion of ideas, feelings and expression – effect on reader – relationship with whole

Part 3   Concluding evaluation
poetic impact of passage
derives from qualities identified in notes on content and style (see Part 2)
final statement of my response to whole

Thinking hard about it, and referring frequently to my notes, it took me about five minutes to work out that plan.

Write the commentary

The vital preparation (study, note-making and planning) has taken about 15 minutes, so there is now half an hour in which to write the commentary and to give it a quick read-through. That is not a lot of time, but it you have prepared thoroughly, you can write confidently. You know what you want to say, and you have worked out the shape of the commentary, so you should not have any major hold-ups while writing.

You may find that you do not use all the material gathered while studying the passage. That often happens and is no cause for alarm. As you write, it becomes clear that some of your points are more readily usable than others. Or you may find that two points are more effective if they are combined. Again, as you write, additional points may occur, or you may want to give greater prominence to one of the points you were already intending to make.

The process of writing stimulates the mind, and you must feel free to adapt your prepared material to your quickening thoughts. A slavish adherence to your notes would cramp your imagination.

But *do not* depart in any major way from your planned scheme for the commentary. Keep a stern eye on any new ideas that bubble up as you write. They may well be illuminating additions, relevant to your overall plan. If so, make use of them. But, do remember, sudden 'inspirations' *can* be wreckers – red herrings – loose ends – will o' the wisps that entice you away from the route you have mapped out so thoughtfully.

Finally, the *style* of your commentary. The examiners are looking for a piece of writing which reflects your own reactions to the passage. How is that personal response to be expressed? You are not breaking any rules if you use 'I', but use it sparingly. Generally, your own views are most effectively put over when they are *implicit* in the wording of your comments. Work hard at this. With practice, you will acquire the knack of phrasing critical statements that clearly but unobtrusively express your own opinions and feelings.

And do try to write in a lively, interesting way. Many candidates adopt what they fondly imagine is a 'correct' style, special to (and officially approved for) critical writing. Their commentaries are cluttered with dead expressions such as: 'Thus it can be seen that'/'It will be appreciated that'/'Critics have often remarked upon'/'Lines 6–13 have been held to be'/'A more than common imaginative capacity is seen to be at work in'/'Strictures have frequently and rightly been levelled at'/'There is also to be noted that characteristic'/'Only William Wordsworth could have written'.

Clichés and 'play safe' formulas drain the life out of a critical commentary – *and* out of the literature that is its subject.

Writing a critical commentary is not easy, so you must practise frequently as you prepare for your examination. Bear in mind the qualities your examiners will be looking for:

- accurate and relevant use of facts;
- sensitive personal response;
- thoughtful opinions, supported by evidence;
- cogent structuring; and
- plain, unpretentious English.

Two critical commentaries on the Wordsworth passage

Notes   Three examples of critical commentaries have been provided in this chapter: one short commentary (12 minutes); one medium-length commentary

(45 minutes); and one extended commentary (60 minutes). Two of the set passages on which those commentaries were based were taken from plays, and the other was taken from a novel. The critical approach adopted in each of those commentaries and the planning and writing techniques employed can be applied equally well to a commentary on a passage taken from a poem.

Because I am trying to show you how to make use of all the advice and techniques supplied earlier, it was helpful to write two commentaries on the Wordsworth extract. Study them both and compare them closely.

Both the Wordsworth commentaries are based on the information given on pages 72–4, and on the preliminary analysis and planning set out on pages 75–7. There is, however, one important difference between them, the result of a decision that I took at the outset. When I wrote the first of these Wordsworth commentaries, I made it my prime concern to explore the contents and the stylistic qualities of the passage and to establish its relationship to Wordsworth's purposes and methods in the poem as a whole. So, without spreading myself extravagantly, I went into all the critical points in considerable detail. When I wrote the second commentary, however, I kept very strictly within the time left to me after the preliminary work on the passage had been completed, just as I would have to in the examination. This was a most useful exercise. Without departing from the critical position expressed in the first commentary, I had to compress and streamline. Yet I still had to explain that position in some detail; and to provide quotations and text references to support my opinions and illuminate my response to Wordsworth's poetry.

It wasn't easy – critical commentaries are never easy to write – but I hope you will find that the second commentary deals adequately with all the essential points that were made at greater length in the first commentary.

Obviously – but I must stress the obvious to avoid any possibility of a serious misunderstanding – under examination conditions, *neither you nor I would have the time to write two versions of a critical commentary.* Having studied the passage, analysing it critically and planning your answer, you must then get on with the commentary you are going to hand in. There is no time for first and second drafts. If you know and understand the set book as you should, and if you have planned your commentary in the way set out earlier in this chapter, you should have little more than a few careless slips to correct when you are reading it through.

Remember, then, that it is the *second* of these two commentaries that represents what would be written in the examination. But, with that caution in mind, I do advise that, from time to time when you are practising critical commentaries, you begin by writing a first version, giving yourself elbow room. Then rewrite the commentary, keeping strictly to the time limit that will be imposed by the examination. As you will see, when comparing these two commentaries, the exercise provides valuable practice in the difficult art of compressing essential material, while yet presenting it clearly and persuasively. It teaches you how to go straight to the heart of the matter, briefly but readably.

First critical commentary

A commentary on the Wordsworth passage, written for practice in expressing text-based critical comments on the poetry, and discussing significant relationships between the extract and the poem as a whole.

In this extract from the closing lines of Book 2, Wordsworth meditates on the significance of the mystical experiences that had irradiated his life by the time his 'seventeenth year was come'. Just before this passage begins, he has recreated the 'visitations' that had made him aware of the oneness of the universe and of his own unity with its spiritual essence. In lines of sustained and intense excitement, he has affirmed the blessings bestowed on him by his communion with 'Nature and her overflowing soul'. He had heard the song that the 'created' sang to 'the Uncreated', and he had been possessed by the spirit of adoration and love that flows through all things. In reliving the mystery of his transfigured life, he exults in the memory of the 'bliss ineffable', of the 'high transport' and of the 'great joy' that were his.

And now, in a quiet passage, he considers the present time, so different from that rapturous period. He considers, too, his own present self. What were the enduring truths imparted by the power then at work in him? What kind of a man has he become? What use has he made of the blessings once 'spread around me like the sea'?

Asking and attempting to answer those questions was not a private, introspective exercise. Here, as always in *The Prelude*, Wordsworth is speaking to Coleridge – a fact made explicit by the direct address to 'my Friend' which immediately follows this extract. For Wordsworth, 'the poem about my early life' was also and equally 'the poem to Coleridge'. That 'wonderful man' would understand what he was saying, and why he needed to write about himself at epic length.

In the first two lines of this extract, Wordsworth concedes that his own direct and intense experience of 'the Uncreated' may not be valid for others. Christianity, or another orthodox religion, may be a more readily acceptable faith. However, as the rest of the passage affirms, 'theological' explanation of the experience is of little importance compared with the spiritual and moral results following from that experience. With deliberate and emphatic repetition ('with grateful voice'/'the gift is yours'/'the gift is yours') he asserts his debt to Nature's beneficent power. To that he owes his experience of God, his highest thoughts, his discovery of an abiding 'principle of joy' to calm the 'uneasy heart'. To that he owes his rejection of materialism, its contentiousness and false values. To that he owes the serene contentment of his quiet, unworldly days.

There was much to make his heart uneasy when he wrote these lines. Like Coleridge and many other Englishmen, he had rejoiced in the French Revolution. Its idealistic early years filled him with hope – 'Bliss was it in that dawn to be alive'. But now, a new French government had reverted to injustice and aggression; and repression was rampant in Britain. He needed all his faith and strength to avoid despair:

in these times of fear,
This melancholy waste of hopes o'erthrown.

His description of the dark days echoes words that Coleridge had used when suggesting that Wordsworth should write about 'the complete failure of the French Revolution'. Friends who had shared their ideals have renegued, disguising their betrayal as a pursuit of 'peace and quiet and domestic love'. Worse, these friends now sneer at the idealism they once professed.

Yet, thanks to Nature's gift, Wordsworth can still believe in human goodness, and encounter the evil days 'with *more than Roman* confidence'. He chose those words carefully. It is not merely a stoical endurance on which he rests his life. He is sustained by a living faith that springs from his own revelationary experience of 'the Wisdom and Spirit of the Universe'. Quietly reflective though this passage is, it insists steadily on the huge claim that he is what he is because he has communed 'with God and Nature'.

The pattern revealed when this passage has been placed in its context in Book 2 is representative of Wordsworth's structuring of *The Prelude* as a whole. In each book – even when, as in Cambridge, London or Paris, the setting is urban – the 'poetic landscape' is that of a mountainous region. Dramatic peaks are separated by meditative valleys, linked each to each by narrative paths.

The ascent of the poetic 'peaks' is an intensely and immediately rewarding experience. Few could ever forget their sensations on first reading, say, the raven's nest or stolen boat episodes, to give just two of the many available examples. We may have problems – and perhaps be rather irritated – if we are told to 'explain the meaning' of such passages. Explanation seems irrelevant to our swift participation in their sheer excitement and austere beauty. In any case, by yielding to the experience, we *know* what Wordsworth 'meant'. In the act of sharing, we discover that all *our* thoughts, like this, 'are steeped in feeling'.

It is the meditative passages, of which this is a characteristic example, that some readers find hard to appreciate. Their difficulties arise, I think, because they do not *listen* to him attentively, sensitive to the sound of his words. The 'song' and the 'message' are one.

Wordsworth's use of blank verse in *The Prelude* is an astonishing technical triumph. The same poetic medium is used throughout, but he speaks in different voices. His subject matter ranged from the 'poetic' to the 'prosaic'. Only by mastering a most flexible use of his verse could he move unobtrusively but surely from one emotional pitch to another – from visionary exultation to thoughtful reflection. Lacking this command of intensity, tone and pace, he could not have established the continuity that holds this great work together, or the variety within continuity that sustains our interest.

Though dominantly meditative in purpose and tone, this passage provides striking examples of the supple verse in which he expresses his varied thoughts and feelings. For instance, in the sad reflection on the falling-off of former friends, there are lengthened intervals between the light stresses; but in the scornful condemnation of the wickedness and 'dereliction' of the time, the beat is heavy and regular.

Comparable variations of the underlying rhythm occur throughout. The basic verse pattern is held – and it holds the passage together. But there is no sense of constraint from the sustaining discipline. Within the pattern. Wordsworth moves easily. At all times, we hear a free and natural voice.

The sentence structure is masterly. There are only three sentences in the 33 lines, but he rides securely on the successive waves in which his thoughts sweep onward to their firm, confident conclusion. A superb craftsman, his artistry conceals the techniques it employs. The second sentence ('If in my youth' to 'thine, O Nature!') exemplifies the controlled eloquence of verse so subtle that we almost forget that it *is* verse. Close inspection reveals something of how it is done: run-on lines; strongly marked, middle-line pauses (often clause endings); clear, thoughtful punctuation; and, always, those delicate changes of stress and pace. Many find that 'reading the score' in that way increases their pleasure; others are better content just to listen to the music.

The comparison with a musical experience is natural, for the sound of this passage is the source of so much of its pleasure. Most memorably, perhaps, when – twice, and with varied repetition – Wordsworth evokes echoes of the winds and waterfalls of his native mountains.

Sound and sense in closest harmony – and not for Coleridge's ears alone. Wordsworth intended the poem primarily for him, but he speaks to us as well. Like Wordsworth – and because we, too, are mortal – we have an uneasy heart and know that we must sometimes live through dark days. His direct experience of 'the Uncreated' and of 'Nature's overflowing soul' may never be ours, but we can share in the gifts vouchsafed to him, if we learn how to listen to him. For there is no language barrier to surmount. As Coleridge said, Wordsworth's language is 'of today and forever'.

But difficulties there are; and it is foolish to ignore them. The intense unity of *The Prelude* – a triumph of the controlling imagination that directed its composition – imposes its own penalties when we read the poem in part. This passage cannot be appreciated unless we bring to it an active recollection of Book 2 as a whole (and of other books, as well, particularly Book 1).

Again, Wordsworth is not an easy poet. At his greatest, he writes with 'an austere purity of diction' (Coleridge); but his concerns are deeply serious – fundamental – human issues. He makes demands, requiring from us a sustained effort of the imagination. He insists that we listen carefully and open our hearts to him. When we accept his challenge, we find great pleasure in his poetry: a pleasure that enlarges our 'human sentiments' and quickens our response to life.

Second critical commentary

A commentary on the Wordsworth passage, written for practice in going to the heart of the critical matters dealt with in the first commentary, within the time available in the examination.

In this extract from the closing lines of Book 2 of *The Prelude*, Wordsworth meditates on the significance of the mystical experiences of his earlier life.

Just before this passage begins, he has recreated the 'visitations' that, by the time he was seventeen, had made him aware of the oneness of the Universe and of his own unity with its spiritual essence. Writing with intense and sustained excitement, he has recalled the 'bliss ineffable' of the 'high transport' and the 'great joy' of the revelations then vouchsafed to him.

Now, in this quiet passage, he considers the present, so different from that rapturous earlier period of his life. He asks himself what he has made of the blessings then bestowed on him by his communion with 'Nature and her overflowing soul'.

Here, as throughout *The Prelude*, Wordsworth is speaking his thoughts to Coleridge, whom he addresses directly as 'my Friend' in the lines immediately following this passage. Though its material was drawn from Wordsworth's own development, 'the poem for Coleridge' (as Wordsworth called what we now know as *The Prelude*) was far from being a prolonged exercise in self-absorbed introspection. It was a strenuous and highly organised attempt to explore universal truths of human life as revealed to him by his own experience. He knew that Coleridge would understand what he was trying to do for, as he says to him in the closing lines of Book 2:

> we, by different routes, at length have gained
> The self-same bourne. And for this cause to thee
> I speak, unapprehensive of contempt. . .

In the first two lines of this extract, Wordsworth recognises that his own revelationary experiences of 'the Uncreated' may not be valid for others whose faith is derived from orthodox religion. However, as he affirms, 'theological' explanations are of little importance compared with the spiritual and moral results of his 'blessings'. Deliberately and emphatically ('with grateful voice'/'the gift is yours'/'the gift is yours') he proclaims his debt to Nature's beneficent power. To that power he owes his highest thoughts and his discovery of an abiding 'principle of joy' to calm the 'uneasy heart'.

There was much to make his heart uneasy when he wrote these lines. He had rejoiced in the idealistic early years of the French Revolution – 'Bliss was it in that dawn to be alive' (*The Prelude*, Book 2). But now, France had resorted to aggression, and in Britain repression was rampant. Friends who had shared his ideals had renegued, disguising their betrayal as a justified pursuit of 'peace and quiet and domestic love', and sneering at the idealism they once professed. He needed all his faith in Nature and in man to avoid despair:

> in these times of fear,
> This melancholy waste of hopes o'erthrown.

Yet, as he says, thanks to his visionary experiences, Wordsworth can still 'Despair not of our nature'. He encounters 'the evil days' with 'A more than Roman confidence'. Those words were carefully chosen. He does not rest his life on a mere stoical endurance. He is sustained by his own visionary experience of the 'Wisdom and Spirit of the Universe' (*The Prelude*. Book 1). Quietly reflective though this passage is, it steadily insists on his huge claim that he is what he is because he has communed 'with God and Nature'.

The structure of Book 2 of *The Prelude* (like that of the other books) is a succession of alternating dramatic peaks and meditative valleys. Many readers who respond at once to the intense poetry of the peaks (such as the raven's nest and stolen boat episodes) find the meditative passages (such as this) harder to appreciate. Yet their qualities are remarkable.

The blank verse of *The Prelude* is an astonishingly flexible medium for greatly varied subject matter, ranging from the inspiringly 'poetic' to the subdued 'prosaic', carrying the reader effortlessly from one experience to another – from visionary exultation to thoughtful reflection or steady narrative. The underlying iambic pattern establishes continuity and sustains unity, while supple variations of that pattern accommodate striking changes of mood and pace.

Though dominantly meditative in purpose and tone, this passage illustrates Wordsworth's ability to modulate his verse patterns as his immediate subject and its attendant emotions demand. For instance, in his sad reflections on the falling-off of friends, there are lengthened intervals between light stresses; but his scornful condemnation of the wickedness and 'dereliction' of the time is reinforced by a heavy, regular beat.

The sentence structure is masterly. There are only three sentences in the 33 lines of this extract, but he rides securely on the successive waves in which his thoughts sweep onward to their firm conclusion. The second sentence ('If in my youth' to 'thine, O Nature!') exemplifies the controlled eloquence of verse so subtle that we almost forget that it *is* verse. His command of technique – run-on lines, strongly marked mid-line pauses, firm punctuation, delicate changes of stress patterns – blends with his plain diction and unobtrusively evocative imagery in a close harmony of sound and sense. Indeed, it is the quiet music of this poetry that most persuades us to listen to its message. It is in its music, too, that so much of its pleasure lies. As, for example, at those memorable moments when echoes of the winds and waterfalls of his native mountains symbolise the free and natural faith that Wordsworth opposes to materialism and despair.

This extract from *The Prelude* typifies Wordsworth's ability to write about his own experience so vividly, so interestingly – above all, so truthfully – that we feel its relevance to our own condition. Like him, and because we, too, are mortal, we have an 'uneasy heart' and must sometimes live through dark days. Though his direct experience of 'the Uncreated' and of 'Nature's overflowing soul' may never be ours, we can – if we learn to listen to his voice – share imaginatively in that experience and in the blessing he received.

There are difficulties when we read *The Prelude* in part. This passage, for example, cannot be appreciated unless we bring to it an active recollection of Book 2 as a whole (and of other books as well, particularly Book 1).

Nor is Wordsworth an easy poet. His concerns are deeply serious. He makes demands, requiring from his readers a sustained effort of the imagination. Above all, he insists that we listen to him attentively and open our hearts to him. But, as this passage shows, if we rise to his challenge, we find great pleasure in his poetry: a pleasure that enlarges our 'human sentiments' and quickens our response to life.

Essay questions

6.1 What these questions test

- Your knowledge of the subject.
- Your ability to see the point of the question.
- Your ability to select, arrange and present relevant material.
- Your ability to sustain an exposition and/or to develop a reasoned argument, at some length, while keeping to the point of the question throughout.
- Your ability to write a well-constructed passage of continuous and connected prose.

Frequently, the subject matter and the wording of a question indicate that the examiners are also looking for

- Evidence that you have made a personal response to the set book about which you are writing.

This requirement is hardly surprising, since all fruitful study of literature is rooted in a meeting between *people*: authors and readers. There is little point in studying books and writers if you do not respond to them in a personal way.

The importance of a personal response when writing critical commentaries was emphasised, and effective ways of expressing it were illustrated, in Section 5.4. The approach and methods discussed and demonstrated in the four examples in that section can be applied with equal success to essay questions of the sort now being discussed. You will find it helpful to refer to Chapter 5 again, before proceeding.

You should also bear the following points in mind as you practise essays:

(i)   Do not be afraid of expressing enthusiasm; but be sure that it is genuine. Overblown endorsements of established views and 'correct' opinions will not impress the examiners. Do not gush, pose or strike attitudes.

(ii)   Do not be afraid of expressing a point of view that differs from the critical opinions generally held, or one that differs from those set out in the question. But do not adopt a contrary opinion just to demonstrate your independence. You will get no credit for airing your prejudices.

The examiners are quick to detect (and to penalise) insincerity on the one hand and narrow-mindedness on the other. They are equally quick to recognise (and to reward) thoughtful expression of a personal view – whether they agree with it or not – provided that it rests on a well-argued case, supported by evidence in the form of brief quotations from and close references to the text.

6.2 The kinds of questions set

The questions test your knowledge; but the knowledge tested is much more than mere information. Accurate information is essential, of course. Without it, you can neither grasp the content of your set books nor put your intellect and imagination to work on them. But the essay questions are designed to test the quality of your understanding and response, rather than the information on which your understanding and response are based. Inaccurate information carries its own penalties. If you have not got your facts right, your case collapses, because your opinions are based on error. But an essay stuffed full of accurate information may be no answer to the question asked.

This point is vital: you must understand the nature of the essay questions you will face, and realise the significance of the formulas that the examiners employ in the wording of their instructions.

The inherent issues that make English a valuable subject for study at an advanced level cannot be examined by setting 'straightforward' questions with 'simple' instructions. For example, 'Give an account of the events that occur between the beginning of the Battle of Philippi and the death of Brutus' would *not* be a suitable A Level question. That simple instruction to carry out a straightforward narrative task invites candidates to show that they have acquired accurate information about *Julius Caesar*. It gives them no opportunity of expressing their understanding of, and their thoughts and feelings about, the deeper issues of the play; or of discussing the ways in which Shakespeare used the events of the play and the motives of the characters to explore those issues. For those reasons, neither the wording of the question nor the contents of a satisfactory answer to it could be considered relevant to the purposes of an A Level course in English.

The formulas generally employed in phrasing essay questions and the subject areas covered by them are designed to provide you with opportunities to express your understanding and appreciation of the literature you have studied. A selection of typical questions illustrates this.

- *Love's Labour's Lost* has been said to be concerned with the rejection of love. Consider the treatment and importance of this theme in the play.
- How far, in your opinion, were Antony and Cleopatra responsible for their own fates?
- To what extent do you think it is necessary to share T. S. Eliot's religious beliefs to be moved by *Murder in the Cathedral*?
- 'Throughout the novel we are constantly made aware of the clash of hostile worlds – for example, ancient and modern, rural and urban.'

Discuss Hardy's description of this 'clash' and its bearing on the tragic theme of *Tess of the d'Urbervilles.*

● 'I describe not men, but manners; not an individual, but a species.' Does *Joseph Andrews* bear out Henry Fielding's claim to portray universal human behaviour?

Although set on different books, all those questions have three features in common:

1. A 'trigger' to fire off the candidate's thinking.
2. A clearly defined subject area.
3. An instruction to write about the prescribed subject in whatever way seems best to the candidate: 'Consider' / 'How far, in your opinion?' / 'To what extent do you think that?' / 'Does *Joseph Andrews*?'. All these instructions (and the frequently used formula 'Discuss and illustrate') simply mean: 'Give your views on the subject, supporting them with evidence from the set book.' You are left free to decide on the best way of setting out your views, but – however the question is worded – you are required to show that they result from close study of the text.

Those features are characteristic of most A Level essay questions, and their implications are explored in detail in Section 6.4. Before studying a complete method of writing examination essays, however, it is useful to look at ways in which a well-prepared candidate might make an *immediate* response to one of the questions just listed.

Love's Labour's Lost has been said to be concerned with the rejection of love. Consider the treatment and importance of this theme in the play.

Immediate response

First, *the 'trigger'*: the statement that *Love's Labour's Lost* is concerned with the rejection of love. It certainly serves its purpose of firing off *this* candidate's thinking: 'Yes, that *is* an issue – and a prominent one – the play opens with an elaborate act of rejection – *but* does it end on that note? – are the lovers parting for ever? – and what is their state of mind? – and what about Armado? – and the songs at the end of the play?'

Next, *the prescribed subject.* 'It's clear that I must stick to these points: the rejection of love as a leading theme in *L.L.L.*; Shakespeare's *treatment* of this theme (how he embodies it in the plot, characters and language of the play); its *importance* (its mental and emotional impact).'

Last, *how to deal with the subject.* 'I'm told to *consider* it. That means I've got to apply the rejection of love idea to the play as a whole, and think it through. Does it accord with my experience of the play? Is this what I see *L.L.L.* as being about? Well, the rejection of love certainly is *a* theme (and very important) – but, somehow, the statement doesn't quite match my view of the play. Why am I not entirely easy about it? I know! – it needs filling out – something like this: *L.L.L.* is concerned with the *consequences* of a vain attempt to reject love (and, therefore, to reject life). That's it! That's what *L.L.L.* says to me – and that's how I'll deal with this question. I'm beginning to see the shape of a good essay on this subject.'

Any attempt to represent spontaneous thinking is bound to seem laborious, taking up much more time than the thinking itself. Allowing for that, what you have just read is a fair reflection of ways in which a candidate might react to that question. There is still a lot to do before the essay can be written, but a good start has been made.

Remember, you will be able to make swift, positive, creative responses to an essay question if (and *only* if) you:

- have studied the set book thoroughly;
- have thought hard about it;
- have made a personal response to it;
- have grasped the nature of A Level questions; and
- have studied past questions and practised answers.

6.3 What you need to know

To be able to write successful A Level essays, it goes without saying that you must build up a fund of detailed and accurate information. But information is not enough on its own. It is the indispensable foundation for something much more important: the thoughtful and sensitive response to texts and authors that A Level essay subjects demand.

In Chapters 4 and 5, the sections headed 'What you need to know about the passage' illustrate the levels of understanding and appreciation that you must attain to be capable of answering the kinds of questions discussed in those chapters. Bear in mind that the essay questions you will have to answer demand the same high standards. You cannot write good A Level essays if your preparation has fallen short of those requirements.

Turn back now and revise those sections carefully. Then revise Section 3.5, 'Background reading'.

The advice and worked examples in this chapter teach you the techniques of essay writing, showing you how to apply the fruits of your set book studies to the kinds of questions you will be asked. But you cannot make use of that help until you have recognised, and done your best to measure up to, the *quality* of the set book study that is expected of you.

6.4 Timing and planning essays

Timing

In the papers set by most of the examining boards, candidates cannot allow themselves to spend more than 45 minutes on each essay question. Only in a few cases is an hour available for each essay. You must practise writing within the time schedule imposed by your own examination – and practise frequently. Unlikely though it may seem to you at first, you will learn to match your pace to the examination clock.

As to length, aim to cover not less than three sides of A4 examination paper (say, 800 words) when answering 45-minute essay questions. (This advice applies to medium-length critical commentary questions, too.) You obviously have more to write when answering 60-minute questions. Though I must stress again that quality is always more important than quantity, nevertheless at A Level you are expected to have quite a lot to say about books and authors studied in detail and over a considerable period.

Planning

Nobody can write a good essay without spending time on preliminary planning. That point has been stressed repeatedly, but it cannot be overemphasised. The worked examples in Chapter 5 took you through the following stages of the planning process.

(i)   Getting to grips with the question – seeing *into* it – grasping its point, so that you understand exactly what you are expected to do.

(ii)   Gathering and selecting material for your essay, testing each item for *relevance*.

(iii)   Deciding on the order of presentation – *shaping* your essay.

Until you have worked your way through those three stages, you do not know *where* your essay is going – or *how* you are going to get it there!

> *Never start to write until you know where you intend to finish.*

A good essay, it has often been said, moves *from* its beginning, *through* its middle, *to* its end. That description is none the worse for being repeated. Practise shaping your essays on the following plan. It provides a sound framework which you can adapt to the requirements of particular questions.

Essay Plan

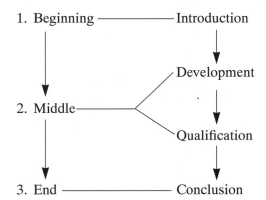

Notes on the plan

Introduction   Go straight into your subject. Get your reader's attention at once by showing that you are at grips with the question. Don't waffle. If you need more than one paragraph for your introduction, it is a sign that you have not thought out your way ahead. A dithering introduction always indicates woolly thinking.

Development   Move on from the introductory paragraph by making your first major point. Follow it with successive and connected paragraphs, dealing with supporting points and illustrations. Confine each paragraph to one topic, and provide links between your paragraphs. (That advice applies, of course, to the paragraphing throughout the essay. Your reader will find it hard to follow ideas that make sudden jumps from one overcrowded paragraph to another.)

Qualification   Turn here to arguments, opinions, facts that must be considered before the line of thought opened up in the development can be carried through to the conclusion. A 'hinge section' at the point where the development closes and the qualification opens will help your reader to share in your thinking. According to the circumstances, the 'hinge' may require one sentence, a few sentences, a separate paragraph. The qualification is not a negative part of the essay. It does not contradict the statements made in the development: it makes a positive contribution to them. The qualification advances the argument of the essay by showing that you have taken a comprehensive view of the subject you are writing about. Another 'hinge section' is needed as you close the qualification and move into the conclusion.

Conclusion   State your final view, presenting it as the outcome of the arguments, opinions and evidence previously set out in the development and qualification. Remember that the conclusion is *not* a repetitive tailpiece or a mechanical summing up. It is the firmly worded culmination of a reasoned case. It is a goal towards which you have been advancing throughout the essay.

6.5 Common mistakes

By following the methods set out in Section 6.4, you can work out a firm plan for each essay before you start to write it; and that is not the only advantage gained. The preliminary planning sharpens your thinking. Your mind is geared to its task. Consequently, you are well placed to avoid the all-too-common mistakes listed below.

Poor writing

- Faulty grammar, punctuation and spelling.
- Weak paragraphing.
- Restricted and/or inaccurate vocabulary.
- Long-winded, pretentious expressions/inappropriate style. (See Section 5.4, page 78.)

Sloppy thinking

(i)   *Waffle*: don't waste words. Come to each point directly, and get on with it. Keep the essay moving.

(ii)   *Irrelevance*: stick to the point you are making and to the subject you have chosen. No digressions – no false starts – no loose ends. Every sentence must bear on the topic under discussion.

(iii)   *Lack of evidence*: supply brief quotations and close text references to support your arguments and opinions.

(iv)   *Failure to do what you have been told to do*. The essence of a good A Level essay lies in its well-informed and thoughtful exploration of the issues raised by the question. Too often, candidates spend much of their time in giving an account of plot or content detail when they ought to be setting out an argument, expounding a point of view, or analysing particular features of a set book. There is no point in telling the examiners what happens in a play or novel, or in describing the substance of a poem. They know that already. Your job is to explore a particular critical issue arising from that play, novel or poem. Your knowledge of plot and content detail is of interest to the examiners in so far as –and *only* in so far as – you use it to express the view that you have taken of the issue raised.

6.6 Worked examples

Note 1   The brief information supplied in the 'Background' for each of the books discussed will help you to follow the working out of the answer. You could *not* write a satisfactory essay if you knew no more than the 'Background' tells you. The kind of knowledge, understanding and appreciation you need to write essays on your set books is indicated in the sections headed 'What you need to know about the passage' in Chapters 4 and 5.

Note 2   You may not agree with every critical opinion expressed in the worked examples. It would be surprising if you did. A Level essay subjects leave room for (indeed, they *invite*) individual responses to the issues they raise. Though careful consideration of the material bearing on those issues may lead different candidates to broadly similar conclusions, some variety of response is both expected and welcomed – differences of emphasis, differing judgements of the significance of this or that fact, different readings of a line of poetry, different reactions to a speech in a play, and so on. The answers suggested in the worked examples are the expression of *my* views, based on *my* interpretation of the evidence that *I* judge to be relevant to the issues discussed. I am not trying to tell you what critical opinions you 'ought' to hold. I am trying to show you how to write essays that express your own opinions effectively.

Note 3   In the first worked example, the preliminary planning gets very detailed treatment because I am trying to represent fully the kind of thinking that went into it. In the others, because you have by then become thoroughly familiar with the planning process, the thinking out is done in brief notes, just as it is when a well-prepared candidate is jotting down and sorting out ideas in the examination room.

1

An essay question on *Hard Times*

Background

Thomas Gradgrind, a leading figure in Coketown, a manufacturing centre, is 'a man of realities . . . of facts and calculations'. He brings up his children, Louisa and Tom, in 'an eminently practical manner', according to his 'system'. which, having no room for the heart, values only the all-sufficient head.

Josiah Bounderby, banker and manufacturer, self-made, pompous, and a tyrant to his factory 'hands', marries Louisa, thirty years his junior. Louisa consents to this loveless match, which her father favours, to further the interests of Tom, who is in Bounderby's employment. Her upbringing has so stunted her emotional growth that – apart from her love for her brother – she knows nothing of 'tastes and fancies . . . and affections'.

James Harthouse, a young man of 'good family', having 'gone in' for politics and statistics for want of anything better to do with his life, arrives in Coketown to be 'taken up' by the 'fellows of the hard Fact school' with a view to becoming their member of parliament. Thrown into Louisa's society, he decides to while away the time by seducing her. He exploits Tom's admiration for him to gain Louisa's good opinion. When she realises what his real intentions are, she returns to her father's house (Stone Lodge) for protection. Gradgrind, at last made aware of the harm that his 'system' has done, shelters Louisa from Bounderby, who then, with the utmost self-righteousness, packs up Louisa's possessions, returns them to Stone Lodge, and 'resumes a bachelor's life'.

Gradgrind and Louisa are comforted in their trouble by the loving presence of Sissy Jupe, daughter of a 'stroller', whom Gradgrind had taken into his house as a servant when her father disappeared. Gradually, during Louisa's married life, Sissy has brought affection into the stony hearts of the inhabitants of Stone Lodge. It is Sissy who confronts James Harthouse and insists that he must leave Coketown, even though he protests to her that he is there 'on a public kind of business' which he has 'gone in for and sworn by' and that he will be placed 'in a very ridiculous position' if he 'takes himself off'. The wealthy and heartless man is forced to recognise that, on this issue, he has been made 'a Great Pyramid of failure' by the moral strength of 'a poor girl, daughter of a stroller'.

Later, it is Sissy who saves Tom from imprisonment. After Louisa has left her husband, Gradgrind discovers that Tom has stolen money from Bounderby's bank and has thrown suspicion on Stephen Blackpool, one of Bounderby's factory 'hands'. Stephen disappears from Coketown but, when he is discovered mortally injured at the bottom of a disused pit shaft, the truth is pieced together from his dying words. With Sissy's help and that of Sleary, proprietor of the travelling circus in which Sissy's father worked, Tom is hurried abroad. Gradgrind then publicly acknowledges Tom's guilt and proclaims Stephen's innocence.

Sustained through their sorrows by Sissy's simple, loving goodness, father and daughter learn new values and a better way of living. Life has taught them both that – as the good-hearted Sleary tells Gradgrind, lisping out his 'philosophy' over a glass of brandy and water: 'there ith a love in the world, not all Thelf-interetht after all'.

Examination question

Discuss the importance of Harthouse in the novel.   (L.)

Get to grips with the task set

This apparently simple instruction requires careful thought. Like any other reader of *Hard Times*, I can judge Harthouse's importance in the novel *only* by considering how his presence affects *my* response to the book as a whole. Therefore, as I interpret it, the instruction tells me to discuss (describe and explain) the ways in which Harthouse's character and actions influence the impact that *Hard Times* makes on my thoughts and feelings. In other words, I have to say what the attitudes and deeds of this man contribute to the experience (emotional, rational and moral) that I receive from reading this book.

Gather material

Harthouse is not present throughout the novel – cf. Bounderby, Gradgrind, Louisa.

He is not a strikingly 'Dickensian' *character* – cf. Sleary and Mrs Sparsit.

He *is* sharply drawn: wealthy, upper class. 'Goes in' for politics. Never doubts his right to be a leader, if he so chooses.

BUT is he chiefly important either as a character, or as a vehicle for satire? Surely, it's what he *does* that matters? His attempted seduction of Louisa brings about her return to her father's house and her separation from Bounderby. So, Harthouse is very important as a plot 'lever'.

Of course, he only does what he does because he is what he is! Character and action are fused.

BUT is his importance to the plot the sole reason for the striking effect of his presence in the novel?

It would be, if *Hard Times* were memorable mainly as a narrative. But it isn't. The impact of the novel – for me –comes from the vivid use of plot and characters to express the *theme*.

And remember the way description is used to embody the theme: Coketown, Stone Lodge, the schoolroom, Old Hell shaft . . . *Careful!* Is this relevant? The essay is about Harthouse and what *he* contributes to the novel.

Concentrate on the *theme* and *his* contribution to it. The theme, as it comes through to me, is: heart opposed to head/love and selflessness opposed to calculation and self-interest/caring opposed to exploitation/the human cost of a heartless society.

Yes – and this is where Harthouse's real importance lies – both as a character and as a plot 'lever' he illuminates the theme.

Dickens introduces him into the Coketown scene. Superficially, he's utterly different from Coketown's leading figures. BUT he's one of them in his nature – he's cold, calculating, *heartless*. So are they.

Gradgrind
|
Louisa —— Harthouse —— Tom
|
Bounderby

He *is* cold, calculating and heartless. And so is what he *does*. He tries to seduce Louisa to while away the time.

Socially, he's of another world: *morally*, he's Coketown, through and through. He's an *exploiter*. He exploits Bounderby, Tom, Louisa. They have no defence against him, because he uses their weapons.

BUT he can't defeat Sissy. She defeats him. Two opposed sets of values come face to face when Sissy confronts Harthouse.

Sissy	*Harthouse*
'I have only the commission of my love for her, and her love for me.'	'He was touched in the cavity where his heart should have been.'
'with a blending of gentleness and steadiness that quite defeated him.'	'only a poor girl – only James Harthouse made nothing of'

Harthouse doesn't change – and the world doesn't change. The odds are still stacked against compassion.

BUT in that interview, Sissy triumphs. *Moral force*. Ties up with Sleary's 'philosophy' expressed near end of novel.

Note   I have taken this stage of the preliminary planning as far as I need to go. By keeping the set task firmly at the front of my mind, I have been able to gather plenty of relevant material. *And*, in the process of gathering that material, I have thought through my subject. I now know what I want to say about Harthouse's importance in *Hard Times*. Next, I must work out a shape for my essay, so that I can present my views clearly and persuasively. I shall waste all the hard thinking that I have put into this subject, if I start to write before I know how I am going to move forward to the conclusion that I have in mind.

Work out the plan

Introduction   Harthouse is in some senses a minor character, but vitally important to the novel as a whole. How? In the answer to that question lies the key to understanding Dickens's intentions in writing *Hard Times*.

Development

(a)   His character – vividly and sharply drawn – satirical elements.
(b)   Plot – his role is crucial – attempted seduction of Louisa and its consequences.
(c)   BUT (a) and (b) do not account for the impact that he makes when we consider book as a whole. (Use this as a hinge section of the essay: the argument now turns to essential qualifying considerations.)

Qualification

(a)   Harthouse is not a memorable 'Dickensian' character. Contrast with other 'Dickensian' characters, including Sleary and Mrs Sparsit. We do not immediately think of him at the mention of *Hard Times*. He doesn't 'live outside the book'!
(b)   Although he is crucial to the plot, plot was not Dickens's major concern. *Hard Times* was not written primarily as a piece of narrative fiction. We do not remember it chiefly for its story.
(c)   The novel lives because every element in it (plot, characterisation and description) is fused with every other to embody its *theme*. (Use this as a

hinge section to indicate that the qualification is closing and leading in to the conclusion.)

Conclusion

(a) Statement of theme: caring opposed to exploitation (see earlier note on theme).

(b) How Dickens uses Harthouse to embody that theme: Harthouse in Coketown – superficially different from Coketown's leading figures, but essentially of the same nature: in what he *is* and what he *does*, he is morally indistinguishable from them.

(c) BUT Harthouse and Sissy: theme of novel encapsulated in his defeat by that 'poor girl' – Sleary's 'philosophy' triumphant.

Note   I concentrated on establishing a clear outline of my argument. There was no need to fill in the details that I shall use when I am writing the essay. Having gathered ample material in stage 2, I've got all the necessary illustrations and supporting evidence in my head. I may modify the plan here and there, as I write. The subject has come alive as I have thought about it; and fresh ideas – better ways of making a point – are always likely to come to the surface as the act of writing the essay quickens the imagination. But, *having worked out where I am going and how I am going to get there*, I shall not risk getting lost by wandering off the main road.

Write the essay

The account of Harthouse's involvement with Coketown occupies very little more than one-third of the book. Compared with Gradgrind, Louisa, Bounderby and Tom, he is a minor character. Yet he makes a dramatic impact on people and events, and he plays an essential part in our experience of the novel as a whole. It is not possible to appreciate Dickens's aims and achievements in *Hard Times* without exploring the use that he made of James Harthouse.

His shallow, selfish nature is established quickly and, apart from the persistent cunning with which he pursues Louisa, we know all there is to be known about him within a few pages of his arrival in Coketown. He is 'a thorough gentleman, made to the model of the time; weary of everything, and putting no faith in anything than Lucifer'. Having tried the army, diplomacy and travel, and found them 'a bore', he has 'gone in' for politics. He comes to Coketown to 'take up' and 'to be taken up by' the 'fellows of the hard Fact school'. He has no 'cause', no commitment to any person or to any issue except the comfort and well-being of James Harthouse. His languid and compliant response to Bounderby's bullying denunciations of the factory 'hands' and of the 'humbugging sentiment' of reformers typifies his attitude. He finds Bounderby disgusting and boring, but his objections rest on purely social grounds. There are no moral contours on Harthouse's map of life.

His contempt for Tom Gradgrind – 'the whelp' – is no bar to cultivating his 'friendship' as the indispensable means of winning Louisa's trust. That gained, he attempts to seduce her – an attempt in which vanity and boredom play as large a part as desire.

There is no need for psychological subtleties in the presentation of this sharply-drawn character. Nor does Dickens develop the satire inherent in his social origins and attitudes. It is sufficient that the reader accepts Harthouse as a credible agent of the changes that his actions bring about in the lives of others. For his attempted seduction of Louisa results in her return to her father's house and her permanent separation from Bounderby. More and heavier troubles lie in store for them, but Gradgrind and his daughter are slowly healed. Painfully and shockingly made to recognise the falseness of their values, they learn to open their hearts to each other and to their fellow creatures.

But neither appreciation of the skill with which his character is drawn nor recognition of his crucial role in the plot is enough to account for the impact that Harthouse makes on the reader of *Hard Times*.

He is not – nor was he intended to be – one of the great 'Dickensian' *characters*, such as those we instantaneously recall on seeing or hearing the titles of the novels in which they appear: for example, Mr Micawber or Betsy Trotwood in *David Copperfield*; Mr Wemmick in *Great Expectations*; Mr Guppy in *Bleak House*. Nobody's first reaction to the title *Hard Times* would be to recall James Harthouse. We would be much more likely to remember Bounderby or Sleary or Mrs Sparsit. Judged purely as ' a character', Harthouse is not outstanding.

Nor does his undoubted importance in the action figure very largely when we take stock of our response to the novel as a whole. For it is not primarily as a narrative that *Hard Times* makes its impact on its readers. Dickens is not simply telling a story. Narration, like characterisation and description, is a means to an end: the vivid and memorable embodiment of a theme. So caught up are we in the lives of his fictitious people – their motives and their deeds, their environment and their values – that we enter their world. And it is in our imaginative response to that experience that we discover what the novel 'means'. Its theme comes home to us.

The theme of *Hard Times* is the price that must be paid for creating a society in which calculation and self-interest cast out love and selflessness. Harthouse's real importance in the book is the contribution that he makes to the expression of that theme.

In Coketown, the exploiters are supreme; and Harthouse – superficially so different from the Gradgrinds and the Bounderbys of that world – is at one with them. He may be bored and disgusted by them, but he is morally indistinguishable from the 'hard Fact fellows'. Moved only by self-interest, he arrives in Coketown to exploit them; and they have no defence against him, for he uses their own weapons. His attempt to seduce Louisa is as cold, calculating and heartless as their treatment of the factory 'hands'.

But their system cannot extinguish simple human goodness. Somehow – and wonderfully – it survives among the poor, the exploited victims of materialism. Sleary's 'philosophy' is not less telling for being lisped out over a glass of brandy and water: 'there ith a love in the world, not all Thelf-interetht after all'.

The story of Rachel and Stephen manifests the love that 'endureth all things'; but the most concentrated and dramatic embodiment of the strength of goodness occurs in the remarkable scene in which Sissy confronts Harthouse – and defeats him. This is no miraculous 'conversion'. He does not change. The man who leaves Coketown at Sissy's command is the same man who arrived there. Nor has the world changed. The odds are still stacked against compassion.

Yet, when Sissy – for Louisa's sake, and armed only 'with my love for her and her love for me' – opposes the cynical, worldly, wealthy man, he is 'touched in the cavity where his heart should have been', and he yields. His adversary is 'only a poor girl, daughter of a stroller', but, momentarily, he recognises a superior moral power, and he is 'made nothing of' by it.

It is then that the reader of *Hard Times* fully understands the importance of James Harthouse.

2

An essay on the poetry of Gerard Manley Hopkins

Background

A *Selection* of Hopkins's poetry is frequently specified as a set book. Extracts from Hopkins's letters, notebooks and journals are usually included. They throw light on his poetic ideals and methods, and on his views on the subjects that inspired his poetry. The editorial introduction and notes provide a starting point for the reader's own exploration of the poems.

It is not surprising that this poet is often studied at A Level, as his work is both challenging and rewarding. Many first-time readers are instantly aware of difficulties and, simultaneously, of pleasures. Few who study him regret the experience. Not every difficulty will be resolved, but imaginative reading brings rich rewards. Much depends on where a start is made. Those who begin with the ' nature poems' (to use a convenient but superficial description) take the best way in. Readers who have experienced, say, 'Inversnaid', 'Spring' and 'Pied Beauty' come to 'The Wreck of the Deutschland' with pleasurable anticipation, even if they know its reputation as a 'difficult' poem.

Hopkins's poetry cannot be appreciated unless – as he insisted – it is read 'with the *ear*'. The definition of poetry as 'memorable speech' is strikingly applicable. Lines, verses, whole poems, lodge effortlessly in the minds of his readers. His style – at once musical and dramatic – is unique. Its distinctive features (daring images, verse forms, diction and syntax) enabled him to explore his chosen themes in his own way and in his own voice. Of no poetry is it truer that *what* is said is inseparable from *how* it is said. Matter and manner are one.

Highly individual (occasionally mannered and eccentric) though he is, his poems enlarge our understanding of the nature of poetry itself. We get nowhere by approaching him 'intellectually'; but once we allow our senses to respond to his language, our emotions and thoughts are quickened too. Reading Hopkins is not only a delight in itself, it is also an experience that makes us better readers of poetry – more perceptive and responsive.

Candidates studying Hopkins need to give thoughtful consideration to the following specific topics.

Subject matter (a) Nature; (b) religion; (c) God and nature – God's

imminence in creation;   (d) God and human nature – love and suffering –
the problem of pain;   (e) the priestly vocation – Hopkins's own fitness for
it.

Content   (a) Expression of 'romantic' attitudes to his subjects – compare
other poems of his in which 'realism' predominates – pessimism? –despair?
(b) Degree to which he makes his experiences universal.   (c) Religious
fervour – does it come between reader and Hopkins? Do we have to be Roman
Catholics to understand and appreciate his poems?   (d) His use of theological
concepts and terms – it is a barrier to our enjoyment?   (e) He includes
unfamiliar ideas drawn from philosophy, science and natural history – how
important are these in our response to him?   (f) Hopkins's own theories (for
example, 'inscape/instress') – does he make poetry of them? – or do they
remain private ideas, expressed in a private language?

Style   (a) Technical devices, such as alliteration, assonance, rhyme,
innovatory metres, especially 'sprung rhythm' – his use of these, and their
effects.   (b) Diction – word coinings, dialect words, obsolete words, words
used in a wholly unexpected way – their startling effects – sense of new-
minted language.   (c) Imagery – rapid and sensuous – again, startling – fusion
of idea with image.   (d) Syntax – condensed – dramatic rapidity of thought
often hard to follow – speech effect.   (e) Nobody quite like him – but echoes
of the Metaphysicals, Keats, Browning – above all, Shakespeare's sonnets and
'final style'.

The poems grouped   (a) 'Simple' nature poems – expressing delight.
(b) 'Ecstatic' nature poems – celebrating God.   (c) The 'terrible' sonnets –
spiritual agony.   (d) Poems about people.   (e) 'The Wreck of the
Deutschland'.

Personal response   (a) What do I enjoy? – and why do I enjoy it?   (b) What
do I dislike – and why do I dislike it?   (c) Do I find him 'difficult'? – where
and why? – analyse – is it my fault or his?   (d) Am I much concerned with
critical arguments about his 'status' ('lesser great poet'/'great lesser poet')?
(e) What has the experience of reading Hopkins taught me about poetry
itself? – about how poets use language?   (f) Does his poetry stay with me?

Note   Not all these topics will be tested *directly* in any one examination
paper. The questions set will refer specifically to two or three of them at the
most. But you cannot write well on any topic unless you have thought about
your set book as a whole. The insight you need cannot be gained by spotting
questions and studying a few topics in isolation. To write well about any one
aspect of a set book depends on the range and depth of the study you have
made of the whole book. Your critical approach must be many-sided.

Examination question

By selecting and analysing examples from TWO poems by Hopkins, show the
characteristics of his poetic style.   (S.U.J.B.)

Get to grips with the task set

Note , *Examples – analyse* – TWO poems *–show characteristics – style.*

This isn't an 'argument' essay – it's an exposition – a demonstration – a 'showing', NOT a discussion. (Must bear this in mind when I'm planning.)

Gather material

Which two poems? How do I make a good choice? I must know them thoroughly. I need plenty of quotations and close references. I must not be vague. Must be *detailed*.

Choose two poems on different subjects and in different moods BUT style of both characteristic of Hopkins.

Rule out 'Deutschland' – its style has all the characteristic features BUT the scale of the poem is wrong for this essay –too big to handle easily *and* out of proportion with any other possible choice.

I'll choose: 1. The 'Kingfishers' sonnet – a joyful celebration of God's presence in all creation. 2. 'Carrion Comfort' – another sonnet, but 'written in blood' (Hopkins) – spiritual agony – bitter desolation.

What am I looking for in the poems? What characteristic features of his style do they illustrate? Voicing of his theme in dramatic speech through the use of: verse form and rhythms – alliteration – assonance – repetitions – daring diction – condensed images – compressed syntax, and so on. I can recall immediately examples of each of these features in the two poems I have chosen.

Work out the plan

Introduction Name poems chosen. Say – very briefly – why. Lead reader straight into the essay.

Development

(a) Verse form and metres.
(b) Diction.
(c) Imagery.
(d) Rhetorical devices.
(e) (*Hinge*) But all these are his stylistic means to his overall stylistic ends.

Qualification

(a) Poems are not just an assemblage of stylistic tricks.
(b) If Hopkins didn't distil a *total*, overall style out of them, he'd be a mere showman.
(c) (Hinge) *Why* he wrote in the way he did.

Conclusion His characteristic and highly individual style is the expression of his response to – and his unique way of voicing – his life's concerns.

Write the essay

Different as they are in theme and tone, the 'Kingfishers' poem and 'Carrion Comfort' both exemplify the characteristic features of Hopkins's poetic style.

The former is a joyous celebration of all creation as a manifestation of God's love. The latter is the agonised expression of spiritual crisis and desolation. Yet, in both, the poetic voice is unmistakably that of Hopkins.

It is his mastery of verse form and rhythms that first strikes the reader's ear, for it is on this mastery that the 'Hopkins sound' chiefly depends. Each poem is firmly based on the Petrarchan sonnet form: an octave rhyming a-b-b-a-a-b-b-a; and a sestet rhyming c-d-c-d-c-d. His disciplined adherence to that sustaining pattern shapes each poem; yet, within the pattern, he moves with the outmost freedom.

'Carrion Comfort' is more daring in its prosody than 'Kingfishers', but its revolutionary techniques are not different in kind. In both poems, the metre is flexible, but it is under tight control. The stresses fall as feeling and thought compel, overriding any constraints that an 'orthodox' scansion would impose. The stress marks that Hopkins inserted above the last two syllables in the first line of the 'Kingfishers' poem reflect his dependence on being read 'with the *ear*'. He disliked 'signposting' his 'unorthodox' stresses, believing that sensitive readers, responsive to the movement of his thought and feeling, would hear them as they read. Occasionally, he felt compelled to mark them. His poetry is damaged if we do not hear it as he meant it to be heard. It cannot reach readers who attempt to impose on it the traditional stress pattern of standard metres.

From first line to last, 'Kingfishers' and 'Carrion Comfort' typify Hopkins's characteristic handling of metres. The opening lines of each poem reveal the essential features:

> As kingfishers catch fire, dragonflies dráw fláme;
> As tumbled over rim in roundy wells
> Stones ring   ('Kingfishers')

> NOT, I'll not, carrion comfort, Despair,
> not feast on thee;
> Not untwist – slack they may be – these last strands of man
> In me   ('Carrion Comfort')

In 'Kingfishers' there are five stresses to each line: in 'Carrion Comfort' there are six. The 'slack' syllables accompanying the stresses vary in number. Thus, the stresses are clustered or spaced out as the expression of emphasised ideas and emotions demands, and not as a standard metre would dictate.

The second line of each poem runs on. The foot (and the sense) begun at the end of that line is completed at the beginning of the next. The new 'turn' of thought/feeling is held off until later in the line. This device – a favourite with Hopkins, and likely to occur at any point in a poem – establishes a second structure within the formal and firmly drawn shape of the verse.

These two features are the essence of the 'counterpointing' to which Hopkins often referred when describing his metrical techniques; and counterpointing is reinforced by other devices that tie word to word and line to line, resulting in a remarkably dense verbal texture.

Alliteration is the most frequently used 'word link', adding point to the stresses:

> To the Father through the features of men's faces
> ('Kingfishers')

> why wouldst thou rude on me
> Thy wring-world right foot rock?
> ('Carrion Comfort')

The 'vowel-chime' of assonance, often in company with alliteration, plays a similar part:

> Deals out that being indoors each one dwells
> ('Kingfishers')

> Hand rather, my heart lo! lapped strength,
> stole joy, would laugh, cheer
> ('Carrion Comfort')

And, as further reinforcement, his strict end-rhymes are backed up with internal rhymes:

> like each tucked string <u>tells</u>, each hung <u>bell's</u>
> Bow <u>swung</u> finds <u>tongue</u> ('Kingfishers')

> <u>Why</u>? That my chaff might <u>fly</u>, my grain <u>lie</u>,
> <u>sheer</u> and <u>clear</u>   ('Carrion Comfort')

Often, these verbal devices are used to create onomatopoeia, directly reproducing sound effects, as in:

> each hung bell's
> Bow swung finds tongue to fling out broad its name
> ('Kingfishers')

Sometimes, the sound confronts us as an emotional experience, as in:

> lay a lionlimb against me? scan
> With darksome devouring eyes my bruised bones? and fan,
> O in turns of tempest, me heaped there ('Carrion Comfort')

Characteristic, too, is the daring diction. Examples have already been given when illustrating other features of his style. It is impossible to isolate a particular feature, for his style is all of a piece. Each feature works with all the others. However, certain elements of his unusual uses of words can be analysed.

Though he can – and often does – speak in the plainest of plain English, he frequently uses obsolete words, dialect words, coined words, and words to which he gives an unexpected sense. In 'Kingfishers' we find 'tucked' (obsolete in the sense used); 'plays' (used as of 'players' – actors). In 'Carrion Comfort', the word 'coil' (in the sense intended) was a dialect survival; 'wring-world' and 'lionlimb' he invented because he needed them.

Similarly, he often makes very simple, direct statements: 'I say more' ('Kingfishers'); 'I can no more' ('Carrion Comfort'); but his syntax is often as daring as his diction. 'Selves' is used as a verb in 'Kingfishers' to mean 'asserts his own individuality'. In the same poem, 'justices' is also used as a verb, meaning 'acts in a just way'. In 'Carrion Comfort', the knotty syntax of 'why wouldst thou rude on me Thy wring-world right foot rock?' is baffling until we realise that the verb is 'rock' and that 'rude' is an adverb. And in the lines beginning, 'Nay in all that toil', the syntactical puzzle is solved only when our imagination is fully engaged with the terrible experience recreated in the rapid language. But the reader of Hopkins must always look for imaginative rather than intellectual ways to perception.

His imagery has the same characteristic compression and energy. He does not explain. The metaphors are condensed. There is no gap – no time lag – between the image and the idea: kingfishers <u>catch fire</u>; God fans (with his flail) the suffering mortal <u>heaped there</u> (on his threshing floor); Despair is <u>carrion comfort</u>.

Characteristic, too, are the rhetorical devices, notably repetitions, exclamations and parentheses: 'Keeps grace: that keeps all his goings graces' ('Kingfishers'); 'I wretch lay wrestling with (my God!) my God' ('Carrion Comfort'). He speaks his poems out loud, directly and dramatically.

These stylistic features all work together to produce the total style that we immediately recognise as his. Were this not their result, he would be a mere showman – a verbal juggler – a word magician.

But Hopkins wrote poetry as the expression of the deepest concerns of his deeply concerned life – as man and priest. Every single feature of his style is bent to the service of that grave purpose. Only by speaking to us directly, urgently, dramatically and memorably could he say what his life's faith compelled him to say. The sound of that distinctive, passionate voice is the most characteristic feature of his poetry.

3

An essay on the poetry and letters of John Keats

Background

Born in 1795, John Keats made his first appearance as a poet with a sonnet published in Leigh Hunt's magazine, the *Examiner*, 1816. His first collection of poems was published in 1817; his last, in 1820 – the year before he died. In that short space of time, his genius developed swiftly and surely. The 1820 volume contained poems that are among the greatest in the English language.

The various *Selections* specified as set books generally concentrate on the 1820 poems, though they usually include extracts from the earlier long poems ('Sleep and Poetry' and 'Endymion') as well as sonnets and 'occasional poems' written at various times. They also include passages from Keats's letters in which he expressed his views about life and poetry. He was an original and profound critic (of his own work as well as that of other poets) whose observations about the nature and art of poetry are essential reading for students of literature. His reflections on poetry are frequently used as the basis of essay questions.

The poems which A Level students are required to study in detail include: a selection of the sonnets (for example, 'On First Looking into Chapman's

Homer' and 'The Human Seasons'); the narrative poems ('Lamia', 'Isabella or The Pot of Basil', 'The Eve of St Agnes'); the four-book (but incomplete) epic 'Hyperion'; and the Odes. These represent his greatest powers and illustrate the nature of his poetic preoccupations and style.

In these poems, he pursued an urgent quest for a perfection of utterance in which he could communicate what he called 'the lore of good and ill'. Life, he said. is 'the vale of soul-making': joy and sorrow are inextricably mingled. Individuals are transient, but 'art offers a type of permanence' amid 'the weariness, the fever, and the fret'. These truths, 'proved on his pulses', he could communicate only if he achieved a style of such intensity that mere argument and explicit explanation – even the delight of decoration – were burned away.

Aware of his mortal illness, he knew that he had less time than most poets. Conscious of his own gift for brilliantly sensuous writing, he knew the temptations of self-indulgence. Yet, so clear was his understanding of his poetic calling, and so courageous was his struggle to be worthy of it, he renounced the style that came so easily to him and strove to discipline his abounding fancy. The 'versifying pet lamb', so given to 'Poesy', became the 'great and mighty poet of the human heart'. In some of his last poems, he attained such mastery of verse form and of the use of symbolic imagery that Matthew Arnold, who began his famous essay on Keats's poetry by asking whether he was anything more than 'abundantly and enchantingly sensuous', acknowledged his greatness in the often-quoted words: 'he is with Shakespeare'.

Candidates preparing to write on Keats will go deeply into the issues touched on in that brief and necessarily unargued outline. Their explorations of Keats's work will include the following specific topics.

Subject matter (a) Love. (b) Nature. (c) Mortality. (d) Art (including sculpture, music and painting, as well as poetry itself). (e) Human transience contrasted with the permanence of art. (f) Human joy and suffering. (g) Beauty. (h) Myth and legend.

Varied treatment of subjects (a) Narrative. (b) Lyric. (c) Epic. (d) Dramatic. (e) Disquisitive.

Development (a) Maturing of thought and emotion. (b) Evolution of his theory of 'acceptance'. (c) Theoretical approaches to art. (e) Style – see below.

Style (a) The decorative impulse. (b) Developing mastery of symbolic imagery, particularly metaphor. (c) Density and variety of sense impressions – the 'fine excess'. (d) Ceaseless experimentation with verse form and metre. (e) Music of verse. (f) The struggle for discipline.

Ways of grouping the poems (a) By chronology. (b) By theme. (c) By subject. (d) By form (for example: sonnets; narrative couplets; narrative stanzas; epic blank verse; odes).

Keats in his setting (a) The spirit of the age. (b) Keats as a 'Romantic' – comparisons with Wordsworth, Shelley and Byron.

Personal response (a) The poems I most enjoy – and why. (b) Poems about which I am less enthusiastic – and why. (c) What has the experience of reading Keats done for me? Do his poems stay with me? (d) What has Keats taught me about poetry?

Examination question

Referring in detail to *two* of the Odes, show how you have been helped in your reading of Keats's poetry by ideas that you have encountered when studying his letters. You are advised to concentrate your attention on not more than two or three of Keats's leading ideas, explaining them clearly and saying exactly how they have influenced your reading of the poems you have selected.

Note The preliminary planning on which the essay was based has been omitted from this worked example. Only the essay itself is printed. If you study it closely, you should be able to describe: (i) the way in which I got to grips with the task set by the examiners, (ii) the criteria I applied when selecting the material used in the essay; and (iii) the plan on which I based the essay. If you cannot give a clear account of all three, either I have not written a good essay, or you have not read it attentively. In assessing its quality, you should also consider: (i) whether the supporting evidence is used effectively; and (ii) whether the essay is clearly, cogently and persuasively written.

Finally, note that the first person is frequently used in the essay – more often than in the earlier essays in this chapter. If you think it is overdone, try to reword the offending passages; but remember that the examiners directed the question to the candidates in an essentially personal way – 'show how *you* have been helped' / 'ideas that *you* have encountered' / '*your* reading of the poems'.

Write the essay

My own reading of 'To a Nightingale' and 'To Autumn' has been influenced greatly by Keats's views about human life and by his thoughts about the language of poetry, as set out in his letters.

Keats's belief that life is 'the vale of soul-making' provided me with the basis of my interpretations of these two poems. Every human being, Keats says, passes through this vale, but only those who attain a state of mind which he called 'acceptance' become intellectually, emotionally and spiritually mature. The 'contraries' of life – its inextricable mingling of joy and sorrow, of delight and pain, of good and evil – must be faced. This inescapable condition constitutes the mystery of life; and that mystery can never be explained away or dodged. Its 'dark passages' must be explored, for that is the only way to attain 'acceptance'.

Keats saw this philosophical position as the supreme quality of the poetic mind; and it was the poet's ordained lot to strive for its possession. 'A man of achievement, especially in literature.' he stated, by attaining 'acceptance' acquired the faculty he called 'negative capability'. And he defined 'negative capability' as the capacity 'of being in uncertainties, doubts, without irritable reaching after fact and reason'.

In other words, he believed that great poetry could be written only by those who had the honesty and courage to accept and depict life as it really is, neither pretending nor wishing it to be otherwise.

In support of this belief, he instances Wordsworth's 'Tintern Abbey' as proof that Wordsworth's 'genius is explorative of those dark passages'. And he claimed that Shakespeare was pre-eminently the possessor of 'negative capability'.

With those as his great examples, he determined to pursue 'the lore of good and ill', and to write poetry that would 'ease the burden of the mystery'. Like his own Grecian Urn, his poetry must be 'a friend to man'.

I have also found his ideas about style very helpful. The essential quality of the style he struggled to master is stated very simply in a letter to his brothers: 'The excellence of every art is its intensity'. In a letter to his publisher, he made a longer statement of his beliefs: 'I think poetry should surprise by a fine excess and not by singularity. It should strike the reader as a wording of his own highest thoughts and appear almost a remembrance'. Then he added, 'if poetry comes not as naturally as the leaves to a tree, it had better not come at all'.

In reading his poetry with those words in mind, it becomes clear that his aim was to fuse the 'content' of a poem and its 'style'. He strove to use language so intensely that the experience of the poem is communicated instantaneously, without need for explanation. The reader is to be 'caught up' into the poet's imagination by the 'fine excess' (the intensity) of the language. There must be no ostentation (no 'singularity') to dilute the essential unity of the poem. No single phrase, line or verse must stick out to draw attention to itself and away from the poem as a whole. Consequently, the highest art of the poet is to conceal his art. The 'fine excess' must *seem* to come 'as naturally as the leaves to a tree'. Nothing must strike the reader as strained or merely decorative.

Keats compressed all his deepest convictions about poetic style into the memorable declaration that great poetry is 'unobtrusive, a thing that enters into one's soul and does not startle it or amaze it with itself but with its subject'.

Those ideas opened a way into the poems that has greatly increased my appreciation. They were especially helpful when I was trying to understand why I found 'To Autumn' a more deeply satisfying poem than the 'Ode to a Nightingale', much as I enjoyed reading the latter.

The 'Ode to a Nightingale' is a superb poem, but it is not wholly and steadily what Keats himself said a poem should be, 'a search after truth'. Though Bacchus is rejected, 'the viewless wings of Poesy' are used to escape from 'the weariness, the fever, and the fret' of life. Keats hides in 'embalmed darkness' from the pain of reality until the forlorn bell tolls him back to the harsh facts of his human life:

> Where palsy shakes a few, sad, last gray hairs,
> Where youth grows pale, and spectre-thin, and dies;
> Where but to think is to be full of sorrow. . . .

In the last verse, at the inevitable end of this unavailing attempt to escape, comes an explicit rejection both of the attempt and of the means he used in making it:

> Adieu! the fancy cannot cheat so well
> As she is famed to do, deceiving elf.

With Keats's letters in mind, we see the significance of the key words in that rejection: 'fancy'; 'cheat'; 'deceiving elf'. That is the escapist language of

'Poesy', not the truthful language of *poetry*. It is that language and therefore, 'Poesy' itself, that Keats is rejecting.

There are lines and whole verses in the Nightingale poem equal in intensity of language to anything he or any other poet has ever achieved. The 'fine excess' of the two verses beginning 'O, for a draught of vintage' and 'I cannot see what flowers are at my feet' is a sure mark of genius. But there *is* 'singularity'. Those two verses stand too much apart. They are poems within the poem. The greatest verse of all, 'Thou wast not born for death', amazes us 'with itself', rather than with its contribution to the *whole* subject of the poem.

I believe that 'To Autumn' more truly realises the poetic ideals that Keats expressed in his letters. When I first read the poem, I seemed to have known it all my life, and I *felt* its truth. Repeated readings deepened those first responses, and soon – with no conscious effort – I found that I knew it by heart. So it was no surprise when I later read Keats's statement that 'Poetry should be great and unobtrusive, a thing that enters one's soul'.

Further reading of the letters provided me with a completely satisfying explanation of the poem's power. It has the intensity that Keats saw as a mark of excellence. It attains a perfect unity, for the 'fine excess' is free from all 'singularity'. Keats's own description of 'the rise, the progress and the setting of imagery' is embodied in the movement of the poem's three verses – from the morning mists, through the noonday warmth, to evening and the closing music of the 'soft-dying day'.

And it was the letters that strengthened my growing realisation that this poem, ostensibly 'about' an autumn day, is more truly to be read as an exploration and an acceptance of mortality. The letters tell us that Shakespeare's treatment of this theme (especially in *King Lear*) haunted Keats's imagination:

> Men must endure
> Their going hence, even as their coming hither;
> Ripeness is all.

It seems to me that 'To Autumn' proclaims a truth about life that Keats had felt 'on his pulses'. He does not have to explain or argue. Symbolised throughout the poem by the imagery, the theme is open and triumphant at the great climax:

> Where are the songs of Spring? Ay, where are they?
> Think not of them, thou hast thy music too.

The 'uncertainties, doubts' of the Nightingale poem are resolved. There is no 'reaching after fact and reason', for 'the sense of beauty obliterates all consideration'.

With Keats's own words as my guide, I see 'To Autumn' as the greater poem, because it 'eases the burden of the mystery' as 'Ode to a Nightingale' does not. If exemplified 'acceptance' in its serene contemplation of life as it is. The poem's beauty is its truth, and its truth is its beauty.

Unseen critical appreciation

Note Six of the examining boards set a compulsory paper of this kind. The others offer it as an option. The term 'unseen' refers to the fact that candidates are neither assumed nor required to have any previous knowledge of the passages or of their authors. When a passage is taken from work by an established author (of the past or of the present), that particular work is not a set book and, usually, the author is not one of those set for special study in that particular year. Often, the passages are taken from work recently published by writers who are not yet widely known, and it is the policy of some boards to print passages without supplying their authors' names. When that is the practice, candidates may well be required to comment on a passage without recognising that it is by an author of classic status. Or they may be required to compare two passages, one by a famous author and the other by an as yet obscure writer, without knowing the identity of either. By denying candidates the assistance (or by preserving them from the prejudice) of previous knowledge of the passages, and/or by concealing their writers' identities, the examiners force them to rely entirely on their own critical resources.

7.1 What these questions test

Obviously, critical appreciation of an unseen passage and critical commentary on a passage from a set book call into play similar mental faculties and writing skills. Turn back *now* to the note on the meaning and implications of the term 'critical' at the beginning of Section 5.1. Revise it carefully. Then revise Section 5.3. Unless you have in mind the points made in those two sections, you cannot make full use of this chapter.

You must also be clear about the meaning of 'appreciation', as used here. In the language of literary studies, an appreciation is an *appraisal*: a judgement arrived at after careful and sympathetic (*not* hostile) consideration of a writer's strengths and weaknesses. As the sample questions we are about to study show, the examiners do not always use the term 'appreciation', preferring sometimes to describe what they want in other terms. For example, in the first question we are going to look at, the instructions begin: 'Write a careful study of the following poem, saying, with reasons, what you like or dislike about it.' But that, in fact, is a precise description of what is meant by 'an appreciation'.

Critical appreciation of a passage of prose or verse tests your ability to:

- Read the passage carefully.
- Respond to it sensitively.
- Analyse your response.
- Identify the various linguistic features of the passage that caused you to respond in the way you did.
- Write a clear, cogent account of your response, stating precisely how the writer's use of language brought it about.

Each of these critical operations will be discussed and demonstrated in later sections of this chapter.

7.2 The kinds of questions set

The examiners' instructions may be worded in different ways, but analysis of past papers shows that questions can be classified into the three main types now listed.

1. Questions in which the instructions suggest or recommend or specify particular matters for inclusion in your appreciation. You must, of course, take careful note of the wording and decide whether you have been offered helpful suggestions or given commands. If the former, you are free to choose which of the particular matters mentioned you can usefully include in your answer. If the latter, you must do exactly what you have been told.

Example 1

(i) Write a careful study of the following poem, saying, with reasons, what you like or dislike about it, and paying close attention to such matters as subject, form and style.

Note Those instructions make it clear that you *must* include the three 'such matters' named, for you are told to pay close attention to them. However, those three matters are identified in general terms ('subject, form and style'), leaving you free to decide how you will approach them, and what particular features you will deal with under each of those broad headings.

Example 2

(ii) Write an appreciation of this poem. If you find that your response to it is influenced by its formal features, you may wish to refer to the abrupt changes of rhythm.

Note The examiners do *not* tell you that you *must* pay particular attention to form in making your appreciation. They *do* give you a strong hint that, in their opinion, the impact of the poem depends very largely on its formal features. They go on to mention a particular aspect of form to which 'you may wish to refer'. It would not be wise to ignore their friendly and helpful advice.

2. Questions in which the instructions are 'open', leaving you to tackle the appreciation in whatever way you choose.

Examples

(i) Write a detailed appreciation of this passage, which consists of the first four paragraphs of a novel.

(ii) Write an appreciation of this poem.

Note Such instructions look easy. There are no restricting conditions, no specified or recommended matters to be covered. In fact there is no practical difference whatever between writing an appreciation for which the instructions are detailed and writing an appreciation for which the instructions are open. As you will see in later sections, a successful critical appreciation must always be based on 'close attention to subject, form and style'. It is always 'a careful study', leading to a reasoned statement of your response to the writer's use of language. Because they provide a check list of what must be done, detailed instructions are easier to carry out successfully than open instructions, which leave you to do all the planning for yourself.

3. Questions requiring you to compare and contrast two (occasionally, more than two) passages. Sometimes both passages are verse, sometimes both are prose. Quite often, there is one of each. The instructions may be either detailed or open.

Examples

(i) Compare the following poems in any ways that seem to you interesting.

(ii) Write a critical appreciation of the poem. Then write a critical appreciation of the prose passage, making any points of comparison or contrast with the poem that seem helpful.

(iii) Write about the poetic craft of both these poems, drawing attention to what you find striking, appealing and interesting in them. If either offers you a more rewarding experience than the other, give a reasoned explanation of why this is so. You may wish to refer to some or all of the following: theme; tone; form (including stanza, sentence and phrase structures; rhythm and rhyme); imagery; diction.

7.3 How to prepare for this paper

Read

The background reading (described and classified in Section 3.5) that provides essential support for set book study also helps you to prepare for the critical appreciation paper; but your general reading is equally important. The wider your experience of the endlessly varied ways in which writers use language, the greater your ability to comment perceptively on the passages the examiners choose. Reading is the basis of success, and you must accept that you will have to give a lot of time to it. But – as I stressed earlier – if you do not enjoy reading, you should not have chosen English as an A Level subject.

However, the quality of your reading is always more important than its quantity. By 'quality' of reading, I do not mean to imply that you should read only acknowledged masterpieces or only the best of contemporary writing. The quality of your reading depends on *how* you read. There is a lot of pleasure and great profit to be got out of reading widely (from 'classics' to 'trash'!) if you read *critically*. Whatever you are reading, try consciously to come to terms with ('evaluate') the experience. Look for the sources of your satisfaction/dissatisfaction, admiration/dislike, interest/boredom – whatever your reactions may be – by studying how the author uses language to present a subject, to convey an attitude to it, to persuade you of its importance, to show you how to look at it differently, to move you – and so on.

If you think about and analyse your response to your reading – not just the books you read in the course of your studies, but *all* the books you read, and newspapers and magazines – you will develop a constructively critical frame of mind (as appreciative of strengths as it is observant of weaknesses) that will increase your pleasure in reading while training you for the examination.

Do not confine your background reading to books directly related to your set books and authors. The passages for unseen critical appreciation may be taken from any period, so it is an advantage to have some knowledge of the ways in which people wrote in the past, when the world and the language were different. You have not got the time to become 'expert' in every period, and nobody expects you to. (In any case, it takes a lifetime – and, even then, all we know is that we know a little.) But, for example, whether you have a set book from the period or not, it may prove useful to understand the senses in which writers in the seventeenth and eighteenth centuries used the words 'nice' and 'wit' and 'science'. Or you may be spared minor but rather worrying problems in the examination if you realise that it was not 'ungrammatical' in Jane Austen's day to write, 'We were so terrible good as to take an extra one in our carriage'.

You will also be better prepared if you know something of the chief characteristics and conventions of the major literary genres: the novel, the epic, lyric poetry – and so on. For example, *Paradise Lost* may not be a set book but, in the appreciation paper, your recognition of the formal features and intended effects of a 'Miltonic' ('epic' or 'Homeric') simile may be very useful.

A good way of acquiring background knowledge of period and genre is to read your way through an anthology of English verse and an anthology of English prose, chronologically arranged. Begin at the beginning, and set yourself the goal of reading one extract from each anthology most days.

But no amount of background information is in any way as valuable as the critical attitudes and aptitudes described earlier.

Discuss

Talk about your reading – with fellow students, lecturers, teachers, members of your family, friends – with anybody you can find who shares your interest in reading. Discussion is a most enjoyable and valuable way of widening experience, developing taste, sharpening judgement and learning to use evidence. It need not be 'bookish' talk, though much of it will be about books. If you talk about your reading, you will not think of 'unseen critical appreciation' as an academic exercise. The examination paper is, in fact, a test of the discrimination (the ability to make reasoned distinctions between more and less valuable experiences) that you have developed as a thinking, feeling – and, of course, reading! – person.

Study technique

Revise *now* the note on 'technical studies' in Section 3.5. It is essential to bear it in mind as you read the rest of this section. Its practical implications were demonstrated in the worked examples in Chapters 5 and 6, and they are featured again in Section 7.7.

Knowledge of the technical terms of literary criticism can be put to good use in two ways: in analysis; and in description. When you are considering your own response to a passage of prose or verse and tracing the linguistic causes of that response, you can *analyse* those causes swiftly and accurately with the aid of the technical terms. When you are writing an appreciation of that passage, you can *describe* your response and its linguistic causes precisely and unambiguously with the aid of the technical terms.

For example, when the examiners suggest that you 'may wish to refer to . . . theme; tone; form (including stanza, sentence and phrase structures, rhythm and rhyme); imagery; diction', they assume that you will make use of a working knowledge of basic literary terms. Similarly, because any appreciation necessarily rests on a close consideration of subject, form and style, even the most 'open' instructions give you the opportunity to put literary terms to good use.

> • You *can* write an appreciation without using literary terms, but it is much easier to be clear and precise if you know how to use them.

It is an unnecessary and self-imposed handicap to take this paper without knowing the convenient, accurate 'shorthand' provided by the basic literary terms.

7.4 Common mistakes

- *Careless reading:* the passage – either in its substance or in its writer's intentions – is misunderstood.
- *Unbalanced judgements.* Nit-picking fault-finding at one extreme; runaway enthusiasm at the other. Or – as often happens – details, treated in isolation, are overemphasised at the expense of the whole.
- *Prejudice:* the critic is biased against the writer's subject or the writer's attitude to it. Opinion is formed on what the critic thinks the writer 'ought' to have said. Or the critic's mind is closed to the writer's originality of style.
- *Failure to support opinions with evidence drawn from the passage* – the 'criticism' consists of a series of dogmatic statements.
- *Insensitivity.* Nuances of meaning and implication are ignored. this fault is most frequent when the tone of the passage is ironical. Ignorance of literary conventions is also a common cause of insensitive responses.
- *Badly planned answers* (see Section 6.4 (Planning) on page 89).

● *Badly written answers:* faulty grammar, spelling and punctuation: clumsy and/or inappropriate style.

**7.5
A critical
method**

What must be done

A critical appreciation is a considered and reasoned account of your personal response to a passage. To produce a good answer, you must do three things:

1. Get clear about the thoughts and feelings that the passage arouses in you.
2. Examine the writer's use of language to discover how it causes you to think and feel as you do.
3. Write a clear, cogent account of your response to the passage, identifying the linguistic features that bring about that response.

The first and second of these tasks are essential preliminaries to the third. Only when you have worked your way through them can you begin to plan and write your answer.

First steps

(i)   Read the whole passage right through at a steady pace, without pausing over details.

(ii)   Jot down a brief note, summing up what you think the passage is about.

(iii) Read the passage again, slowly. Puzzle out the meaning of anything you did not understand when you first read it. You are concerned with details now. The meaning of words and phrases that you did not understand at first usually becomes plain during this second reading. You have already got an understanding of the overall meaning, and troublesome details are cleared up when you see them in relation to the whole.

(iv)   Re-read your first statement of what the passage is about. Revise it, if necessary, in the light of your second reading. You should now be confident that you understand what the writer is saying.

● Discover *what* your writers say;
● Then, *why* they say it in this way.

Looking for clues

(i)   Read the passage again, slowly and very attentively. Listen to the writer's *tone of voice*, just as you listen to a speaker's tone of voice when you are trying to decide exactly what is going on in his/her mind. Very often, it is not so much *what* is said as *how* it is said (the *tone*) that reveals the writer's frame of mind.

Here are just a few examples of the many different tones of voice that may be noticed, and to which you must pay close attention if you are to arrive at a true appreciation: ironic, hostile, loving, reverent, contemptuous, friendly, urbane, grave, flippant, witty, cool, passionate, detached. Remember that the tone comes through in the way language is used, and you can hear it only if you listen.

(ii)   When you have tuned in to the tone, you know what the writer's *attitude* is. Suppose, for example, you are reading a poem about war. It is the tone of voice and what it implies that tell you whether the writer's attitude to that subject is earnest, mocking, patriotic, indignant, admiring – and so on.

(iii)   It is your awareness of tone and attitude that enables you to enter fully into the experience that the writer is trying to convey. The importance of making an imaginative effort to share in that experience and to respond to it *in the way the writer intended you to* was demonstrated in Chapter 2 (see especially Guided Practice 1 on pages 17–21). Here, it need only be repeated that when making a critical appreciation you should:
* Show that you have understood what the writer was trying to do.
* Show that you have formed your opinion of the literary qualities of the passage by considering whether the ways in which the language is used are well suited to achieve the purposes the writer had in mind.

Forming your judgement

You are required to make 'a careful study of the subject, form and style' of the passage (see Section 7.2). Study the subject of the passage in the way outlined in 'What must be done' and 'First steps' above. Then proceed to the study of form and style in light of what you have discovered about the tone, the attitude and the intention.

Under each of the general headings 'form' and 'style', individual linguistic features may require detailed analysis because they make an important contribution to the overall effect of the passage.

For example, under the heading 'form', you need to look at the structure of the passage, as a whole and in detail. If it is a prose passage, consider such matters as its *shape* (has it a beginning, a middle and an end?); and its *unity* (are there digressions and loose ends?). Individual paragraph, sentence and phrase structures may play an important part in contributing to (or detracting from) the strength of the overall structure. You may need to comment on the writer's skill (or clumsiness, or negligence) in linking part to part, and in connecting part to whole.

All these matters are raised by verse passages too, with the additional requirement to look closely at the particular verse form used, and the skill with which it is used; blank verse/couplets/stanza structure/sonnet – and so on.

Under the heading 'style', in both prose and verse passages, you should examine the diction (choice of words), and the use of imagery and figures of speech. When considering poetry, special attention should be given to 'versification' (for example, the use of metres of different kinds, and rhyme patterns), linking your observations to the particular verse structure used – which you have already noted when considering the form of the passage. The rhythms of a prose passage can be of critical importance, as the writer may reinforce the argument and/or increase the emotional impact with skilful variations of sentence length and structure.

Close and perceptive attention to linguistic detail is essential, but good judgement finally depends on *the use you make* of your careful observation. Since the passage as a whole is to be assessed by its success (or failure) in carrying out the writer's intention, it follows that:

- You should include details of form and style in your critical appreciation *only* when you can bring out their contribution to (or their detraction from) the overall effect of the passage.

7.6 Timing and planning answers

Practise answering questions within the time limits imposed by your own examining board. Typical requirements are: two questions to be answered in a 2-hour paper; two questions to be answered in a $2\frac{1}{2}$-hour paper; three questions to be answered in a 3-hour paper. This more generous time allowance (as compared with that given to essay questions) does not indicate that the examiners expect longer answers. It reflects their intention that candidates should have adequate time for reading, thinking and planning.

In no other paper is it more important to spend time on careful preparation before starting to write the answer.

The passages set for critical appreciation are not short. A poem of seven or eight verses, *together with* a prose passage of anything from five hundred to a thousand words is a quite usual length. The critical process set out in Section 7.5 (repeated readings to ensure full comprehension, followed by the elucidation of tone, attitude and intention, and close analysis of linguistic features) cannot be completed quickly.

And when all that has been done, you still have to arrive at a considered, reasoned evaluation of the passage (or passages), and then think out the shape of your answer. Like a critical commentary or the answer to an essay question, a critical appreciation tests your ability to write good prose. You are expected to express your findings in a clear, coherent, continuous piece of writing.

Whether the instructions are open or detailed (see Section 7.2), and whether the question centres on a single passage or on a comparison of two or more passages, the nature of the task is essentially the same. That fact suggests the outline of a plan on which a good answer can be based. To be sure of including all the necessary material and setting it out in a clear and logical sequence, the contents and shape of your answer should mirror the critical method used to explore the passage or passages. Think of your answer as the 'writing up' of the results of your critical enquiries.

Answer plan

1. *Beginning* *Subject of passage*
   (a) Meaning.
   (b) Tone.
   (c) Attitude and intention.

2. *Middle* *Form of passage*
   (a) Overall structure.
   (b) Details of structure.
   Style of passage
   (a) Diction.
   (b) Imagery and figures of speech.
   (c) Sentence and phrase rhythms (prose)/versification (poetry).

3. *End*   *Evaluation of passage*
Your assessment of the writer's success or failure: measured by the degree to which the uses of language you explored when considering the form and style helped to achieve the purposes for which the passage was written.

Revise *now* the account of critical method given in Section 7.5. It provides an essential commentary on that plan, filling in the details needed to make it work. Pay special attention to these three points:

1. You will not always find material in the passage corresponding to every item listed in the plan. For example, a rhythmic pattern of sentences and phrases by no means always plays a prominent part (or even any part at all) in a prose passage; nor does every poem contain figures of speech.
2. Never drag material into your answer just to match the headings in the plan. For example, it is pointless merely to refer to images that you have noted. They have no part to play in your answer unless you can bring out their contribution to the overall effect at which the writer was aiming.
3. Although it is advisable to base your appreciation on the sequence set out in the plan (subject → form → style → evaluation), you must not feel constrained to treat each as a separately paragraphed section. Method is essential, but try to avoid a mechanical presentation. Aim at a smooth-flowing, progressive account of your findings. It is often effective to combine various aspects of your material. For example, versification or prose rhythms may be best treated as aspects of both form and style, and examined in that way. And you are certainly not obliged to write about stylistic features in the order in which they are listed in the plan. The metrical brilliance or subtle rhyme patterns of a particular poem may strike you as its most telling stylistic feature – the chief of the various ways in which language is used in that poem to bring about its overall effect. If that is the case, start your assessment of its style there, leaving diction and imagery until you have commented on the versification.

The plan is not a strait-jacket. It is a guide to help you to decide what to include in (and how to arrange the contents of) a critical appreciation. Use it flexibly, fitting it to the passage, not the passage to it.

7.7 Worked examples

Note 1   The thinking and planning that must be done before an unseen critical appreciation can be written is set out in full detail in the first of the worked examples. Neither you nor I would need to write our notes out at such length in the examination, but I wanted to give you a complete demonstration of the methods that I advise you to use. This necessarily took up a lot of room. The notes on preliminary thinking and planning have been omitted from the second worked example (on the 'Menelaus and Helen' poem). However, as you study my appreciation of that poem, you will realise that it is based on exactly the same critical approach as that set out in the notes made while preparing to answer the first question.

Note 2   Study each of the appreciations (on pages 116–32) closely. Then rewrite each, observing the following word limits: 'I Remember, I Remember' –

about 800 words; the extract from *Cider with Rosie* – about 700 words; 'Menelaus and Helen' – about 900 words. Make use of critical points you agree with, but use your own words. This is an exercise of the kind that was demonstrated in the two commentaries on the *Prelude* passage. You may therefore find it an advantage to revise pages 78–84 before you start to compress and streamline the extended critical appreciations provided for practice material here.

1

Time: 2 hours
ANSWER BOTH QUESTIONS

1. Write an appreciation of the poem.
2. Write an appreciation of the prose passage, making any points of comparison or contrast with the poem that seem to you interesting.

I Remember, I Remember

Coming up England by a different line
For once, early in the cold new year,
We stopped, and, watching men with number-plates
Spring down the platform to familiar gates,
'Why, Coventry!' I exclaimed. 'I was born here.'

I leant far out, and squinnied for a sign
That this was still the town that had been 'mine'
So long, but found I wasn't even clear
Which side was which. From where those cycle-crates
Were standing, had we annually departed

For all those family hols? . . . A whistle went:
Things moved. I sat back, staring at my boots.
'Was that,' my friend smiled, 'where you "have your roots"?'
No, only where my childhood was unspent,
I wanted to retort, just where I started:

By now I've got the whole place clearly charted.
Our garden, first: where I did not invent
Blinding theologies of flowers and fruits,
And wasn't spoken to by an old hat.
And here we have that splendid family

I never ran to when I got depressed,
The boys all biceps and the girls all chest,
Their comic Ford, their farm where I could be
'Really myself'. I'll show you, come to that,
The bracken where I never trembling sat,

Determined to go through with it; where she
Lay back, and 'all became a burning mist'.
And in those offices, my doggerel
Was not set up in blunt ten-point, nor read
By a distinguished cousin of the mayor,

Who didn't call and tell my father *There*
Before us, had we the gift to see ahead –
'You look as if you wished the place in Hell,'
My friend said, 'judging from your face.' 'Oh well,
I suppose it's not the place's fault,' I said.

'Nothing, like something, happens anywhere.'

Philip Larkin

I was set down from the carrier's cart at the age of three; and there with a sense of bewilderment and terror my life in the village began.

The June grass, amongst which I stood, was taller than I was, and I wept. I had never been so close to grass before. It towered above me and all around me, each blade was tattooed with tiger-skins of sunlight. It was knife-edged, dark, and a wicked green, thick as a forest and alive with grasshoppers that chirped and chattered and leapt through the air like monkeys.

I was lost and didn't know where to move. A tropic heat oozed up from the ground, rank with sharp odours of roots and nettles. Snow-clouds of elder-blossoms banked in the sky, showering upon me the fumes and flakes of their sweet and giddy suffocation. High overhead ran frenzied larks, screaming, as though the sky were tearing apart.

For the first time in my life I was out of sight of humans. For the first time in my life I was alone in a world whose behaviour I could neither predict nor fathom: a world of birds that squealed, of plants that stank, of insects that sprang about without warning. I was lost and I did not expect to be found again. I put back my head and howled, and the sun hit me smartly on the face, like a bully.

From this daylight nightmare I was awakened, as from many another, by the appearance of my sisters. They came scrambling and calling up the steep rough bank, and parting the long grass found me. Faces of rose, familiar, living; huge shining faces hung up like shields between me and the sky; faces with grins and white teeth (some broken) to be conjured up like genii with a howl, brushing off terror with their broad scoldings and affection. They leaned over me – one, two, three – their mouths smeared with red currants and their hands dripping with juice.

'There, there, it's all right, don't you wail any more. Come down 'ome and we'll stuff you with currants.'

And Marjorie, the eldest, lifted me into her long brown hair, and ran me jogging down the path and through the steep rose-filled garden, and set me down on the cottage doorstep, which was our home, though I couldn't believe it.

That was the day we came to the village, in the summer of the last year of the First World War. To a cottage that stood in a half-acre of garden on a steep bank above a lake; a cottage with three floors and a cellar and a treasure in the walls, with a pump and apple trees, syringa and strawberries, rooks in the chimneys, frogs in the cellar, mushrooms on the ceiling, and all for three and sixpence a week.

I don't know where I lived before then. My life began on the carrier's cart which brought me up the long slow hills to the village, and dumped me in the high grass, and lost me. I had ridden wrapped up in a Union Jack to protect me from the sun, and when I rolled out of it, and stood piping loud among the buzzing jungle of that summer bank, then, I feel, was I born. And to all the rest of us, the whole family of eight, it was the beginning of a life.

But on that first day we were all lost. Chaos was come in cartloads of furniture, and I crawled the kitchen floor through forests of upturned chair-legs and crystal fields of glass. We were washed up in a new land, and began to spread out searching its springs and treasures. The sisters spent the light of that first day stripping the fruit bushes in the garden. The currants were at their prime, clusters of red, black, and yellow berries all tangled up with wild roses. Here was bounty the girls had never known before, and they darted squawking from bush to bush, clawing the fruit like sparrows.

Laurie Lee, *Cider with Rosie*
(S.U.J.B.)

Note Although the first task set by the examiners is to write an appreciation of the poem, it is advisable to start by reading both passages right through. The instructions for the second task – an appreciation of the prose passage – refer to 'points of comparison or contrast'. This indicates that each passage throws light on the other, so you will be more perceptive of the poet's attitude to and treatment of his subject if you read the prose passage before you get down to close study of the poem.

Studying the poem

Subject

What it is about

The poet (the 'I' of the poem), travelling in a train, suddenly realises that they have stopped at Coventry, his birthplace. He 'squinnies' out of the window and can hardly recognise what was once a familiar scene. The train moves on. He recalls his childhood. From the look on his face, his companion supposes that his memories are painful, and that he blames the place. The poet doesn't tell him what his memories are, but he answers enigmatically that the place is not to blame: the 'nothing' of his childhood, like the 'something' of other people's, might have happened 'anywhere'.

Details of meaning

Some things I didn't understand at first are clearer now that I've made an outline of the contents. 'Nothing' is the key word – the negation at the heart of all the memories that the place recalls. Larkin says that his 'childhood was *unspent*'. That's because 'nothing' happened. Similarly, he 'never ran' to 'that splendid family', and he 'never trembling sat' in 'bracken' with a girl who 'lay back'. His juvenile verse ('doggerel') wasn't published in the local newspaper to the admiration of 'a distinguished cousin of the mayor'. Nor was his father made proud of his achievements. The 'blinding theologies of flowers and fruits' that he didn't invent refer to the mystical or religious insights into life's meaning that nature did *not* inspire in him. The fact that he 'wasn't spoken to by an old hat' tells us that he had no exciting experiences of 'the magic of childhood', so often celebrated by so many writers.

Minor details that were difficult at first are also plain now. 'Men with number-plates' refers to car delivery men getting out at the station, having returned by train after taking Coventry-made cars to customers. 'Blunt ten-point' refers to the typeface in which his 'doggerel' would have been printed (if it had been!) on the presses of the local newspaper.

Looking for clues

Tone

The tone comes through unmistakably and insistently as I listen to the succession of quietly spoken – rather flat – disillusioned negatives. He doesn't sound bitter about his 'unspent' childhood. He speaks of it calmly. He's resigned to his memories of it, because he didn't, and doesn't, expect the experience to be anything other than it was. He doesn't waste time and energy rebelling against or resenting what was as it had to be.

Attitude and Intention

He is completely unromantic about his childhood, and looks at it very steadily and honestly. He's quiet about it. There's no shouting or rhetoric, but he's set on making us see it as he believes it was. The deliberate echoes of a very different point of view – 'blinding theologies of flowers and fruits'; 'an old hat' that speaks to a child; 'that splendid family' and 'their farm' – effectively debunk the attitudes of writers who express visionary views of childhood. Larkin writes in full ironical awareness of what others have said – and he rejects it. He stands the image of the 'prophet child' on its head. 'Come off it,' he says, 'childhood wasn't like that for me.' And, at the end, he asserts firmly that his experience is just as valid as romanticism. The final words have the ring of an axiom. That epigrammatic last line sums up what he sees as an alternative truth. He wants his readers to face it, even if they are not permanently converted to it.

Larkin's title provided me with an immediate clue to his attitude, because I happen to remember a poem of the same title, written by Thomas Hood. Hood's poem – 'I remember, I remember, the house where I was born' – is a wistful, nostalgic reminiscence of the sweet delights of childhood, as recalled by a saddened adult. It was plain that, by using Hood's title, Larkin emphasised the ironical contrast between his memories of childhood and those of his predecessor. But I didn't *need* my knowledge of that poem to enable me to discern Larkin's attitude and intention; and I don't think Larkin expected all his readers to recognise the allusion. Even if Larkin's title is taken at face value, the poem itself provides all that is necessary to make a sensitive reader fully aware of the writer's attitude to his subject, and to persuade the reader to share it, even if only for a time.

Form

Overall structure

Seven five-line stanzas, followed by one separate line. An underlying iambic metre frequently rises to the surface (as in line 2 of stanza 2). Strong and often close rhymes are a feature (as in stanza 3), but the rhyme pattern varies. For example, stanza 1 rhymes a-b-c-c-b, and so does stanza 7, but stanza 2 rhymes a-a-b-c-d, and stanza 5 rhymes a-a-b-c-c.

Details of structure

When the details are examined, the variations just noted are seen to be typical of the freedom with which Larkin handles the form. There *is* an overall and strong structure, as already described, but within that shape, he changes metres and rhyme patterns as the sense dictates. The utterance runs on from line to line (for example, lines 3 and 4 of stanza 1), and from stanza to stanza (for example, the last line of stanza 4 leads without an end pause into the first line of stanza 5). In effect, he lengthens and shortens his lines just as freely as he varies metres and rhymes, but he never loses his way. Every variation is a controlled movement within the overall shape.

Style

Versification

There are no fireworks. Nothing is flamboyant or obtrusive, because every subtle variation has a purpose to which it is always subordinated. For example, that last line would stand in perilous isolation, looking contrived and theatrical, if it were not linked to the rhyme pattern of the final stanza. What might look like an 'outcrop' is, in fact, the sixth line of the final stanza – its climax, *and* the climax of the whole poem. Not only does it rhyme with the first line of stanza 7 ('There'/'where'), but it is a continuation of the direct speech with which stanza 7 ends.

It would be wholly inappropriate to read this poem as a series of 'stanza-based' instalments. The poet talks the experience out, using the whole of the poem as his voice. The stanzas are interwoven by the run-on lines and the changing rhyme patterns. The metres (as, for example, in the last line of stanza 5 and the first line of stanza 6) flow *through* the poem, their varying 'wavelengths' carrying the shifts of thought and feeling.

Diction

Precise, plain language. Larkin wastes no words. He aims for a low-key sincerity of expression. His deliberate quotation of the hackneyed 'all became a burning mist' highlights his own resolute determination to say what he wants to say as simply and directly as possible. This bare diction packs a tremendous punch.

Single words carry a lot of meaning – for example, the juvenile, slangy abbreviation 'hols' ('all those family 'hols' – stanza 3) perfectly conveys the remembered emptiness of those annual events. This is typical of his restrained, laconic utterance – designed to persuade us of the truth of the experience he is sharing with us.

Imagery and figures of speech

None! And their absence is one of the most striking and telling stylistic features of this poem. Larkin's attitude and intention, as I perceive them, are fittingly expressed in plain statements. His uncompromisingly unromantic view of childhood would be less convincing if he relied on anything but the most direct of language.

Evaluation

I find this 'unpoetic' poem very satisfying. The poet's attitude to his subject is refreshingly original, and its expression is pleasing and persuasive. I like the quiet irony. I admire Larkin's refusal to pretend that life is different from what his experience leads him to believe it is. He's never solemn, but his light (often humorous) touch and directness of language say something that he's serious about. It's the honesty of the poem (both in what he says and in how he says it) that I find most impressive. He leaves me feeling that even if childhood isn't like this for everybody always, it's like this for somebody often! I'm quite sure that the poem as a whole will stay with me; and some lines are instantly memorable:

> And here we have that splendid family
> I never ran to when I got depressed,
> The boys all biceps and the girls all chest . . .

The thoughts and emotions the poem compels me to share are concisely voiced in that quiet final statement: 'Nothing, like something, happens anywhere'.

Note   I have now completed a careful study of the poem. Because I have followed the critical method set out in Section 7.5, I am satisfied that I have: (i) sorted out my response to the poem; (ii) explored the poet's use of language to discover how it causes me to respond in the way I do. And – again because I have followed that critical method – I am clear about the shape of the appreciation that I shall write. I know how to give it a beginning, a middle and an end (see Section 7.6). As I write, I am free to add points to or to omit others from those I set down in my notes; and, of course, I can change or use their wording as seems helpful. But, although I am not bound to use the notes exactly as I set them down, they provide me with a sound basis for my written answer, and I shall not make any major changes.

Studying the prose passage

Subject

What it is about

The writer recalls his experiences on arriving at the new home to which he was taken as a child. He describes the garden and the house, and the exciting things that happened to him. He also gives some account of his sisters' activities and feelings.

Details of meaning

There are no difficulties in understanding the passage. Closer study of its contents does not cause me to revise the outline I made after my first careful reading. Directly and indirectly, we are supplied with a lot of details, from which we gather the following information. He was three. It was a hot June day in 1918. The overgrown garden was full of birds, flowers, fruit and grass. There were eight people in his family. His sisters were older and bigger than he. The eldest, Marjorie, had long, brown hair. They were loving, happy, active, noisy creatures, red-faced, healthy (despite the broken teeth!). It was a country cottage 'with three floors and a cellar', damp, but cheap – the rent was only three and sixpence a week. Life here was in every way a change from their previous experience, which had been urban.

Looking for clues

Tone

Exuberant! He's excited and noisy.

Attitude and intention

That day was magic, he insists; and he intends his readers to experience the magic. 'Look, listen, taste!' he says. 'Share the remembered intoxication with me.' Generally, he sees the momentous occasion through the eyes of an adult. He recalls every detail, reading meaning into and out of it. Occasionally, his standpoint seems to change from the adult's to the child's. Then, his vision gets blurred. For example, he seems to suggest – without, I think, meaning to – that the child of three saw each blade of grass 'tattooed with tiger-skins of sunlight'. When he does this it's not easy to share in the experience he's trying to convey. I find myself questioning the value of what he's asking me to share, because I can't accept the truth of the child's reactions, as they are depicted.

Form

Overall structure

A straightforward succession of well-managed paragraphs, taking the reader through that first day. The passage is neatly rounded off with a reference to its beginning.

Details of structure

Word groups are varied in length and syntax to sustain the particular meaning and emotional impact of each. Compare, for example, the direct simplicity of 'I had never been so close to grass before' with the piled-up structure beginning: 'Faces of rose'. The latter consists of a series of phrases, added one to the other, with no finite verb – but effective.

Style

Imagery and figures of speech

The passage teems with figurative language. Grass is 'tattooed'; green is 'wicked'; grasshoppers are 'like monkeys'; the sun hits 'like a bully'; a summer bank is 'a buzzing jungle' – and so on.

Diction

Colourful, rich, emphatic: 'bewilderment', 'terror', 'sweet and giddy suffocation', 'smeared', 'dripping', 'springs and treasures', 'bounty' – and so on. One or two plain statements, but the overwhelming profusion of the language is – overwhelming! (*Do* larks 'scream'?) It's like eating too much plum pudding, and getting indigestion.

Evaluation

I do recognise the energy of the writing, and the richly sensuous detail. The language is vivid – full of fireworks. But it draws attention to itself. I admire it in bits; but, on the whole, it's too deliberately contrived. And, at times, I simply do not believe in that little boy of three with his highly developed sensibilities. The passage doesn't convince me that this magical experience ever took place – certainly not in the way it is described. Even if it did, it belonged to Lee's own private world, and he doesn't persuade me that the experience has anything very much to do with me. The torrent of language washes through my mind and leaves me quite unmoved.

Note That completes my preparation for writing an appreciation of the prose passage. The material used in the appreciation will be used in the same way as the material gathered while studying the poem. (See note on page 121.)

Question1

Write an appreciation of the poem

Looking out of a carriage window, Larkin realises that the train has stopped at Coventry, his birthplace. As it moves on again, he recalls his childhood 'unspent' there. That one word epitomises the negative quality of all his memories.

He is not sure which side of the station is which, or from which platform they used to depart 'for all those family hols'. And, even when he has 'clearly charted' his childhood places, it is only to remember everything that did *not* happen: those magic, mysterious, wonderful experiences that so many other writers have celebrated as the child's 'birthright'.

For the boy Larkin, there were no 'intimations of immortality', no 'great formative experiences', such as are described by those who believe that their imaginative life was rooted in the rich soil of childhood. Larkin recalls that he 'did not invent blinding theologies of flowers and fruits'. He 'wasn't spoken to by an old hat'. He did not roam into a countryside fertile in characters and sex, for he 'never ran' to 'that splendid family' or 'their farm'; and he 'never trembling sat' in 'bracken' with a girl who 'lay back'. Nor did the local newspaper print his youthful 'doggerel', and so amaze 'a distinguished cousin of the mayor' that he congratulated the boy's father on his son's budding genius.

From the look on his face, Larkin's travelling companion supposes that his memories are painful, and that he blames the place for them. But Larkin replies that the place is not to blame, adding enigmatically that 'Nothing, like something, happens anywhere'.

Throughout, he speaks in a quiet, unexcited tone of voice. He uses no rhetoric, and he seems neither angry nor bitter. His descriptions of all the wonderful experiences that others claim to have had, but that never happened to him, are ironical. In a series of flatly worded, disillusioned negatives, he stands the conventional image of the 'prophet child' on its head, effectively debunking that romantic conception. 'Come off it', he says, 'childhood wasn't like that for me.' And the last line sums up his refusal to falsify his experience or to modify his unromantic view of childhood. The 'nothing' of his memories is just as valid as the 'something' that others have recalled and celebrated as a visionary and universal truth. His 'nothing' – like their 'something' – 'happens anywhere'. Their romantic ideal of childhood is one way of looking at life. His is another.

Larkin's plain, matter-of-fact attitude finds expression in a form that has no obtrusive 'poetic' features. The overall structure of the poem is perfectly adapted to his low-key approach to his subject, opening with a brief account of a very ordinary incident, moving on to the memories it stirs, and ending with a laconic comment on those memories.

The firm shape – seven carefully built stanzas – gives the poem a distinct and individual identity. He talks us purposefully through a unified experience without rambling or losing the thread. He is completely in control, saying no more and no less than is required to carry us along.

And within that disciplined structure, he moves with an easy freedom. The varied rhyme patterns (compare the a-b-c-c-b pattern of stanzas 1 and 7 with the a-a-b-c-d of stanza 2 and the a-a-b-c-c of stanza 5) shift the rhymes to emphasise sense and feeling. For example: 'plates'/'gates' signals the moment of recognition; 'depressed'/'chest' underlines the ironically humorous recall of what never took place.

The run-on lines strengthen the impression that we are listening to a quiet, confidential account of remembered experience. The formal line pattern is never allowed to check the murmur of the voice, which pauses only when a particular utterance is complete:

> Coming up England by a different line
> For once . . .

> where I did not invent
> Blinding theologies . . .

Metre is used as flexibly as line lengths and rhyme patterns. The stresses fall to reinforce sense and feeling, not to fit into a rigid metrical scheme. An underlying iambic beat frequently comes to the surface, and – just as frequently – is overridden by clustered or spaced-out stresses, emphasising a change of mood or idea. The second stanza provides a typical example:

> I leant far out, and squinnied for a sign
>
> That this was still the town that had been 'mine'
>
> So long, but found I wasn't even clear
>
> Which side was which.

And the stanzas themselves are interwoven by the same skilful but unobtrusive use of technical devices. Stanza run-on bears the flowing voice forward. For example, the last line of stanza 4 leads into the first line of stanza 5 without an end pause. The metres (as in the last line of stanza 5 and the first line of stanza 6) flow through the poem, their varying and uninterrupted 'wavelengths' carrying the shifts of sense and feeling over what would otherwise be gaps between stanzas.

Larkin is in firm and purposeful control of all the varied devices he uses. His poetic craft is most strikingly demonstrated in the way he brings the poem to its memorable end. The last line would stand in perilous isolation, appearing contrived and theatrical, if it were not so subtly, yet firmly, linked with the final full-length stanza. It rhymes with the first line of that stanza ('There'/'where'), and it is a continuation of the direct speech of its last line. What might look like an 'outcrop' is, in fact, the sixth line of the final stanza – its climax, *and* the climax of the whole poem.

No sensitive reader of this poem would attempt to chop it up into a series of stanza instalments. The poet talks the experience out, using the whole poem as his voice.

His choice of words unfailingly matches his purposes. The language is precise, plain, unadorned – like the experience it communicates. An unromantic attitude is expressed in unromantic words. There is no decoration and no redundancy. He aims at, and achieves, a low-key, honest exactness. It is the truth of the experience that he searches for,. Two examples typify the effectiveness of his diction. His deliberate quotation of the hackneyed expression 'all became a burning mist' highlights his own determination to use simple, direct, truthful language. The falseness of the quoted words contrasts strikingly with the honesty of his own. The juvenile, slangy abbreviation 'hols' ('all those family hols') perfectly conveys the remembered emptiness of those annual events. It exemplifies the power of his restrained, laconic utterance.

This same restraint is evident in the total absence of imagery and figures of speech. To me, this is one of the poem's most telling stylistic features. His resolutely unromantic view would have been less convincing if he had relied on anything but the most direct of language.

This deliberately 'unpoetic' poem is deeply satisfying. A refreshingly original attitude to a subject so often overwritten is pleasingly and persuasively expressed. I enjoy the irony, and admire Larkin's refusal to pretend that life is different from what he believes it is. He is never solemn, but his light (often humorous) touch and directness of language say something serious about a subject that is of universal interest.

It is the honesty of what he says, and of how he says it, that I find most impressive. He leaves me reflecting that even if childhood is not like this for everybody always, it is like this for everybody sometimes.

I am quite sure that the poem will stay with me. Many lines have that immediately memorable quality that I look for whenever I read a new poem. For example:

> . . . I did not invent
> Blinding theologies of flowers and fruits

> And here we have that splendid family
> I never ran to when I got depressed,
> The boys all biceps and the girls all chest . . .

The art with which Larkin ruefully explores his own deeply-felt experience gives me great pleasure. His words reverberate in my mind, quietly but insistently – and nowhere more so than when he voices the stoical conclusion of his poem in that epigrammatic final statement: 'Nothing, like something, happens anywhere.'

Question 2

Write an appreciation of the prose passage, making any points of comparison or contrast with the poem that seem to you interesting

Philip Larkin and Laurie Lee are writing about their childhoods. That is where comparison begins – and ends. All the other points that I want to make are contrasts.

The two passages could hardly be more different in tone and attitude. The poem is quiet, but the prose is noisy. Laurie Lee's exuberant celebration of his childhood wonderland is shouted out at the top of his voice, 'Look, listen, taste, smell!' he thunders. 'Wasn't it all marvellously exciting?'

His attitude to childhood is intensely romantic. If the little boy he recalls did not 'invent blinding theologies of flowers and fruits', it is only because the passage ends before the visions start. And if he 'wasn't spoken to by an old hat', he did experience terror in a garden where the grass and the birds and the insects threatened him under a bullying sun and a splitting sky.

It would be easier to enter the experience if the writer presented it from a consistent standpoint. Whereas we always know where we are in the poem, the prose passage does not look steadily at its subject. Generally, it is clear that the writer is recalling what happened when he was three, and writing about that experience from his adult perspective and in his adult language. But, too often, he writes as if the child, at that moment, was feeling and thinking as the adult writer does when recalling and interpreting his childhood experience.

When the writer gets carried away like that, his representation of the child's responses is simply not credible. Did a child of three see blades of grass 'tattooed with tiger-skins of sunshine'? Did that child see his sisters' faces 'hung up like shields between me and the sky'? Did he think of his sisters as 'genii'? At moments like those, the writing does not ring true.

I realise, of course, that Laurie Lee did not intend such expressions to be taken as a literal rendering of the child's mental processes and linguistic powers. Even so, a writer who was clear about his chosen standpoint, and in control of his words, would not lay himself open to objections of this kind. Lee's enthusiastically romantic attitude, as reflected in this passage, is not sustained by the clear thinking and disciplined feeling that are so evident in Larkin's austerely unromantic attitude.

The two passages also present striking contrasts in their formal and stylistic qualities. Subtle handling of form as a means of expressing thought and feeling is always more readily available in verse than in prose. So it is not an adverse judgement to say that brilliant techniques are not a feature of Lee's prose, as they are of Larkin's poem. The passage is shaped to suit its writer's purposes. A succession of well-made paragraphs takes the reader through the events of the summer day; and the well-judged 'return' (at the beginning of the last paragraph) rounds the passage off in a satisfying way. The sentences, skilfully varied in length and syntax, express the ideas and emotions fluently and confidently.

My difficulty in accepting Laurie Lee's attitude to his subject as a valuable extension of my own experience springs chiefly from his prodigal way of using words. The passage teems with figurative language: metaphor piled on metaphor, simile jostling simile. Grass is 'tattooed'; green is 'wicked'; larks 'scream'; grasshoppers are 'like monkeys'; the sun behaves 'like a bully'; a summer bank is 'a buzzing jungle'. And on and on he goes, breathless with excitement, intoxicated with his own inventions. The imagery is incessant, overdone – and, therefore, self-defeating.

Nor is there restraint or sense of proportion in the choice of words. His vocabulary is excessively rich, colourful, emphatic. There are very few plain words; and no examples of simple, telling language, such as the poem uses. He wastes his talent in spendthrift extravagance, going right over the top in describing that magical garden with its 'bewilderment' and 'terror', and 'sweet and giddy suffocation', where mouths are 'smeared' and hands are 'dripping', and the child's new world is full of 'springs' and 'treasures' and 'bounty'. It is to be hoped that the currants with which the sisters said they would stuff the little boy proved more digestible than the 'poetic' words with which the writer stuffs this passage.

I do recognise the energy of the writing and the vividly sensuous detail. The passage is full of fireworks, but the language is self-conscious and obviously contrived. It draws attention to itself. I admire it in bits, but – as a whole – the passage leaves me cold. It adds nothing to my experience.

The controlled artistry with which the poem is written contrasts sharply with the undisciplined ebullience of the language used in the prose passage.

2

Note This was the first (and compulsory) question in a three-hour paper. In addition, candidates were instructed to write one other appreciation, and were given two passages from which to choose. Equal marks were allocated to each appreciation. Allowing for the reading time needed before making their choice, candidates could spend about 80 minutes on each of the two questions they had to answer.

Write a careful study of the following poem, paying close attention to such matters as subject, style and total impression, and indicating whether or not you like it.

Menelaus and Helen

I

Hot through Troy's ruin Menelaus broke
    To Priam's palace, sword in hand, to sate
    On that adulterous whore a ten years' hate
And a king's honour. Through red death, and smoke,
And cries, and then by quieter ways he strode,
    Till the still innermost chamber fronted him.
    He swung his sword, and crashed into the dim
Luxurious bower, flaming like a god.

High sat white Helen, lonely and serene.
    He had not remembered that she was so fair,
And that her neck curved down in such a way;
And he felt tired. He flung the sword away,
    And kissed her feet, and knelt before her there,
The perfect Knight before the perfect Queen.

II

So far the poet. How should he behold
    That journey home, the long connubial years?
    He does not tell you how white Helen bears
Child on legitimate child, becomes a scold,
Haggard with virtue. Menelaus bold
    Waxed garrulous, and sacked a hundred Troys
    'Twixt noon and supper. And her golden voice
Got shrill as he grew deafer. And both were old.

Often he wonders why on earth he went
    Troyward, or why poor Paris ever came.
Oft she weeps, gummy-eyed and impotent;
    Her dry shanks twitch at Paris' mumbled name.
So Menelaus nagged; and Helen cried;
And Paris slept on by Scamander side.

Notes

1. The abduction of Helen (wife of Menelaus) by Paris was the cause of the ten years' war between the Greeks and the Trojans.
2. Scamander – a river near Troy.

(L.)

The poem tells how Menelaus, pressing on towards Priam's palace, stormed through the battle in which Troy was overwhelmed. Intent on achieving his long-nourished revenge for the dishonour that Helen's adultery with Paris had brought upon him, he forced his way into the quiet room where, untouched by war, she sat in splendour. Disarmed by her beauty, he threw his sword aside and knelt in homage, kissing her feet.

Then came the drawn-out, disillusioned years of their life together. Childbearing and boredom turned Helen into an ageing, shrill-voiced scold. Menelaus, deaf and garrulous, filled his days with boastful, repetitive stories of his own exploits. And memories of the dead Paris haunted them both, as their lives drained away in mutual recriminations.

As far as it goes, that is an accurate outline of the subject matter, but it excludes the deeper levels of response suggested throughout the poem. The contrasts by which the total experience is conveyed present a succession of conflicting attitudes. Situations and relationships take on different perspectives as both the poet and the people in the poem see things from changing standpoints and in changed times.

Part I is heroic. Menelaus, 'flaming like a god', and 'white Helen, lonely and serene', are legendary figures. In Part II, we hear the nagging, scolding voices of two old people whose greatness is long past. That stark, basic contrast shapes the poem, establishing a framework within which we respond to the experience it embodies. Yet, different as it is in tone and attitude, Part II develops out of Part I. The continuity so affirmed plays a major part in the total impression made by the poem.

In Part I, the dramatic confrontation and the equally dramatic reunion of the long-estranged husband and wife are shot through with irony. False feelings and dubious motives undermine Menelaus's heroic attitudes and exalted sentiments. Poised for revenge, he is instantly disarmed by beauty's spell. The 'adulterous whore' is magically transformed into an idol; and godlike Menelaus poses in a tableau of his own staging – 'the perfect Knight' kneeling to 'the perfect Queen'.

And 'the perfect Queen' passively goes along with the charade. The role she has played before serves her well. Men will always kneel to 'white Helen'. As yet, she has not been called upon to pay a price greater than she is ready and willing to pay.

But 'the long connubial years' are foreshadowed at the very instant of Menelaus' renewed enthralment. As we read the words, 'And he felt tired', we see through the illusions that blind them. Their self-deceptions content them momentarily, but appearance cannot long be mistaken for reality.

In Part II, the painful truth of their life together is sharpened by tormenting reverberations of past deeds and past hopes. 'White Helen', no longer 'serene',

bears

Child on legitimate child, becomes a scold,
Haggard with virtue.

Her once-golden voice, now shrill, burdens a deaf husband, who monotonously recalls his heroic past in bragging recitals:

Menelaus bold

Waxed garrulous, and sacked a hundred Troys
'Twixt noon and supper.

King Menelaus and Queen Helen are defenceless against age and age's ills. The instability of a relationship based on illusions makes them helpless victims of time's onslaught. Self-knowing and mutually trusting human beings may hope to endure with dignity, but these two people capitulate ignobly, diminished in every way. 'The perfect Knight' harps on about the infidelity of his 'perfect Queen'. 'Gummy-eyed and impotent', she weeps, while he mumbles over his own wrongs. He wonders why he bothered to go to Troy, and what ill-chance brought 'poor Paris' to his kingdom – and, having brought him, made him fall in love with her. The murderous hatred that once raised Menelaus' avenging sword has dwindled into a senile resentment at having been put to so much trouble.

My growing realisation of how much this poem was saying to me was accompanied by an increasing awareness of (and pleasure in) the skill with which the poet uses language. Appreciation of meaning and style went hand in hand, for I found that I could account for my understanding of and response to what was being said only by paying close attention to *how* it was being said.

Only 28 lines long, the poem re-creates a complex human relationship, working so powerfully on our imagination that we share in and are moved by the experience. That result is brought about by a remarkable command of style, every feature of which sustains the overall purpose for which the poem was written.

The shape of the poem embodies the developing situations and relationships, as I pointed out when commenting on the contrasting subject matter and attitudes depicted in Parts I and II. But there are further divisions within that two-part design.

Each part is itself split into two. The first eight lines of each part are concerned with an event or situation in the lives of Menelaus and Helen. Then, after a pause, the next six lines comment on or suggest an attitude to that event or situation.

The first eight lines of Part I tell of Menelaus' hot pursuit of revenge. The next six lines comment on the action just described by providing an ironical account of its outcome.

The first eight lines of Part II depict the dreary reality of the years that followed their reunion. The next six lines are concerned with their thoughts and feelings.

The distinctive function of each group of lines is emphasised by the sharply different rhyme schemes that distinguish the two eight-line groups from the two six-line groups. The eight-line groups have similar rhyme patterns. Their first four lines rhyme a-b-b-a; and though their rhyme schemes diverge in the next four lines, neither uses rhymes that occur in either of the six-line groups.

In other words, each of the two parts is written in sonnet form; and the whole poem consists of a sequence of two sonnets, firmly based on the Petrarchan pattern: an octave (the first eight lines), followed by a break, followed by a sestet (the next six lines). The strict discipline of this form, by which strong emotions and serious thoughts are controlled and compressed, makes a major contribution to the poem's impact.

Changes of pace and emphasis, brought about by variations of line length and stress patterns, direct attention to the developing action, attitudes and motives. For example, Menelaus's hatred and violence are emphasised in the strongly stressed opening lines. The first line has seven stressed syllables to only two unstressed. The rapid action is then carried forward in a regular iambic metre until, after the words 'And a king's honour', a mid-line pause checks the first movement.

The second movement begins violently ('Through red death and smoke'). It ends in a clash of discordant noise, sense and sound working together on the reader's imagination, for the sound is part of the sense. The comma pause after the unstressed, drawn-out second syllable of 'bower', and the 'missing' stress in the last line, throw the words 'flaming like a god' into heightened prominence. Poised for revenge, Menelaus is frozen in an incomplete (and never-to-be-completed) action.

After the octave/sestet break, all is changed. Helen, 'lonely and serene', waits for him and he succumbs. Hesitant at first, as Menelaus pauses and remembers, the metre then moves smoothly into the bland regularity of the last lines: 'He flung the sword away . . . the perfect Queen'.

Part II is equally remarkable for the skill with which the versification reinforces the sense and feeling. The dreariness of 'the long connubial years' – each as empty as the next – is the subject of the octave, in which six of the eight lines run on. The phrasing – at once economical and evocative – and the structure work together to convey the monotony of a life in which two people are carried helplessly along on time's uninterrupted current.

The contrasting shape of the sestet (it has only one run-on line, and a closer rhyme scheme) supports a changed perspective, the establishment of which I consider to be the poet's finest achievement in this fine poem. I see the last lines as the intellectual and emotional fulfilment of all that has gone before.

In what I have written so far, I have tried to justify my admiration of the poem. Directly and indirectly, I have commented on its fusion of style with meaning: the unfailing selection of the right word to produce a large effect; the compressed power of the sparingly used images (generally expressed through the metaphorical meaning of single words); the subtle support that the versification gives to sense and emotion; the structural and verbal contrasts that embody meaning and communicate attitudes.

But unless I now attempt to account for the impact of the ending, I cannot do justice to the total impression that the poem makes on me.

When, at the beginning of Part II, we read the words 'So far the poet', we recognise that, at one level, the poem is satirical. The poet referred to is not the poet we are listening to. He is Homer himself, perhaps, or any other poet writing about Menelaus and Helen in traditionally heroic vein. His identity is not important. What *our* poet is saying is this: 'The story I have just told you in Part I is the conventional account – though I have suggested my own way of looking at it – of how Menelaus and Helen met amid Troy's ruin, and of how they were reunited.' He then points out that the poet who told their story like that was so blinkered by the conventional view that he could not concern himself with the inevitable sequel to the high romantic moment – 'How should he behold?' *That* poet 'does not tell you'; but *our* poet goes on to tell us what the heroic account omits.

In describing their life together – as I have tried to show earlier – there is no attempt to excuse Menelaus and Helen. They lied to each other and to themselves. Their mutual misery was self-inflicted, and they paid the price that deception exacts.

If the poem ended there, its qualities could still be admired: its poetic craft, its clear-sightedness. But, in the last lines, the theme is enlarged. As Menelaus mumbles over 'poor Paris', and 'gummy-eyed and impotent' Helen weeps, troubled by a feeble stirring of former passion, we are moved to pity them. Our compassion for suffering fellow creatures lifts them above satire. No longer remote figures, from whose want of moral fibre lessons can be drawn, they come closer to us – and we are moved by them. Denying nothing of their folly and guilt, the closely rhymed incisive statements of the sestet in Part II enclose us in the prison of their sad minds.

And then, right at the end, in the final memorable couplet, the full irony of life is borne in upon us. One thing Menelaus and Helen still share: the memory of a dead man. And the dead man, for whose fate they – in their different ways – were responsible, has been less harshly dealt with than they, the sad survivors of a long-gone past.

It is this last perspective, in which their transient lives are proportioned against oblivion, that brings this superb poem right home to me. I am reminded of our common lot and of my kinship with all three:

> So Menelaus nagged; and Helen cried;
> And Paris slept on by Scamander side.

8 Comprehension and varieties of English

Note The different kinds of examination questions discussed and worked out in previous chapters test particular areas of knowledge and understanding and particular skills, as defined in the syllabuses of the various boards. The contents and the emphasis of the separate papers differ accordingly. Nevertheless, the focal point of English A Level studies is *English*. That is why, whatever its immediate 'targets', each paper is necessarily a test of:

1. Your understanding of the varied ways in which language works.
2. Your ability to give a clear and reasoned account of how individual writers make language work, whether in the prescribed texts you are studying or in the unseen passages that the examiners select for critical appreciation.

It is to emphasise the crucial importance of a language-based approach to English studies that some boards set special questions, or special papers, consisting of comprehension tests and/or exercises in the identification and analysis of varieties of English.

8.1 Comprehension

The meaning of 'comprehension'

The verb *to comprehend* means 'to grasp with the mind'; 'to take in'. Comprehension is a deep and full understanding, arrived at by close, accurate and imaginative reading of the passage set.

Statement and implication

To understand *what* is said, you have to pay close attention to *how* it is said. Revise *now* Section 7.5 – 'Looking for clues'. The points made there about tone, attitude and intention are as relevant to the answering of comprehension questions as to the writing of critical appreciations. A writer's implied meaning may extend, reinforce, modify – even negate – the stated meaning. Comprehension – deep and full understanding – is attained when you are aware of the interplay between statement and implication, and bring the two into balance according to your judgement of the writer's overall intention.

8.2 The kinds of questions set

The passages

It is the practice of some boards to combine comprehension tests with exercises in appreciation by setting questions or papers variously described as 'Comment and Appreciation' or 'Comprehension and Appreciation'. Since, as you are by now fully aware, you cannot appreciate without comprehending, or comprehend without appreciating, that practice requires no further explanation. Both verse and prose passages are set in questions and papers of this kind. The methods of working out appreciations have already been demonstrated in Chapter 7.

Our concern here is with those questions and papers in which comprehension is tested explicitly. The passages set for this purpose are generally in prose. Often, the subject matter is related to literary studies, but do not count on this. The passages are drawn from a great variety of sources, present and past: exploration, philosophy, political thought, science, religion, fiction, biography, history – to instance some of the subjects featured in recent papers. Tone, attitude and purpose are similarly varied. Humorous, satirical, factual, subjective, objective, narrative, dramatic, impressionistic, discursive passages – all are grist to the examiners' mill. The range is limited only by their view of the degree of difficulty an A Level candidate can be expected to surmount.

It is obvious that a candidate who has read widely will be better placed than one who has read only set books. Even so, the nature of the passages and of the questions justifies this advice:

- Do not panic if you know nothing about the subject of the passage: previous knowledge of it is not required.
- Remember that all the questions are within your intellectual capacity *if* you read the passage and the questions carefully.
- Remember that all the facts needed to answer factual questions are contained in the passage.
- Remember that the non-factual questions are designed to draw out answers based on an intelligent and imaginative response to the language – statement and implication again!

The questions

The questions test your ability to understand the passage, to think about it, and to use your imagination.

You are expected to:

- draw logical conclusions from stated facts;
- develop a line of argument; and
- respond imaginatively to the implications of the contents and the style.

You must therefore be able to recognise the point of each question. Study the following classification; not all these kinds of questions will be set on every passage, but some will be.

(a)   Questions about the subject matter of the passage – its *content*. These questions ask you to show that you have understood *what* the writer said.

Examples

(i)   Basing your answer on the information supplied in the first paragraph, outline the legal points at issue in the dispute.

(ii)   For what reasons does the writer disagree with the conventional account of the minister's downfall?

(b)   Questions about the language of the passage – its *style*. These questions ask you to show that you appreciate *how* the writer says what is said in the passage.

Examples

(i)   What stylistic techniques are used to present the argument forcefully?

(ii)   Discuss the effect of the two short sentences at the end of the first paragraph.

(c)   Questions about the writer's choice of words – the *diction*. These questions may direct attention to matters of content or to matters of style. You may be asked to explain the meaning of unusual or difficult words; to comment on ordinary words used in an unusual way; to discuss the accuracy and/or appropriateness of individual words prominently placed in the passage.

Examples

(i)   Express in your own words the meaning of the following words and phrases, as they are used in the passage: dubiously acquired; incunabula; pirated books.

(ii)   Bring out in your own words the full force of the word 'scant' in the third sentence.

Note 1   Whether explicitly instructed to do so or not, always explain the meaning of words and phrases *as the author uses them in the passage*.

Note 2   If you are instructed to suggest a one-word equivalent for a word used in the passage, supply a word with the same grammatical function as the word you are explaining. For example, the word 'scant' (see above) might be used as either an adjective or a verb. Your synonym should be the same part of speech as the word used in the passage.

(d)   Questions that require an imaginative response to the passage. Such questions are designed to test your awareness of *implications* and shades of meaning.

Examples

(i)   How seriously are we intended to take the plan of action set out in the third paragraph? Give reasons for your answer, relating that paragraph to the passage as a whole.

(ii) If you think the writer's attitude to the character described here is ambiguous, point to at least two features of the writing that lead you to take that view.

(e)   Questions that test your ability to *reason*: to draw conclusions, and to use *evidence*.

Examples

(i)   Do you think that the writer is justified in dismissing the argument set out in the first paragraph? Consider the reasons given in paragraphs two and three and the conclusion of the passage.

(ii) Outline in not more than fifty of your own words the position that the writer takes in the final paragraph. Say, with reasons, whether you agree with it or not.

8.3 Method

Although the examiners are not looking for the full-length critical evaluations called for in appreciations, you should study the passage set for comprehension in the same closely analytical way. Revise *now* Section 7.5 – 'A critical method'.

The following additional hints are to help you to apply techniques specially suited to exercises that test your ability to comprehend lengthy passages of prose.

(a)   Read right through the passage to discover its general sense. Do not at this stage puzzle long over details, but read on steadily. Do not read the questions set on the passage before you have gained an overall view of its contents.

(b)   Jot down a short statement of the gist of the passage, using your own words. Something like this is what is needed: 'The writer questions the reasons usually given for Britain's economic decline between 1919 and 1939.'

(c)   With your summary of the main point of the passage in mind, read through the passage again, very slowly and carefully. As you do so:
(i)   Check the accuracy of your brief summary.
(ii) Analyse the structure of the passage, noting the development of the writer's ideas and arguments – puzzle out the meaning of anything that you did not understand at first reading.
(iii) Note key words and phrases indicative of tone and attitude, so that you fully understand the writer's intentions and enter into the spirit in which the passage was written – note also details of ways in which the writer uses language to bring about the desired response from the reader.

Note   By now, you should have *comprehended* the passage, in the true sense of that term. You have been 'reading between the lines', noting *what* is said and *how* it is said. You have entered into its spirit and grasped its full meaning and purpose.

(d) Now read through *all* the questions set on the passage. Do *not* start to answer until you have read them all. Many marks are lost in these tests through misunderstanding the meaning and point of the questions. You will find that each question throws light on the others.

(e) Now start to answer. Work through each question in order. Do not spend too long over a question that puzzles you at first. Leave a space, and go on to the next. Very often, a baffling question seems easier when you have thought about later questions. The answer emerges as you work on the others.

Note   The time allowed for comprehension questions – rarely less than one hour – permits you to draft your answers on rough paper. You are strongly recommended to do so. On the whole, short answers are required, so you have time to correct and polish your drafts before writing them out in their final form.

8.4 Common mistakes

- *Factual blunders* – the result of careless reading.
- *Misinterpretations of the writer's tone, attitude and intention.*
- *Falsifications (accidental or deliberate) of the writer's meaning* – usually the result of strong disagreement with the writer's views.
- *Failure to grapple with the issues raised by the questions.*
- *Failure to supply reasons for answers* when told to do so.
- *Badly proportioned answers*, in which minor points (even irrelevancies) are treated at length, while the main point is merely touched on.
- *Badly written answers* – faulty grammar, punctuation and spelling, limited vocabulary.

Year after year, the examiners' reports comment on the poor standard of answers to comprehension questions. The remarks of one examiner identify the root causes of failure: 'Whenever it was tackled, usually in a 20-minute rush, the optional comprehension question was atrociously done, without organisation, subtlety, or lucidity of analysis.'

In other words, candidates did not study the passage closely and carefully. They did not make a clear analysis of its contents and style. The method set out in this chapter is designed to enable you to do both.

The resulting growth of reading skill is a benefit not restricted to answering comprehension questions. The quality of all your reading – set books, background books, leisure books, newspapers, magazines – will be improved as you practise the analytical methods that comprehension questions demand.

8.5 Worked examples

Read the following passage and then answer the questions.

The Breath and Spirit of All Knowledge

'The future of poetry is immense, because in poetry, where it is worthy of its high destinies, our race, as time goes on, will find an ever surer and surer stay. There is not a creed which is not shaken, not an accredited dogma which is not shown to be questionable, not a received tradition which does not threaten to dissolve. Our religion has materialised itself in the fact, in the supposed fact; it has attached its emotion to the fact, and now the fact is failing it. But for poetry the idea is everything; the rest is a world of illusion, of divine illusion. Poetry attaches its emotion to the idea; the idea *is* the fact. The strongest part of our religion today is its unconscious poetry.'

Let me be permitted to quote these words of my own, as uttering the thought which should, in my opinion, go with us and govern us in all our study of poetry. In the present work* it is the course of one great contributory stream to the world-river of poetry that we are invited to follow. We are here invited to trace the stream of English poetry. But whether we set ourselves, as here, to follow only one of the several streams that make the mighty river of poetry, or whether we seek to know them all, our governing thought should be the same. We should conceive of poetry worthily, and more highly than it has been the custom to conceive of it. We should conceive of it as capable of higher uses, and called to higher destinies, than those which in general men have assigned to it hitherto. More and more mankind will discover that we have to turn to poetry to interpret life for us, to console us, to sustain us. Without poetry, our science will appear incomplete; and most of what now passes with us for religion and philosophy will be replaced by poetry. Science, I say, will appear incomplete without it. For finely and truly does Wordsworth call poetry 'the impassioned expression which is in the countenance of all science' and what is a countenance without its expression? Again, Wordsworth finely and truly calls poetry 'the breath and finer spirit of all knowledge': our religion, parading evidences such as those on which the popular mind relies now; our philosophy, pluming itself on its reasonings about causation and finite and infinite being; what are they but the shadows and dreams and false shows of knowledge? The day will come when we shall wonder at ourselves for having trusted to them, for having taken them seriously; and the more we perceive their hollowness, the more we shall prize 'the breath and finer spirit of all knowledge' offered to us by poetry.

Matthew Arnold

*A poetry anthology for which Arnold wrote this passage as the introduction

(i)   State in your own words Arnold's claims for poetry as set out in this passage.   (15 marks)

(ii) What stylistic devices does Arnold employ to make his arguments more compelling?   (10 marks)

(iii) Say, with reasons, whether you agree or disagree with the claims that Arnold makes for poetry.   (15 marks)

Note   The time limit is one hour. When I was starting work, I estimated that the preparatory reading and note-taking would take about 20 minutes. In fact, I spent 25 minutes on it. (The passage is not easy to comprehend. An abstruse argument is advanced in a series of eloquent statements that demand concentrated attention and careful analysis.) I then had 35 minutes in which to answer the three questions set. The first and third were harder than the second (and they each carried more marks), so I spent about 13 minutes on (i), 8 minutes on (ii), and 13 minutes on (iii).

Comprehending the passage

Make a brief summarising statement of its contents

Arnold states that religion and philosophy are discredited, and that poetry will take their place. He says that poetry will also be seen as the essential completion of science.

Analyse the structure and the use of language

Structure	*Language*
Development of thought and argument	*Key expressions (indicating tone, attitude, intention) – use of language to bring about desired response*
1. Long quotation (whole of 1st para.) from A.'s own works announces main idea: poetry has a truth that religion lacks – religion has based its claims on 'facts' now discredited – poetry rests solely on ideas it embodies – not dependent on so-called 'facts' – moves us by its ideas – what survives of religion is the poetry that clings to it	Gravity of tone (e.g. 'immense'/'high destiny'/'ever surer and surer stay') – A. is intensely serious about his subject – almost 'preaching' – wants to 'convert' reader by force of his 'message' – use of long quotation of his own words indicates confident reliance on his own reputation as a thinker
2. Links big idea just announced to immediate purpose of passage (intro. to anthology of poetry)	Metaphor (stream and river) used to illustrate relationship between main idea and immediate task
3. Returns to main theme: supreme importance of poetry in our lives – it follows that we must learn to think of poetry in a new way – a way that recognises its spiritual function	'Governing thought'/'conceive of it worthily'/'highly'/'higher uses'/'higher destinies' – A. is lifting subject up – elevating it – wants it to inspire reader – *conceive* used 3 times in 3 lines
4. Begins to define function of poetry – compares it with those of religion, philosophy and science – poetry will replace religion and philosophy, taking over their functions – it will be seen as completion of what science leaves incomplete.	Careful – exact – choice of words: 'to *interpret* . . . to *console* . . . to *sustain*' – these are the traditionally accepted functions of religion and philosophy – A. firmly and precisely asserts that poetry does all these things
5. Returns to point about science and poetry – recognising that idea he is advancing will strike many readers as new (perhaps strained), he deliberately repeats it	'Impassioned expression . . . countenance . . . science': 1st quotation from Wordsworth intended to bring authority of great poet into the argument on A.'s side: poetry puts living expression on face of science –

i.e. it brings science into relationship with human life and feeling – without poetry, science would be cold, blank, inhuman

6.   Returns to religion and philosophy, demolishing their claims to have a continuing value – the 'evidences' for religion are such as only ignorant and unthinking people ('the popular mind') accept – philosophy busies itself with pedantic distinctions ('causation and finite and infinite being')

2nd quotation from W. (same purpose as 1st) enlarges claim for poetry – poetry is 'breath' (inspiration) and 'finer spirit' (distillation – essence of spiritual truth) of *all* knowledge (not only religion, philosophy and science) – the claim is all-embracing now – NB emotive phrasing: 'religion *parading* evidences'/'philosophy *pluming* itself'/'*shadows* and *dreams* and *false shows* of knowledge' – A. wants readers to feel the absurdity of these boastful and empty claims to continuing validity

7.   Ends by predicting that someday people will be astonished that the claims of religion and philosophy were ever taken seriously – and the more their emptiness is realised, the more highly will poetry be prized.

Use of emotive language noted in (6) continues – A. emphasises *folly* of taking r. and p. seriously – 'hollowness' is the key word here – they are shams – part of 2nd W. quotation repeated to ram argument home

Note   I tried to be objective as I made that close study of the passage. I did not agree with all that Arnold was saying, nor did I think that his method of arguing was always effective; so I was often tempted to make subjective comments in my notes – even to alter his views to suit my ideas. I resisted the temptation. My job was to understand *what* he was saying and to study *how* he was saying it. If the questions ask me to give my views on the passage, that will be the time to put forward my own opinions and arguments.

Answering the questions

(i)   Arnold claims that poetry is the supreme achievement of the human mind. It is destined to replace religion and philosophy, and it is an essential completion of science.

His belief that the study of poetry brings spiritual and moral benefits which cannot be derived from either religion or philosophy is based on the claim that poetry is true where religion and philosophy are false.

Religion has relied on belief in certain facts. The emotions it aroused and the faith it demanded were dependent on the truth of those facts; but they are now discredited. Religious faith and emotion have been destroyed with them.

But poetry does not rely on facts. The emotions that poetry arouses are fused with the ideas that it embodies. Ideas *are* the facts of poetry. It is, therefore, immune from change, for ideas are eternal.

Philosophy has tried to reveal truth by making reasoned distinctions between abstruse concepts that are of little interest to anyone who is not a philosopher. But poetry is not concerned with such pedantries. Its truth is the truth of the whole of human life.

For those reasons, poetry is the one true source of the interpretative, consolatory and sustaining powers once ascribed to religion and philosophy.

And poetry is a higher thing than science. The truths of science are coldly objective. Therefore a scientific account of life is incomplete. Poetry denies none of the undoubted facts of science, for it is not concerned with facts. Poetry is an essential completion of the scientific view. It relates the truth of science to the emotions and aspirations of humanity.

(ii) The stylistic techniques are those of an orator. Arnold uses quotations here, rather as a preacher uses scriptural texts. Quoting Wordsworth twice and himself once, he seeks to add authority to his arguments and to increase their emotional appeal, for his three quotations make firm pronouncements and are deeply felt.

He also uses emphatic repetitions: 'Without poetry our science will appear incomplete'/'Science, I say, will appear incomplete'. The word 'conceive' is used three times in as many lines; 'finely and truly' appears twice. The second Wordsworth quotation is repeated as part of the climax with which the passage ends.

The oratorical effect is increased by the use of rhetorical questions: 'what is a countenance without its expression?'/'what are they but?' Inversions add to the 'speech-making' impression: 'For finely and truly does Wordsworth'.

His diction is carefully selected for its persuasive powers. The grave language of the opening sounds the keynote. Then he indicates the elevated nature of his theme ('conceive of poetry worthily'/'higher uses'/'higher destinies'). The exalted function of poetry is described eloquently: 'to *interpret* life for us, to *console* us, to *sustain* us.'

Again, like an orator, he reserves the grandest effect for the end, exploiting the emotive qualities of words in a fine flourish. The scornful rejection of religion ('*parading* evidences') and of philosophy ('*pluming* itself') leads into the powerful, rhythmic denunciation of 'the shadows and dreams and false shows' of their 'hollowness'.

(iii) I agree with his claim that poetry can 'interpret, console and sustain'. I can think of many poems that do all those things for me.

I agree that the truth of poetry is independent of facts. Poetry is concerned with imaginative, not factual, truth.

I agree that the visionary power at work in some poetry is an essential element of human experience, complementing the rationality of an objective, scientific view of life. But I think Arnold makes too rigid a distinction between poetry and science. The work of *great* scientists is illuminated by imagination, inspired by 'vision'.

That leads me to my chief reservations about Arnold's claims. I think it was a mistake to argue that poetry is a rival to – and the inevitable displacer of – religion and philosophy. His anxiety to substitute poetry for religion was the product of his own intellectual history and of the circumstances of his time. It all seems rather a sterile argument now.

Things have not gone the way he thought they would. Religion retains the poetry he saw as its one surviving strength; and (to name just one world religion) organised Christianity adapts its theology to new discoveries. On a broader view than Arnold took (he seems to have had only the Church of England of his own day in mind), some of the other world-wide religions maintain their hold on their followers without giving so much as a nod in the direction of science and rationality.

And, of course, poetry survives – 'a friend to man'; but without absurdly aspiring to function as some sort of nebulous universal 'creed'. I think Arnold was carried away by his salvationary theory of poetry. He writes as if every poet must be a preacher. The 'pleasure principle' does not seem to play any part in his thinking. I read poetry for the pleasure it gives me. Any 'lessons' it 'teaches' me arise out of that.

My own experience of poetry makes me disagree with Arnold's main claim. I am much more in tune with the point of view that Keats expressed when he said: 'What shocks the virtuous philosopher delights the chameleon poet'.

8.6 Varieties of English

Directing attention to the ways in which language is used in the passages set for comment, the questions require candidates to:

- analyse the linguistic features; and
- write objective, evidential accounts of those features.

They may also be required to identify the particular variety of English used in each passage.

8.7 The kinds of questions set

The passages

Drawn from varied sources, the passages may be examples of spoken or written English – literary or non-literary. (It is the practice of some examining boards to refer to passages drawn from written English as 'texts', whereas passages drawn from spoken English are referred to as 'transcripts'.)

Recent papers have included passages drawn from the following sources: transcripts of radio and television interviews; transcripts of everyday conversations on various topics (for example, blood sports, fashion in clothes, pop music and rural transport); transcripts of cross-examination in a court of law; written and spoken answers to questionnaires issued by market research organisations and political parties; articles and headlines in 'quality' and 'popular' newspapers; advertising copy; car maintenance manuals; knitting instructions; cookery books; novels; plays; memoirs; letters; transcripts of political speeches.

Diverse as those passages were in subject matter and origin, each provided candidates with opportunities to comment on the ways in which a particular speaker's or writer's language was influenced by and adapted to the purposes for which, and the situation in which, it was used. It was this common feature that made them suitable material for an examination paper on varieties of English.

The questions

Matters to which particular attention should be paid may be specified, or the instructions may be worded in more general terms. Here are three typical questions, in the third of which the candidate is left to decide which linguistic features should be included in the answer.

1. The following extracts from various newspaper accounts of a parliamentary occasion contain some striking differences in the description of events and in the attitude to the occasion which they reveal. Discuss these differences and how they are manifested in the structure of the passages, the choice of words and the handling of grammar.

2. Identify the variety of English which each of these extracts illustrates. Then say how you recognise it, by describing in detail the linguistic features which provide the clues to its identity. You may wish to refer to items of vocabulary, layout on the page, word-forms and grammar, together with any aspects of meaning and context of use that seem relevant.

3. These passages were taken from the autobiographies of two scientists, both eminent in the same field. Show how the different ways in which language is used reflect the different purposes each writer had in mind when giving an account of his early work.

Whether guidelines are provided or not, the questions cannot be answered successfully unless a detailed linguistic analysis of the passage is made, close attention being paid to the features listed in the following section.

8.8 What to look for – and how to look for it

As you read a passage through for the first time, concentrating on its meaning, its linguistic features are making an impression on you. You are aware – however vaguely, at this stage – that the words chosen and the arrangement of those words are telling you something about the purposes for which (and the situation in which) this particular speaker or writer used language in this way.

Linguistic analysis of the passage begins when you follow up the clues provided by those early verbal signals. As your investigation proceeds – and you will find that one clue leads to another – you are collecting the facts on which to base a full, objective account of the ways in which language is used.

You cannot write a factual, evidential report on the language unless you study it methodically. Think of the linguistic categories listed at the end of this section as providing a set of analytical 'filters'. Then practise putting various examples of speech and writing through each 'filter'. You will find that the evidence so gathered builds up into a collection of detailed information about a speaker's or writer's use of language.

Information collected by one 'filter' may well be repeated as the language is put through another. But that is to be expected, since any utterance is much more than a mere assemblage of separate 'bits' of language. Close analysis identifies the various linguistic features present in any passage. It also establishes how they relate to each other; *and* how they all relate to the overall purpose for which, and the situation within which, language was used in a particular passage.

Here is a check-list of points to which you may need to pay attention when analysing the ways in which language is used.

Linguistic features

- Spoken or written.
- Formal or informal.
- Personal or impersonal.
- Standard English or non-standard.
- Vocabulary – for example: plain/coloured; simple/difficult; accurate/inaccurate; everyday/remote; racy/restrained; slangy/formal.
- Phrasing and sentence construction – for example: economical/verbose; direct/circumlocutory; active/passive; short sentences/long sentences.
- Feeling language or factual language – words used emotively (to convey and to arouse feelings – to suggest); words used referentially (to emphasise factual content – to state); words used pseudo-referentially (pretending to be concerned with facts, but really intended to arouse emotion).
- Paragraphing.
- Grammar, punctuation and spelling. Pause marks in transcripts.
- Layout on the page – for example: headline layout; tabloid or broadsheet layout; advertising copy layout; verse layout.
- Typographical features – for example: italic/roman; capitals; spacing; indentation; half-lines.

Function

- Narrative.
- Descriptive.
- Dramatic.
- Discursive (argumentative or controversial).
- Impressionistic.
- Practical (transactional).

Purpose

- To inform; or to elicit information.
- To give instructions or commands.
- To make requests or to grant them.
- To communicate facts.
- To convey and/or to arouse feelings.
- To convince by statement and reason.
- To persuade by suggestion and emotion.
- To entertain.

- To express the speaker's or writer's personality.
- To convey an attitude to the subject and/or to the listener or reader.

Situation

The linguistic situation is often called the 'context of situation' or the 'context of use'. Both terms emphasise that any spoken or written utterance takes place *within a particular set of circumstances*. Those circumstances are dominant influences on the ways in which language is used; and the matters so far listed relate to them. For example, the use of formal vocabulary and grammar indicates the speaker's or writer's perception that s/he is using language in a formal situation. Speech or writing having a narrative function indicates the speaker's or writer's perception that s/he is using language in a 'story-telling' situation.

The context of situation or context of use, within which a spoken or written utterance is made, includes the subject matter and the purpose of that utterance. It also includes *the kind of relationship* that exists between the speaker/writer on the one hand and the listener/reader on the other. The speaker's/writer's awareness of the kind of relationship s/he has with the listener/reader is called 'sense of audience'; and sense of audience plays a most important part in determining how language is used.

According to particular circumstances, any or all of the following considerations contribute to sense of audience:

- Relative ages of speaker/writer and listener/reader.
- Relative status.
- How well (or how little) they are known to each other.
- The presence or absence of an emotional connection between them; and – if a connection exists – its nature: warmth, coolness, hostility, and so on.
- The speaker's/writer's attitude to the listener/reader – assumptions made about listener's/reader's intelligence, and/or about the nature of the listener's/reader's interest in and knowledge of the subject matter.
- The size of the audience addressed. Is this a one-to-one utterance? Or one-to-several? Or one-to-many?
- The degree to which the utterance is intended to be private or public.

8.9 Timing and planning answers

Timing

As a rule, these are 3-hour papers, and candidates are required to answer two questions. About 10 minutes should be spent in reading through the whole paper and choosing questions. Of the 85 minutes then available for each question, about 30 minutes will be needed for close study and linguistic analysis of the passages set for comment. Do not begin to write your answer until that essential preparatory work has been completed.

Planning

In answering these questions, you should show that you have made a detailed study of the ways in which language is used in the texts or transcripts you have selected. The examiners may specify particular matters (of vocabulary, grammar, and so on) for your special attention. Or they may give you more general instructions, leaving you to judge for yourself which linguistic features of the passage are of special importance. In either case, you should work out a plan that covers all the essential points.

Remember too that the examiners are looking for an answer that:

- makes detailed reference to the passage under discussion to support your statements;
- *and* is written in good, clear English, and with orderly presentation.

These requirements are a stiff test of your ability to organise your answer. The kinds of problems posed, and ways of tackling them, are demonstrated in the following section.

8.10 Worked examples

1

In providing sharply contrasting descriptions of the day's events, these four reports of a Royal Wedding reveal that their writers' attitudes towards the wedding were very different. Discuss the four different descriptions and attitudes, paying special attention to the vocabulary and grammar employed by the writers in presenting them.

A

Royal Romance Blows the Clouds Away

A Royal Wedding is a regal enactment of a universal ceremony, holding us all in thrall. When – as yesterday, at the altar of St. Paul's – the royal couple stumble over their words, that touch of nature makes the whole world kin. Mr and Mrs Smith are moved to smile at each other in
(5) reminiscent sympathy, recalling how, on their wedding day, she, too, spoke his baptismal names in the wrong order, and how he, too, forgot to endow her with his worldly goods.

In clouded times, and for a nation bowed beneath a cross weighty with economic ills and political anxieties, it was a day of exuberant romance,
(10) bright and celebratory. For all our friends in the free world, it signified no less, and gladsome were they in sharing the joys of an ancient kingdom.

Not that the harsh facts of the daily round could be entirely hidden, however tactfully the armed policemen were deployed along the processional route. Crack shots perforce perched high overhead; detectives
(15) dispersed watchfully among the throngs. Two of the 'footmen' riding stately coaches were, if truth be told, armed policemen in the livery of the royal household.

Yet the day closed with no unseemly events to mar its brightness. The missing were shepherded safely back into their family folds; and in the
(20) whole teeming City just one person was apprehended – a minor transgressor of the huckstering byelaws.

People had teemed into London from the three corners of the world. They came from far flung countries whose denizens still rejoice in their allegiance to the Throne – an allegiance nominal in law, perchance; but,
(25) cherished in their warmly beating hearts, no mere and legal fiction.

From past colonies they came. Republicans from the USA – royalists to a man – were taking their places along the route a full twenty-four hours in advance, clustering eagerly by St. Paul's, where – as everywhere – every vacant nook and cranny was occupied.

(30) Red, white and blue favours dazzled our eyes and made glad our hearts. We whiled away the waiting hours by cheering all that moved – let it be peeress or policewoman, rifleman or refuse cart.

And then, how the tumultuous cheers rang out for Lady Diana Frances Spencer in her Glass Coach! A breath-taking vision in her wedding gown
(35) of lace and taffeta, its spectacular brilliance fully manifest only when the waterfall that was its train poured down the great flight of steps, she proceeded into the cathedral on her father's arm to join her waiting bridegroom and to meet her royal destiny.

And, as always on that magic day, Mr and Mrs Smith were at her side –
(40) her subjects and her kin.

B

Britain's Biggest Security Operation

What was described as 'Britain's biggest security operation' was mounted for the royal wedding yesterday.

No one realised that a footman on the Queen's coach and another on Prince Charles' were armed policemen in disguise, and the congregation
(5) did not spot the armed policewoman in St. Paul's.

The Horseguard escorts for the royal procession had practised their own anti-terrorist drill. They rode very close to the coaches with the horses' heads blocking the view.

Apart from some 4,000 uniformed police, many of whom turned their
(10) backs on the royal procession to peer into the crowd, anti-terrorist SAS troops were also on the streets.

The £750,000 police helicopter, complete with electronic eye, seen on many London demonstrations, hovered low over. And armed detectives and Special Branch officers mingled with the crowd.

(15) Lists of people who occupied vantage points at windows and on stands were checked while uniformed officers – some using dogs – examined possible hiding places for explosives.

Manhole covers and drains were inspected and even the insides of scaffolding poles used for stands and crowd barriers were probed.

(20) Police were also in ITN's Goodyear airship keeping an eye on the crowd.

Police marksmen were also seen on roofs the length of the procession. There were four arrests for pick pocketing, said the police.

C

Why Do I Want to Go to Royal Wedding?

Early yesterday morning the narrow pavements of the Strand and Fleet Street were only impassable in some places. For most of the route the flag sellers, souvenir programme vendors, and bystanders in search of a better vantage point, walked easily.

(5) But the petty entrepreneurs didn't appear to be making a killing from the punters, who were stacked only two or three deep in places. By 8.30 souvenir programmes price £1 were still not selling for 50 pence. Periscopes in red, white and blue stripes were being knocked down from £2.99 to £2, to £1 to 50 pence, or even free with 40 cigarettes.

(10) Behind the procession route in Covent Garden, stall holders like Peter Luff in his Union Jack hat were getting ready for the end of the ceremony. 'If it's a lovely day it'll really bring 'em out,' he wished aloud.

Advertisers were less discreet in their wishes, with a keen eye on the multitude of television cameras scanning the route from beginning to end.

(15) Messages galore in delicate royal type-faces above giant block letters declaring company names and telephone numbers, wished the couple well. So the sheltered Lady Di will know the name of a good scaffolder or insurance company should she need one.

But what the Tory Consumer Minister Sally Oppenheim has called 'the

(20) tourist attraction of the century' didn't quite come off for others. The London Tourist Board admitted 'there is tremendous public interest in the wedding, but it is not reflected in hotel bookings'.

But the last word must go to a lonely old lady, wandering the back streets of Covent Garden, talking loudly to herself. 'Royal wedding?' she

(25) questioned. 'What do I want to go to a royal wedding for?'

D

Court Circular

Buckingham Palace
July 29: The Marriage of the Prince of Wales with the Lady Diana Spencer was solemnised in St Paul's Cathedral this morning.

The Queen and The Duke of Edinburgh, with Queen Elizabeth The

(5) Queen Mother and other members of the Royal Family, drove to St Paul's Cathedral in a carriage procession escorted by a Sovereign's Escort of the Household Cavalry, with two Standards, under the command of Lieutenant-Colonel Andrew Parker Bowles, The Blues and Royals.

The Queen and The Duke of Edinburgh, Queen Elizabeth the Queen

(10) Mother and other Members of the Royal Family, were received at the steps of St Paul's Cathedral by the Right Hon the Lord Mayor (Alderman Sir Ronald Gardner-Thorpe) and at the West Door by the Dean and Chapter, the Bishop of London and the Archbishop of Canterbury.

A procession was formed and Their Majesties and Their Royal

(15) Highnesses were conducted to their places.

The Prince of Wales, with The Prince Andrew, drove to St Paul's Cathedral in a carriage procession escorted by a Prince of Wales' Escort of the Household Cavalry under the command of Major Anthony de Ritter, the Life Guards.

(20)   The Prince of Wales, with The Prince Andrew (Supporter), was received at the West Door of the Cathedral by the Dean and Chapter, the Bishop of London and the Archbishop of Canterbury.

Having been joined by The Prince Edward (Supporter), a procession was formed and Their Royal Highnesses were conducted to their places.

(25)   The Earl Spencer and The Lady Diana Spencer drove to St Paul's Cathedral in the Glass Coach and were received at the West Door by the Dean and Chapter, the Bishop of London and the Archbishop of Canterbury.

The Service was performed by the Archbishop of Canterbury, assisted
(30)   by the Dean of St Paul's.

At the conclusion of the Service the Registers were signed in the Dean's Aisle.

The Bride and Bridegroom were conducted to their carriage and, escorted by a Prince of Wales' Escort of the Household Cavalry, drove to
(35)   Buckingham Palace.

Working out the answer

Note   Candidates were allowed $1\frac{1}{2}$ hours for this question. That provided sufficient time for thorough study and detailed planning before starting to write the answer.

Collecting your material

(a)   Read through all four passages, gathering first impressions of their contents and their style.

(b)   Study each passage closely. Concentrate on the matters specified in the examiners' instructions:

   (i)   the differences in the descriptions of events;

   (ii)   the different attitudes to the wedding indicated by the different descriptions;

   (iii)   the ways in which those different descriptions and different attitudes are brought out by each writer's choice of words and use of grammar.

(c)   Make notes as you investigate those matters. Bear in mind that a mass of unsorted notes won't be of much help when you come to plan your answer, so sort out your material as you collect it. Write your notes on each passage on a separate sheet of rough-work paper. Put down one of the three headings you need on each sheet ('description' – 'attitude' – 'vocabulary and grammar') and enter each note under the appropriate heading.

(d)   Don't copy out chunks of the original passages when you are making your notes. Keep them brief. Line numbers, short quotations and precise references are what is needed. For example:

Passage A
Vocabulary and grammar
gladsome – perchance – huckstering – inversion (1.14) – sentences (ll. 5–9)
Passage C
Attitude
compare Consumer Minister (ll. 25–27)/L.T. Board (ll. 27–30)

Planning your answer

(a) When writing your answer, you must try to carry out all the examiners' instructions in an orderly way. If you don't work out a firm structure before you begin to write, you'll overlook important points and get in a muddle.

Think hard about your plan, and be prepared to look critically at the first ideas that spring to mind. They may need a lot of revision before they can be put to good use.

When I was planning my answer to this question, my first idea was to arrange it in four main sections, with three sub-sections in each. Like this:

Passage A
(i)   Description of events.
(ii) Writer's attitude as revealed by description.
(iii) Vocabulary and grammar used in presentation of description and attitude.

I intended to repeat that pattern as I dealt with B, C and D in turn.

(b) On further thought, I saw the dangers of that plan. It would enable me to present my analysis of each separate passage clearly, but it would make it difficult for me to carry out all the examiners' instructions in a clear, orderly way. Those instructions call for *discussion*. The key words are: 'Discuss those different descriptions and attitudes . . . [and] the vocabulary and grammar employed'.

If I dealt with each passage in a separate section of my answer, I couldn't see how I was going to make comparisons and contrasts between each passage and the others without being repetitive and clumsy.

The trap I foresaw was this. At the end of my section on A, I'd have to draw B, C and D into the discussion *before* I'd presented my findings on them. Then, at the end of my section on B, I'd have to refer back to A and forward to C and D. My section on D would be easier to handle because I'd have made my points about the other passages by the time I got to D, but that wouldn't rescue the earlier sections from muddle.

There was an alternative. I could deal with A, B, C and D as planned. Then I could add a final comparison and contrast section. But that would have to include a lot of expository material set out earlier in the answer.

All in all, I was not happy with my first ideas. If I proceeded along those lines, I'd be constantly stopping and restarting. My answer would be fragmented. It would not progress purposefully.

(c) I went back to the instructions for guidance, trying to reason out a structure that would meet their demands.

The examiners' introductory comments on the passages state that the writers' attitudes are revealed *through* their descriptions; and the instructions expressly *connect* vocabulary and grammar with the presentation of descriptions and attitudes.

I concluded that I was expected to explore the *connections* between (the *interplay* of) descriptions, attitudes, vocabulary and grammar, while at the same time comparing and contrasting the four passages.

That is why my first plan was a mistake. It separated passage from passage and feature from feature much too rigidly.

(d) This is the plan I finally worked out. I judged that it would enable me to maintain a *continuous* and *progressive* discussion of the four passages, paying the required attention to descriptions, attitudes, vocabulary and grammar as I went along.

Plan

Introduction   Comment on the four headlines, showing that they indicate the writers' very different interests and attitudes. (This provides a crisp lead-in to the body of the answer.)

Body of answer

(i)   Differences of description in all four passages.
(ii)   The different attitudes thus revealed.
(iii)   The different uses made of vocabulary and grammar in the presentations of description and attitude.

Note   Provide frequent cross-references to sustain *continuous* discussion of all four passages. Keep the comparisons and contrasts going all the way through. Link idea to idea and paragraph to paragraph so that no one topic gets isolated from the others.

Conclusion   Round answer off with a *brief* statement of main conclusions drawn from close study of these four very different uses of language.

Answer

The headlines prepare us for the writers' strikingly different descriptions of and attitudes towards the wedding. Passage A gushingly announces a romantic story. B grimly highlights potential violence. C coolly questions whether the wedding was of any interest at all. D (not, strictly speaking, a 'headline') flatly states its origin, thus establishing its authority and implicitly promising a factual record, without 'slant' or 'colour'.

Each headline is followed by selective descriptions of the day's events. Passage A concentrates on three: the assembling of the crowds; the bride's arrival at St Paul's; the bride and bridegroom at the altar.

B spends little time on either the wedding or the procession, preferring to offer a catalogue of security precautions. The wedding gets a mention because of the armed policewoman in St Paul's. The procession is of interest to B only because of the disguised and armed policemen on the coaches and the use of the mounted escorts as anti-terrorist shields.

C reports a lot that was going on but, like B, shows little interest in the procession and the wedding. Unlike B, however, C is not concerned with the policing. With one exception – the 'lonely old lady' (lines 31–34) – C's subjects are the street traders, the advertisers and the tourist industry. What A describes as a 'magic day' is reported by C as a day on which a lot of people intended to make money – and were disappointed.

D's account of the day is completely different from all the others. A's emotional reporting, B's relentless record of security arrangements, and C's ironical description of thwarted commercial enterprises are poles apart from this plain, factual detailing of who did what. D provides a schedule of events from which future organisers of a similar operation could reconstruct the machinery that got the principal personages and their proper attendants to the wedding, through it, and back again. The actions and emotions of the onlookers, the threat of disorder, and the money-making opportunities are of no interest to the writer of the Court Circular.

The four writers' different attitudes, so clearly revealed through their selective reporting of events, are presented by their contrasting choices of vocabulary and grammar. It is not only *what* they choose to write about, it is also *how* they choose to write about it that shows how very differently they think and feel.

Passage A shines up the 'exuberant romance' of the day with fulsome expressions. For example: 'Red, white and blue favours dazzled our eyes and made glad our hearts'. The language of the other reports is drab in comparison. B and D use no colour words at all. C gives a straightforward description of 'periscopes in red, white and blue stripes', but points out that they were being given away with cigarettes because nobody would buy them. And A's breathless report of the teeming crowds in lines 28–39 does not accord with C's sober statements in lines 1–5.

In general, A's use of words is loose and hackneyed. For example: 'Republicans from the USA' are said to be 'royalists to a man'. How does the author of A know that? (And what about the women?)

The bride's appearance is described in hollow generalities. She is a 'breath-taking vision' in the 'spectacular brilliance' of her wedding gown. The attempt to invoke past imperial glories in lines 29–35 is similarly enfeebled with cliché and imprecision.

All this make-believe is set against the background of 'clouded times', but the 'joys of an ancient kingdom', shared with 'all our friends in the free world', lighten the weight of 'a cross'. The choice of metaphor is both silly and offensively out of place.

Reluctantly, A admits that the national (and international) love feast might have been disrupted by violence, but presents the 'harsh facts' without upsetting anybody. The possibilities of murder and mutilation are passed off as 'unseemly events' – of which, of course, there were none. Armed police were 'tactfully deployed'. (According to B, there was nothing very 'tactful' about the scale and nature of the security arrangements.) The day 'closed'. The missing (sheep?) were safely 'folded'.

A's use of words is at its worst in describing the royal pair at the altar. When they get their lines wrong, we are presented with a whimsical picture of 'Mr and Mrs Smith' (that stereotyped couple of 'ordinary folk') smiling in loyal and loving sympathy as they recall their own wedding day and their own nervous mumblings on that happy occasion. It is instructive to compare D's blunt and objective statements in lines 38 and 39. The Court Circular sees no reason to mention mistakes, and feels no compulsion to pretend that the royal bride and bridegroom were simple, ordinary people at heart – or in head.

'Mr and Mrs Smith' appear again at the end of Passage A, strangely described as the bride's 'subjects', and miraculously transformed into 'her kin'. Since the bride was 'on her father's arm' at that moment, the word 'kin' is absurdly misplaced.

Passage A uses some involved sentences (lines 45–51, for example), presumably to bolster the 'eloquence' of the writing. But the intended 'flow' is checked at times by peculiar grammatical uses that draw attention to themselves. The 'quaint' inversion in line 14 is just one example.

There are, too, some odd and stilted expressions (for example: 'let it be' – 'perforce' – 'huckstering byelaws') which strain unsuccessfully to create a 'romantic' effect.

The graceless style of B matches its contents. Single-minded concentration on the potentially violent measures taken to combat a potentially violent situation is expressed in a crudely monotonous succession of staccato sentences and truncated paragraphs, typical of tabloid writing and layout.

The vocabulary is restricted to the writer's unflattering estimate of the reader's intellectual capacity, just as the contents reflect narrow assumptions about what will be of interest.

B's standards and attitudes are made plain in line 16 ('The £750,000 police helicopter'). The cost of the machine is of no importance whatever in this context – but that is of no importance to B. Cramming the reader with facts and figures – true or false, relevant or not – makes the writer seem so well informed, so sensible, such a no-nonsense, trustworthy reporter.

The reference to 'many London demonstrations' is intended to conjure up visions of hordes of malcontents and subversives against whom, on this occasion as on so many others, a massive deployment of the forces of law and order is required. Item is piled on top of item: '4,000 uniformed police – anti-terrorist SAS troops – helicopter – electronic eye – airship – Special Branch – dogs'. And on it goes.

B seems disappointed to have to report that, after all these precautions had been taken, there were so few arrests, and those for such trivial offences. A more sensitive writer would have avoided the ludicrous anti-climax at the end ('Police marksmen' followed immediately by 'There were four arrests for pickpocketing'.) But, then, a sensitive writer would not have inserted the redundant preposition 'over' in line 18. Where else would a helicopter hover?

C is written in a much more lively way than the others. Direct speech, colloquialisms and an uninhibited choice of words result in an easy, everyday style of utterance, in keeping with the writer's attitude to the royal occasion. 'It was,' says C, 'an opportunity for petty entrepreneurs, and some big ones, to make money; and I am not going to fool myself, or you, by pretending that it was anything else'.

So A's thrilled onlookers are C's 'punters'. B describes 'Britain's biggest security operation', but C describes 'the tourist attraction of the century' that didn't come off. The street traders, the advertisers, the tourist board and the Tory

Consumer Minister are more in evidence than the 'bystanders in search of a better vantage point'. And though, according to A, the magic day was shared with 'the three corners of the world', C's 'lonely old lady' saw no point in leaving 'the back streets of Covent Garden' to glimpse the great ones as they passed. Like B's policemen, though for a different reason, she turned her back on the royal procession.

The conversational style appropriate to C's commonsensical, mildly amused attitude alternates with expressions of a sharper scepticism. For example, the word 'sheltered' (line 23) points the satirical supposition that C's 'Lady Di' (A's 'Lady Diana Frances Spencer' and D's 'the Lady Diana Spencer') might ever have need of 'a good scaffolder or insurance company'.

C's handling of vocabulary and grammar is so well geared to the writer's purposes and attitude that the broken English of the headline is surprising. Presumably, it was lack of space that forced the sub-editor into a fault that the writer would not have committed.

D is well written – and very boring. But, since its sole purpose was to provide a factual record of the order of procedure and a list of the principals and their entourages, it did not attempt to excite or amuse. Its interest, such as it is, lies solely in its efficient performance of a severely practical function.

Its vocabulary is correct and formal. Its sentences are short, and its paragraphs are strictly measured out to accommodate one item at a time. Each stage of the proceedings gets a paragraph to itself, even when (as in line 40) it consists of just one short sentence.

It is interesting to compare D with B because – superficially – they have features in common. Each is written in a series of short sentences and very short paragraphs. But the contrasts are more instructive. The unadorned, strictly practical use of language in D is justified, where B's deliberate 'brutalism' is not. D uses restricted language for a restricted purpose, and with complete honesty. B uses deliberately impoverished language to appeal to readers whose minds are assumed to be incapable of anything but an impoverished response.

The result of studying the varieties of English used in these passages is a sense of astonishment that four writers reporting the same occasion could produce such different accounts. A cynic might well recall the familiar saying: 'Never believe anything you read in the papers'.

Assess the quality of that answer by applying the tests that the examiners would use when marking it:

(i)   Does it bring out the differences in the four descriptions of the day's events?

(ii)   Does it bring out the different attitudes to the wedding?

(iii)   Does it show how the writers' descriptions and attitudes are presented by their choices of vocabulary and grammar?

(iv)   Does it use evidence convincingly?

(v)   Does it present a sustained discussion in an orderly fashion and in good, readable English?

2

When the article printed below appeared in *The Guardian* on 30 June 1994 many people who could – or who bothered to – remember the event described in Question 1 saw it in retrospect as having been the ironical prelude to a period during which the British public's enthusiasm for royal persons, and for the monarchy itself, diminished rapidly. The writer of the article describes a television programme in which the Prince of Wales attempted to answer his critics. He argues that it did little to repair the Prince's damaged position or to strengthen his future role as a constitutional monarch; and he advises the Prince to adopt a different strategy.

King for a TV Day

There now, can we all (including the Prince of Wales) settle down? Last night the torrent of hype – with 15 million electric tea kettles boiling at commercial breaks around the nation – became a thinner rivulet of reality. The King-to-be said a lot; much of it earnestly positive, very little of it worth a big headline. Perhaps, at the close, we understood his problem better: but it was not *our* problem. That sense of distance, at Wagnerian length, made the programme like some extended Finnish movie about marital angst and good intentions. You wished you could care more – but all you really cared about was another cup of coffee.

So, neither a triumph nor a disaster: more a bizarre dislocation. What was it, all of it, there *for*? Not, surely, for a few muttered sentences about adultery. What, after the Squidgy tapes, is interesting about that? Not for princely words about the kind of disestablished monarchy he'd like to run when, at 65 or 75, he makes it to the throne. The point had to be more immediate than that. The point was to say that, after rather a bad time, here was rather a good chap. No contest. He works hard. He presses the flesh. He supports worthy causes. He uses his influence shrewdly and beneficially. He strives for the vision thing. The once and continuing story of the last 25 years.

But – and here, in turn, comes the angst – does he know what *he's* there for? The role of a constitutional monarch is simply to be there, because that's all one requires: a conservative succession which society deems less fuss (and better for tourism) than the Presidential elections of Tony Benn's dreamings. You don't need to be a philosopher king or a telly star: you need to be born at the right time to the right mother. Future events may unhinge such inert arrangements, to be sure. But Charles isn't running for election or top spot in the latest *Sun* readers' poll. It's sadly irrelevant whether he 'cares more deeply' about the future of this country than 'some politicians'; or whether he speaks up for 'the ordinary person'. His ultimate job is to exist and, maybe, adjust the nature of the future role to something more modest and relaxed. Of that there was scant sign last night. The Prince clearly feels trapped: trapped by frustrated ambition, by convention, by a miserable marriage, by the weight of supposed responsibility, by the goldfish-bowl press. He's striving to get the inner him across. Alas, the wrong response to the wrong question. Show quietly, don't tell. The way for the Royal family to survive is to become less important. Prince Charles would rather chain us to our TV sets to unveil a different sense of importance. But it punctures on inquiry – because it is simply not the job fate has promised him.

What do the ways in which language is used in that article tell you about the writer's attitude to his subject and to his readers? Consider the linguistic features of the writing and their appropriateness to the function of the article and to the writer's purposes.

Note   Revise pages 143–6 and then study the following commentary before you start to answer that question. Use the commentary as a guide, *not* as a 'blueprint'. It draws attention to matters you will need to consider when you are working on the question; and it demonstrates methods you will find it helpful to adopt. In particular, it shows you how to make a detailed analysis of the content and the style of the article (or of any other passage of writing). Think about the views expressed in the commentary but do not accept them uncritically. It is your own views – and, of course, the *reasoning* on which they are based – that you should give when answering this question – or any other question of a similar kind.

Commentary

A brief summary of the content of the article   The writer discusses the personal and the constitutional aspects of the problems facing the Prince of Wales. He argues that the Prince does not understand the true nature of his difficult situation and that, in consequence, his attempts to restore his popularity are misconceived.

The structure of the article and the development of the argument   The writer sets his argument out in three paragraphs. In paragraph 1 he derides the TV programme in which the Prince tried to woo public support. In paragraph 2 he develops the point (introduced in paragraph 1) that the programme failed because so little of its content was relevant to the real issue. It drew attention to the Prince's thoughtfulness and to his conscientious performance of his duties; but those, says the writer, are matters of minor importance and in any case they are not in serious dispute. In paragraph 3 he argues that public relations exercises are inappropriate ways of bolstering the Prince's present position and his future role. By the accident of birth, he is 'the King-to-be'. It is pointless for him to try to win understanding and sympathy by revealing his inner self. All that is required of him is to be there when the time comes for him to succeed to the throne as a constitutional monarch. Meanwhile, he would best serve his own interests and those of his country by continuing to perform his public duties ('Show quietly') and resisting the temptation to explain himself and justify his actions ('don't tell').

The writer's attitude to his subject and to his readers   As that outline of the writer's argument makes clear, he is concerned with two conflicting views of how the Prince can repair his damaged position. On the one hand, there is the view taken by the Prince and his advisers (and exemplified by the TV programme), that things will improve if he can put himself across as 'rather a good chap' who works hard. On the other hand, there is the view taken by the writer that the best course of action for the Prince is to go about his duties quietly and to keep silent about his personal life and qualities.

The writer uses language in ways that convey unmistakably his attitudes to each of those points of view. The opening sentence ('There now,') dismisses the TV programme as a trivial interlude. The tone is such as an adult might adopt when admonishing naughty children: 'Come on! You've had your fun. Now let's get on with something important.' The programme is described as a showbiz exercise: a 'torrent of hype – with 15 million electric tea kettles boiling around the nation'. The writer's disdain for the content and style of the programme and for the misguided activities of those who planned it and took part in it is apparent.

That attitude to what he regards as a frivolous approach is sustained throughout the article and conveyed by the language he uses when commenting on it and on its results. The deliberate use of clichés in paragraph 2 is a striking example: 'No contest . . . presses the flesh . . . the vision thing'. So is 'telly star' (in paragraph 3). These smart, modish, claptrap terms aptly express his scornful rebuttal of the shallow thinking manifest in the TV programme.

In contrast, when he is explaining the nub of the matter and advocating an appropriate strategy for dealing with it, the tone of the language is well suited to convey a serious and constructive approach. (That point is developed later in this commentary.)

Notice, too, how the writer suggests that he and his readers are of the same mind. An identity of view is established in the first paragraph and then – without the need for further justification – tacitly maintained while he develops his argument to its conclusion.

The writer's attitude to his readers is made clear when he says, 'Perhaps, at the close, we understood his problem better: but it was not *our* problem.' By italicising 'our' he unites his readers with himself. We were at one, he claims, in finding the programme remote from our concerns. We were exasperated by its trivial approach. We were exasperated, too, because we had wasted our time watching the long-drawn-out frivolity.

His subsequent use of the pronoun *you* (in the sense of 'one') emphasises that he is indeed speaking on behalf of his readers (and of all 'right-minded' people!): 'You [that is to say, "You, my readers, and I"] wished you could care more – but all you really cared about was another cup of coffee.'

The writer's confident assumption that he knows how his readers responded to the TV programme springs from his equally confident belief that they are well-educated, well-informed and lively-minded people. They share his vocabulary. They will have no difficulty in understanding his references. They will respond appropriately to the nuances of his style and to the finer points of his argument.

That he believes he is addressing readers whose interests, attainments and attitudes are similar to his own is made apparent by the allusive style in which much of the article is written. Knowing that he can rely on their apprehension, he describes the TV programme as dealing 'at Wagnerian length' with 'marital angst and good intentions' in the manner of an 'extended Finnish movie'. Later, he refers to 'the Squidgy tapes'; to 'the Presidential elections of Tony Benn's dreamings'; to the fact that 'Charles isn't running for election or top spot in the latest *Sun* readers' poll'.

His consistent approach to his readers as intelligent and literate people is affirmed by the incisive language in which he expresses key points of his argument – for example: 'a bizarre dislocation' – 'The once and continuing story of the last 25 years' – 'Future events may unhinge such inert arrangements' – 'adjust the nature of the role to something more modest and relaxed' – 'But it punctures on inquiry'.

The linguistic features of the writing: their appropriateness to the function of the article and to the writer's purposes   It was necessary to examine some of the chief linguistic features of the writing when considering the writer's attitude to his subject and to his readers. Another important point must now be made. Although it is a passage of *writing*, printed in a newspaper for people to read, this article has many of the linguistic features of a *spoken* utterance. It is, of course, a 'text' and not a 'transcript' (see page 142) but it frequently 'sounds' like speech – very well-organised, controlled, thought-out, fluent, stumble-free speech. Contractions (e.g. 'he's' – 'you don't need' – 'isn't running'), compressed grammatical constructions (e.g. 'So ... dislocation' – 'Alas ... question'), familiar turns of phrase (e.g. 'to be sure' – 'maybe') contribute to that effect and reinforce the prevailingly conversational tone in which the discussion is conducted.

The subject is treated seriously and, as pointed out earlier, the writer asks his readers to think it out with him; but he presents it in a relaxed manner. He wrote the article in a racy, colloquial style because he wanted it to be easy to read; but he also wanted it to be seen as a constructive contribution to the debate. Consequently, he had to try to maintain the spontaneous tone of the writing while putting forward a thoughtful argument. So, when dismissing the trivial aspects of the subject he tried not to sound flippant; and when discussing its serious aspects he tried not to sound ponderous.

Clearly, the purposes that the writer of such an article has in mind are very largely determined by its function. A leader writer has (or should have) expert knowledge of his subject. He is, therefore, well equipped to describe, explain, analyse and recommend. More than that, he should have a sensitive awareness of his audience (see page 145) and he should be able to write clearly and persuasively for them. He is, to some extent, their mouthpiece; but he is also their opinion-former.

By virtue of his position (as a leader writer for their newspaper), he should know his readers. By virtue of his expert knowledge, he should be able to provide them with information that they have neither the time nor the means to acquire for themselves. By virtue of his experience in his specialised field, he should be able to suggest ways of approaching the subject and policies for dealing with it that might not occur to them.

But he must not get too far ahead of them. He is trying to throw light on the subject he is discussing and to persuade them to consider it in the ways he suggests. He will not succeed if he addresses them from a superior height or speaks to them across a gulf.

With the help of that commentary (and bearing in mind the advice in the note on page 140) study the article closely. Then answer the question printed on page 156.

Problem solving

The essay-writing problems singled out for discussion in this chapter are those most frequently identified in examiners' reports as giving candidates the greatest trouble and causing them to lose marks. Ways of tackling these particular difficulties are suggested in the notes and outline answers, which demonstrate how problems can be overcome by applying the methods of question analysis and answer planning set out in previous chapters.

The examination questions tackled here may refer to material (set books, for example) not specified in your syllabus. This does not lessen the value of studying the questions and the suggested ways of answering them. In their wording and scope, the questions are representative of those set in English A Level papers, and the methods of tackling them put forward here get to grips with problems that confront all English A Level candidates, of whichever examining board.

1

'Love, sacred and profane, has never been so ruthlessly analysed as by the Metaphysicals.' Indicate the range of experience and attitude to love of both kinds shown by *at least two* poets in your selection, excluding Donne.

(S.U.J.B.)

Notes Anthologies present particular problems as set books. The number of writers and the variety of work represented (even when linked by membership of one literary 'school') make considerable demands on the student, who must be familiar with the identity of each writer and the individuality of his/her work, while appreciating shared characteristics. One anthology of Metaphysical poetry that is often set contains the work of 38 different poets. Other Metaphysical selections specified as set books range as widely over the field, representing not only the considerable number of these poets, but also the development of the 'school' from its early to its later stages.

Many boards permit candidates to take copies of set texts into the examination room, but this is of little help unless they have studied the texts thoroughly beforehand. The time allowance for the question now considered was 40 minutes. Unless candidates know what to look for and where to look, they cannot, in that short time, get to grips with the question, gather relevant material, plan an answer, write it, and read it through.

The 'trigger' of the question (see Section 6.2) is the quotation with which it begins. The key words in that quotation are: 'Love, sacred and profane . . . ruthlessly analysed'. The key words in the instructions are: 'Indicate . . . range of experience and attitude to love of both kinds . . . *at least two* poets . . . excluding Donne'.

Since John Donne (whose poems exemplify so outstandingly the qualities specified in the question) is ruled out, the material for the answer must be found in the work of at least two other poets who analyse sacred and profane love, covering a range of different experiences and expressing different attitudes. Clearly, if sufficient material is to be found, they must be poets who are represented at some length in the set book. Candidates who know the text well will think immediately of the following possibilities: Henry King, George Herbert, Thomas Carew, Richard Crashaw, Richard Lovelace, Andrew Marvell. Their poetry explores an ample range of experience in, and attitudes to, both kinds of love. Which two or more of those poets are finally chosen is a matter of individual decision, based on confident understanding of and lively personal response to their work built up during the English A Level course.

Before the plan for the answer can be worked out, further thought must be given to the 'command' word in the examiners' instructions. *Indicate* means 'point to, point out, make known, show'. The examiners are looking for an *exposition*, not a critical discussion. They require candidates to *demonstrate* that two or more poets in the anthology (other than Donne) have as their prime concern the subject matter detailed in the question, and that they treat it in the manner described there.

With all those considerations settled, a plan can be worked out. Something along these lines will provide a sound basis for the answer.

Plan

Introduction   Respond to the 'trigger' of the question – comment briefly on Metaphysicals' choice of love as a theme – their interest in its psychology – their fusion (through statement and imagery) of sacred and profane love in exploring both.

Body of answer: development

(i)   State which two (or more) poets have been selected.

(ii) Demonstrate the varied facets of 1st poet's analysis of sacred love, making brief comments on particular poems – ensure that detailed references and quotations supporting those comments are drawn from different experiences and from different attitudes to those experiences: hope, despair, faith, doubt, joy, sorrow and so on.

(iii)   Deal with 1st poet's profane love poetry in similar manner – again, ensure that variety of experience and attitude is illustrated: joy, sorrow, union, separation, distrust, confidence, jealousy, revulsion and so on.

(iv)   Deal with 2nd poet's work as in (ii) and (iii).

(v)   Deal with 3rd poet, if chosen.

Body of answer: qualification

(i)   Briefly point out that chosen poets do write on other subjects: their contemporaries, public events and issues, scientific and philosophical matters – name one or two poems.

(ii)   Round off qualification by stressing their commitment to love themes – intensity of their interest in and treatment of their dominant subject – (this is a swift lead-in to the conclusion).

Conclusion

(i)   Take up reference in question to ruthlessness of poets' analysis of love (this is a key point in the trigger quotation not, so far, covered in the answer).

(ii)   Ruthless qualities: single-minded, dramatic concentration on central situation treated in each poem – vivid honesty of presentation explores essence of lovers' experience unsparingly.

(iii)   Above all, ruthless because no distinction is made between sacred and profane experiences – poets' sole concern is to explore physical, mental, spiritual effects of love, as manifested in different situations, whether humanly or divinely inspired.

2

'*Much Ado* comes too near to tragedy quite to succeed as comedy.' Discuss.

Notes   This question requires a discursive (a 'reasoned-out') answer. Candidates are expected to take the quotation as their starting point, and then to present a reasoned argument for agreeing with or rejecting the proposition that it puts forward.

Whether candidates agree with or reject the proposition is of less importance than the quality of their argument (its clarity, its logicality, its cogency, its use of evidence).

When answering the question candidates should define the senses in which the key terms ('tragedy' and 'comedy') are used in the essay. An argument of the quality expected cannot be put forward unless that is done at the outset.

Briefly, these are the points to be considered.

(i)   Is the term 'tragedy' used in the question (and should it, therefore, be used in the answer) in the simple and popular sense of a sad play with an unhappy ending? *Or* is that term used in the question (and should it therefore be used in the answer) in the more complex sense in which it is employed in critical discussion – of, for example, the experience conveyed by *King Lear*?

(ii) Is the term 'comedy' used in the question (and should it therefore be used in the answer) in the simple and popular sense of an amusing play with a happy ending? *Or* is that term used in the question (and should it, therefore, be used in the answer) in the more complex sense in which it is used in critical discussion – of, for example, the experience conveyed by *Twelfth Night*?

The quality of the essay will be judged by the clarity and persuasiveness of the argument it sets out. That is why it is essential to explain the senses in which the two key terms are used – and to use them consistently in those senses throughout the essay.

3

Discuss Lawrence's description of places and his use of symbols in his treatment of the relationship between Paul and Miriam.

(J.M.B.)

Notes   Candidates often fail to detect that questions worded like this (and it is a formula often used) give precise instructions. A schematic presentation makes clear what must be done.

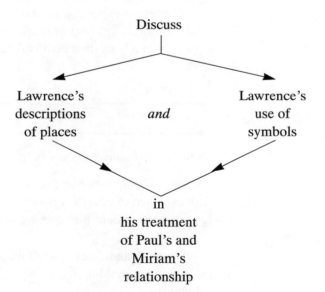

Each of the key terms used in the instructions must be carefully considered.

discuss   = say what you think about this subject and provide evidence from the text to support your opinions.

treatment   = how D.H. Lawrence explores their relationship, making it seem interesting and important to the reader – involving the reader in their lives – communicating what they meant to each other and why it matters.

relationship = Paul's and Miriam's thoughts about and feelings for each other –
their attitudes to each other – how they behaved to each other.

Note that the features of the novel from which material is to be drawn for the purposes of this discussion are stipulated clearly: the author's descriptions of places, and his use of symbols. Only discussion based on those two features and illustrations derived from them will be considered relevant. Note, too, that the examiners make a distinction between Lawrence's use of descriptions of places and his use of symbols. They expect candidates to observe this distinction and to discuss each as making a distinctive contribution to the novelist's treatment of the relationship.

Clear thinking is required, because Lawrence's symbols (the wild rose bush, for example) are often embedded in his description of a place. Other equally potent symbols (the broken umbrella, for example) are derived from sources other than his place descriptions.

Again, long descriptive passages (the contrasted 'purity' of farming country and the 'taint' of encroaching industrialisation, for example) have a symbolic function, but cannot be classified accurately as symbols.

Thorough knowledge and understanding of the book, and careful thought about the nature of Lawrence's art are, of course, prerequisites for a good answer; but, as these notes have demonstrated, the wording of the question must be considered very carefully. Candidates must analyse the examiners' requirements, think out the details of the material they will use in their answer, then plan that answer accordingly.

The question also poses (and sharply) the recurring essay problem of how to handle text references and quotations. The set book to be discussed is in prose (always harder to quote from than poetry), and two distinct subject areas are stipulated. Frequent use of evidence is required to support the opinions expressed, but much of the evidence consists of (or is embedded in) sustained passages of description, which candidates can neither carry in their memory nor find time to write out in full. That difficulty is compounded by the fact that evidence drawn from Lawrence's use of descriptions of places and evidence drawn from his use of symbols must be clearly distinguished as relating to one or the other of the two different topics specified for discussion.

Make brief and very precise references to any long passages used as evidence, so that the examiners recognise them at once and appreciate the purposes for which they are being brought into the discussion.

Quote key words whenever possible. For example, Lawrence's description of the countryside through which Paul passed to his first meeting with Miriam plays an essential part in his treatment of their relationship. The significance of that description can be brought out swiftly and economically by quoting a few telling words – 'on the fallow land the young wheat shone silkily' would be an effective choice. In this way, the whole passage can be used as evidence in support of the argument.

Again, if making the point that Paul was leaving one environment for another and that they represent forces and tensions inherent in his relationship with Miriam, that point could be established by referring to the colliery that 'waved its plumes of white steam, coughed, and rattled hoarsely'.

Just a few words from the text (easily memorised during the course of study) bring clarity and authority into the discussion of Lawrence's artistic aims and methods.

Similarly, the identity and function of 'pure' symbols can be established quickly and clearly by using Lawrence's own words. For example, Paul's and Miriam's recognition of hitherto unrealised elements in their relationship (and the candidate's appreciation of Lawrence's treatment of this) could be brought out effectively by quoting the last words of the broken umbrella incident: ' "Come on," he said. "I can't do it"; and they went in silence along the road.'

4

'In Shakespeare's plays, love is generally a disease.' Discuss.

(O. & C.)

Notes   Several examining boards set questions which, like this, require candidates to draw on their wider reading. Clearly, it would be foolish to attempt this question without having some detailed knowledge of several of Shakespeare's plays, in addition to the two or three generally set for close study.

The wording of this question is deliberately provocative. It is tempting to react to it in a dismissive way, because – at first sight – it seems an outrageous statement. However, the purpose of all English A Level questions is to stimulate thought about literature and language, and this question is no exception. Though little sympathy may be felt for the opinion expressed, it must be considered carefully and judiciously. A summary, out-of-hand rejection will not do. The grounds on which the opinion rests must be probed, and the evidence in its favour must be weighed. Only then can a reasoned refutation, based on text evidence, be advanced. During the careful preparatory planning of the answer, it is important to strike a balance between the space to be given to the proposition and the space to be given to the refutation. The main emphasis must be placed on the arguments rejecting the proposition and putting forward a sounder opinion, but sufficient attention must be given to the proposition to show that it has received due consideration.

Balance does not preclude the expression of firmly held and well-substantiated opinions. A contentious question should not receive a wishy-washy, 'there's-much-to-be-said-on-both-sides' answer. There is usually something to be said on one side, but more to be said on the other.

Nevertheless, a cool tone and clarity of expression are the requisite features of good writing on contentious subjects. However carefully they have thought out their answer, candidates who feel that the proposition is wrong-headed often become excited – even intemperate – when writing. Precise language and strictly controlled sentence and paragraph structures pay off handsomely.

A more detailed consideration of the issues involved in this particular question illustrates the importance of the points already made in the notes in this chapter. Here are the preliminary stages of gathering material and planning an answer. They are set out in the form of rough-paper jottings, such as a candidate might make when coming to grips with the question.

The case for the proposition: love as a disease

(i)   *Hamlet* – his love for Ophelia described in disease images – extended to include all love – the 'nunnery' scene – she 'spies' on him – betrayal – disillusionment – diatribes against women, especially his mother – her adultery – 'rank corruption'

(ii)   *Othello* – 'I loved not wisely, but too well' – corroding effects of jealousy – love blinds Othello – 'animal' nature of love stressed by imagery

(iii) *Macbeth* – influence of Lady M. – worked on M.'s love to trap him into murder – love = death

(iv)   *King Lear* – cold self-seeking of Goneril and Regan – the nature of Lear's 'love' for them – possessive, demanding, self-deluding and self-destructive

(v)   *Antony and Cleopatra* – their love destroys them – and deceives them – and leads them to deceive others – Antony's tormented denunciations of the 'spell' and of the 'enchantress'

(vi)   The 'Dark Comedies' – Cressida betrays and destroys Troilus – cynicism of *All's Well* – ambiguities of *Measure for Measure*.

The case against the proposition: love as the 'sovereign flower' – the redeemer of the individual – the bond of personal and social unity – the health-giving spirit

(i)   Early comedies – for example, *L.L.L.*, where the young men rail against love, but accept it *and* approach maturity through it.

(ii)   The 'golden comedies' – *Much Ado* and *As You Like It* in particular – Beatrice and Benedick, sanity and health – the most clearsighted and truest of lovers – the church scene – Rosalind and Orlando – 'just as high as my heart' – 'how many fathoms deep in love' – the healing power

(iii) Especially the Last Plays – love the redeemer – the life force – young lovers in each bring salvation to a dark world – love is truth and health

(iv)   Even in plays which offer some support to proposition, case is not sound – it won't stand up to close examination – it's a very partial interpretation of people, events and motives – Ophelia is not the cause of Hamlet's defeat – Desdemona is innocent – Othello's 'love' is more self-love than real love – he's immature, incapable of trust – if Lady M. is partly responsible for M.'s first crime, he plans all the rest, and not for love of her – love has ceased to play any part in his nature – his tragedy is the denial of love – Cordelia triumphantly embodies love's healing power, and Lear knows it at last – Antony and Cleopatra lose the worldly might of Rome and the flesh-pots of Egypt, but they die more nobly than Octavius lives – she confident of their immortality and future union: 'Husband, I come: Now to that name my courage prove my title'.

Line of argument to be deployed

(i)   State what can be said for proposition

(ii)   Demonstrate weakness at its base: its reliance on partial, tendentiously selected evidence in support of dubious arguments

(iii) Deploy positive arguments against proposition. **NB** include 'Dark

Comedies' here to turn a main point of proposition's case against itself – stress that Last Plays are a development out of 'Dark Comedies' – the final act, as it were, that gives them proportion – stress continuity – many elements of 'Dark Comedies' appear at beginning of Last Plays, but compressed as prelude to restoration through love – out of darkness, light.

(iv) Conclude by gathering together separate elements treated in (iii) to provide final refutation.

This material, gathered and sorted, forms the basis of a well-reasoned refutation of the proposition. There are still details to be worked out, but the plan emerging in the 'Line of argument' section could be completed very quickly, leaving adequate time for writing a clear, firmly argued answer to this contentious question.

Further reading

Note Individual requirements for further reading are conditioned mainly by your own syllabus. Your lecturers and the editorial matter (introduction and notes) in your copies of the prescribed texts will provide you with the titles of books and articles that you should read to fill out your set book study.

Chapter 3 of this book (Section 3.5) makes detailed suggestions to help you to organise your extra reading and – while giving it all the time you can – to keep it within manageable limits.

In addition to the further reading that stems directly from your own set texts, the specialised help provided by the books in this short list of further reading will be of benefit to all English A Level candidates.

Standard reference books

The Oxford Companion to English Literature (OUP)
Brewer's Dictionary of Phrase and Fable (Cassell)

Histories of literature

The Cambridge History of English Literature (CUP)
The Macmillan History of Literature (Macmillan)
The Pelican Guide to English Literature (Penguin)

Unseen critical appreciation

S. H. Burton, *The Criticism of Poetry* (Longman)
S. H. Burton, *The Criticism of Prose* (Longman)
Richard Gill, *Mastering English Literature* (Macmillan)

The technical terms of literature and criticism

J. A. Cuddon, *A Dictionary of Literary Terms* (Penguin)
Patrick Murray, *Literary Criticism: A Glossary of Major Terms* (Longman)
John Peck and Martin Coyle, *Literary Terms and Criticism* (Macmillan)

Study guides

Until fairly recently, books of this kind were rarely of much value. 'Notes' – on this book, that book, and the other – weighed down the bookshop shelves with their stodgy comments and dull exercises. Nowadays, however, there are many lively and thought-provoking 'Study Guides' offering factual but imaginative critical comments on individual books and authors. An hour's browsing in your local bookshop will show you how wide a choice is provided by several leading publishers who, between them, issue titles corresponding to most of the set texts specified by the various examining boards. *Macmillan Master Guides* are particularly useful; and they introduce their subjects in an interesting and stimulating way. Each contains a carefully chosen and up-to-date list of further reading from which you can plan a programme to meet your examiners' demands.

English language

S. H. Burton and J. A. Humphries, *Mastering English Language* (Macmillan)
S. H. Burton, *Mastering English Grammar* (Macmillan)

Index